The Mountain

THE MOUNTAIN

Journeys in High Places

Robin Patten

THE UNIVERSITY OF UTAH PRESS
Salt Lake City

Library of Congress Cataloging-in-Publication Data
Names: Patten, Robin, 1962- author
Title: The mountain : journeys in high places / Robin Patten.
Description: Salt Lake City : The University of Utah Press, [2025] |
Includes bibliographical references. |
Identifiers: LCCN 2024050260 | ISBN 9781647692261 paperback | ISBN 9781647692278 ebook
Subjects: LCSH: Patten, Robin, 1962---Travel | Mountains--Philosophy | West
(U.S.)--Description and travel | Women naturalists--West
(U.S.)--Biography | Naturalists--West (U.S.)--Biography |
Scotland--Description and travel | LCGFT: Autobiographies
Classification: LCC F595.3 .P38 2025
LC record available at https://lccn.loc.gov/2024050260

For EU safety / GPSR concerns:
Email: gpsr@mare-nostrum.co.uk

Physical address:
Mare Nostrum Group B.V.
Mauritskade 21D
1091 GC Amsterdam
The Netherlands

Cover photo from Assynt, Scotland, with the remnant of
a nineteenth-century trail in the foreground, by the author.

Errata and further information on this and other titles available at
UofUpress.com

For my parents, who created possibilities

~~~

Across the planet are mountains, physical places found on a map.
There is also the Mountain.
The Mountain is an idea, a thought,
a memory of something from another time,
a symbol, an icon.
The Mountain situates the human in the greater cosmos.
The Mountain is Meaning. The Mountain is what we seek but cannot know.
It is what some hope to find in mountains.
~~~

CONTENTS

INTRODUCTION

The fell-field ridge leading to Monument Mountain's crest is rocky and near barren yet still holds life: scattered cushions of moss campion and alpine forget-me-nots, mats of creamy petaled mountain avens, the occasional pika bleating to remind any passerby of the local residents. That day, the alpine flowers were in full bloom, bursting with color and scent to attract their pollinators during the brief growing season. I walked upward along the ridge, pausing to kneel beside the flowers, bending down as if in prayer to inhale their fragrance, then rising to look up into an endless sky that stretched beyond the horizon outward and upward to realms only imagination could follow.

The ridge took me to the summit thousands of feet higher than the sea, a rounded top that unfolds from the rocky fell-field into an expansive alpine meadow swathed in green and a wildflower brilliance of golden cinquefoil, maroon shooting stars, white bistort, magenta lousewort, azure bluebells, dark-blue lupine. All the blooms were of short stature but with flowers the size of their low-elevation cousins, a bounteous garden of color clinging to the ground yet seeming to weave into the clear sky so close overhead. I lay in the meadow with eyes closed, drowning in abundance, drenched with sunlight, and infused with scent. I sat up to watch how the slight breeze brushed the grass and swayed the garden. I stood and walked over to a lichen-splashed boulder and perched on it, arms raised with the utter joy of being.

A peregrine falcon flew over, circling, gliding slowly over toward my perch. I imprinted the markings into memory, dark head, barred chest, checkered underwings, wanting to positively identify the bird later. As the raptor spiraled above, sweeping by again, my thoughts abandoned rational analysis, my mind floating with the bird till the falcon descended, stretching out talons to alight on a neighboring rock, eyeing me. Looking down to steady my feet, seeking stillness to hold that moment, I noted tiny bones, bloodstains, creamy streaks of excrement on the very rock where I stood. It seems my perch was the peregrine's dining table. The falcon tilted her head, fixing her eyes on mine in an unblinking stare. Human and peregrine, perched side by side, under that sky, within that meadow, those eyes looking into me with the stare of a creature holding wild in its veins and the heavens in its grasp. My existence shrank, my self reduced to something less than those minuscule bones at my feet. Yet I was there, part of the flow of that event, of that narrative that has no beginning and will not end.

I stepped down from the falcon's rock, moving off slowly. The falcon's wings spread, the bird lifting into the sky to disappear into the airy distance, leaving that moment behind—something I have never done, being the human who I am.

~~~

The world is restless, not so static as it may appear in our brief human lives, its skin twitching as its plates move, driven by churning magma far below: they pull apart, slide past each other, crash together, folding the earth and crumpling the land, lifting bits of the globe closer to the sky. With this tectonic motion, the wandering plates have decorated the entire planet with high mountains, magnificent sculptures of rock and stone where life takes hold and thrives where it can, dwindling in the highest zones beyond good habitat and human dwellings, though we go there anyway. Some of these mountains are young and still rising, jagged and edgy like the Tetons of Wyoming; some are older and rounded, more a function of erosion than uplift, like the Cairngorms of Scotland; others emerged in a fiery uprising of magma from below, like Ngauruhoe of New Zealand.

The mountains rise above us, pulling our eyes upward, drawing us toward their heights even as they stir trepidation for what we cannot fully understand. They have shapes and summits, a beginning in their low slopes and an end in their highest points, and so a foothold in the earth and a hand in the heavens. Many have followed their call,
~~~

traveling into the peaks in physical and in spiritual quests, while others do not simply journey within the heights but make them home, as a retreat and as part of community.

What is sought by those who go to the mountains varies and cannot easily be categorized. There are those intent on conquest of a particular summit, those who seek solitude or pilgrimage, and many who walk the heights for reasons even they cannot articulate. When Peter Matthiessen set off into the mountains of Nepal with George Schaller, the expedition's outward goal was to study Himalayan blue sheep with hopes of seeing a snow leopard. But when asked his reason for trekking into the high peaks, Matthiessen acknowledged, "I did not know. How could I say that I wished to penetrate the secrets of the mountains in search of something still unknown that, like the yeti, might well be missed for the very fact of searching?"[1]

The Mountain holds that unknown, cradling knowledge in its valleys and running truths along its ridges. I write of the "Mountain" as something different than a mountain or mountains, something beyond the geographic physicality or verticality of the thing. Spend enough time in the mountains, stand in the high places with vastness all around, and the Mountain might rise up and forever shift the soul. There are many who set out to climb mainly for physical reasons, only to have that numinous Mountain experience, an intuited sense of something beyond what can adequately be described in words. Countless mountaineering narratives are threaded through with such epiphanies and spiritual musings.

Scotland's W. H. Murray described his high mountain experience in *Mountaineering in Scotland and Undiscovered Scotland*, the first draft of which was written on toilet paper while Murray was imprisoned in a World War II POW camp. Perhaps in such horrific conditions, Murray found soul sustenance in remembering such moments as this, when he had just reached a summit at sunrise.

> The mind fails one how miserably and painfully before great beauty. It cannot understand. Yet it would contain more. Mercifully, it is by this very process of not understanding that one is allowed to

> understand much: for each one has within him "the divine reason that sits at the helm of the soul," of which the head knows nothing. Find beauty; be still; and that faculty grows more surely than grain sown in season. However, I must be content to observe that here, for the first time, broke upon me the unmistakable intimation of a last reality underlying mountain beauty; and here for the first time, it awakened within me a faculty of comprehension that had never before been exercised.[2]

In a longer process, Nan Shepherd (see chapter 5) confides in *The Living Mountain* that she too initially climbed in the Cairngorm mountains for "sensuous gratification," the thrill of the heights, the excitement of distance and effort; she went for her own pleasure, only discovering "the mountain in itself" over time. She had her inspirational moments and flashes of insight, but it was over the years that the Mountain wrought change and brought her to a deeper sense of being: "I am not out of myself, but in myself. I am. To know Being, this is the final grace accorded from the mountain."[3]

It is the way of mountains, shaping us, transforming a person's worldview, weaving insights into a culture. Mountains reach into our psyche, their presence and power evoking a deep response. Even for those who seek "something still unknown," the Mountain may not answer questions so much as pose them, illuminating their significance—and so can cause a rumbling shift in worldview.

The Mountain can change a person.

But why? How is it that mountains affect us so strongly, and how does that mesh with what we carry into our meetings with the high places of the earth? For any relationship *with* the mountains is also a function of what is brought *to* the mountains.

Within each waking moment lies the potential for experiential learning, an ongoing process stitched through with received knowledge: mentors speak to us, study informs us, culture infuses us. We weave together our experience with that received knowledge and cultural heritage, process it through rational thought, emotion, spirit, intuition—only to have it reshaped by further experience and further learning. Mountain experiences can be powerful, but they too are infiltrated with other learnings and experiences, even as they instill their own lessons, and so a dialogue may arise between mountain and person as well as mountain and culture. As Nan Shepherd so aptly put it, "What more there is lies within the mountain. Something moves between me and it. Place and mind may interpenetrate till the nature of both is altered."[4] Obviously, it is not the physical mountain that is altered but the Mountain one holds in their mind and feels in their spirit.

This relationship between humanity and mountains has been studied, considered, and contemplated in many fields and disciplines, in and out of academia. From such study, Denis Cosgrove and Veronica Della Dora conclude in their geography anthology that "height, then, is much more than a question of scale or altitudinal measure, just as place is much more than geographical location; it denotes a relationship between location and human experience."[5]

Yet paths of learning mix and meld in different ways, while experiences and emotions are never identical, meaning no two individuals nor even two cultures will have the same fusion of elements in their ways of knowing. The result is that across individuals, populations, societies, and cultures there are many different ways that mountains are understood, myriad ways of "knowing" mountains. Cultures drape them with personae from hellish to heavenly, think of them as hermitage or playground, view them as natural cathedral or tap them as natural resource. Individuals know their own mountains in their own ways, gazing up or striding across, walking them in pilgrimage or ascending them in conquest. Mountains are experienced in prayer and in song, in silent thought or jubilant celebration, in so many ways that I can't imagine, for I am just one individual among many who have journeyed within the mountains. And always there is the possibility for inspiration, even illumination.

Deserts, the ocean, even the Arctic hold qualities that can stir a response similar to that of mountains. Stand in the midst or even on the edge of these places, and they pull your eye out toward infinity. In the face of such immeasurability, you might shrink to nothingness even while engaging with a sense of leaning into an abyss that could carry you . . . just where? Among others, women writers akin to Nan Shepherd have told of these places, providing a glimpse of the mystique they hold: Mary Austin's *The Land of Little Rain* (desert), Rachel Carson's *Under the Sea Wind* (ocean), and Christiane Ritter's *A Woman in the Polar Night* (Arctic). Like *The Living Mountain*, these are all slim, powerful books that portray these places in ways that stretch one's perspective. Mountain, desert, ocean, Arctic: they all draw one simultaneously inward and outward, challenging one with existential questions and metaphysical musings.

What makes the mountain different? Perhaps it is simply that the mountain rises up, extends into another sphere closer to the larger cosmos, its summit's reach an essential and compelling characteristic. It may be that this form allows humans to find meanings in mountains that are not so easily ascribed to other inspiring landscapes; with an identifiable shape that creates an individual unit, the mountain may be perceived not only as a symbol but also as an entity, even an animated being. The Māori know the mountains as their ancestors.

That verticality also creates intriguing physical diversity with geologic narratives in stone, dramatic climatic and biotic gradients, and a challenging environment that affects visitors, climbers, and those who reside there. But the mountain's impact goes far beyond the physical: the reach into the heavens, the *elevated* vista, makes a difference to how the mountain is experienced. As Robert Macfarlane wrote, "Great height gives you greater vision: the view from the summit empowers you. But in a way, too, it obliterates you. Your sense of self is enhanced because of its extended capacity for sight, but it also comes under attack—is threatened with insignificance by the grand vistas of time and space which become apparent from a mountain-top."[6]

Through time and across the planet, the mountains' connection to the elevated realms has led people and cultures to draw significance from the peaks. As just one example, David Hinton describes the ancient Chinese philosophy associated with the heights in *Hunger Mountain*:

> Referring to [the Cosmos's] two most fundamental elements, they called it "heaven and earth," and they recognized in mountain

landscape its most dramatic manifestation, for they saw the generative powers of heaven and earth mingling there: heaven's male yang mingling with earth's female yin. Sky with its mist and cloud seethes down and vanishes among mountains, while mountains in turn vanish into that mist and cloud, only to reappear churning up into sky. This is a primary reason the ancients were perennially drawn to mountain landscapes—either as visitors wandering there and staying in mountain monasteries, or as recluses living among summits and ridgelines.[7]

More simply, Edwin Bernbaum's first sentence in the *Sacred Mountains of the World* states, "As the highest and most dramatic features of the natural landscape, mountains have an extraordinary power to evoke the sacred."[8] I would suggest "sacred" can be felt in many ways, without any religious context, a concurrent feeling of both insignificance and belonging within something greater than our own small, ephemeral lives.

Still, I believe there is more to the mountain beyond the awe arising from the immensity and stretch of space felt in many high places. That drama alone seems not enough to explain the Mountain. It seems the other direction may play an integral role, that the humbling vastness of the mountains is related to an awareness of the minuscule alongside the monumental and all the stretch between the two, micro to macro, the Mountain setting the seemingly delicate minutiae before one in an environment that can challenge as easily as delight, even as it pushes the infinite and eternal into sight. And there you sit within it.

Ecophilosopher Arne Næss mused upon this idea. After long observation of alpine flowers at his *hytte* (hut) in the Norwegian mountains, he wrote:

> A microcosmos... I have learned an admiration for the minute, to say it very simply: Where others see adversity, I see the Self-realization of tiny beings in nature.... There is a kind of equal status of organisms at extremely different levels of development. You see the tremendous importance of bacteria, or nonvertebrate animals. All these extremely beautiful one-celled animals, they get a prominent place

> in nature, and not just crocodiles and other spectacular animals. You get to appreciate the ecosystems, and you see yourself as part of these ecosystems. I found a kind of rational basis for this feeling of belonging to this rich world of animals and plants and rocks.[9]

This he found in the alpine rigors of Hallingskarvet.

On the day I stood on the peregrine's perch under the infinite stretch of sky, my feet rested on rock formed from minerals of stardust, decorated with the ancient life-form of lichen. That moment held tiny bones and a drop of blood nestled on the stone, ephemeral petals of delicate blossoms, the arc of a wing on a creature whose evolutionary lineage is much longer than humanity, all present in that single, solitary nanosecond when *wild* reached into me from the bird's hunter-eye, meshing outer and inner. Time and space collapsed, time and space stretched, cycles of life and death, the unity of micro to macro and all things in-between, an entire cosmos, just there, on the top of that mountain. At that ineffable moment, I felt as a participant in something greater than my self; I was nothing and everything, reduced yet belonging, one small part of a grand, mysterious whole.

In such moments, the Mountain presents the infinite fractal cosmos. This is why I have never left behind that moment with the peregrine, being a human who contemplates such things. Could such a feeling happen in other places? Yes. But nowhere else does one stand so close to the cosmos that surrounds this small planet as on top of the Mountain on a cloudless summer day, with all that it holds there at your feet and above your head.

Perhaps it is just this feeling—that mountains are grounded in our own earthly place even as they are hung from the sky—that allows the micro-to-macro spatiotemporal stretch to be so strongly felt; you can pick up the stone, hear the bird, smell the flower even as you look out and up and also *down* to the reaches below. It is there in those alpine and rocky expanses where earth brushes against sky, where mountains expose us to that unbounded realm even as a flower petal anchors us to the earth: it is there that many fall into a simultaneous sense of insignificance and of belonging. There on the Mountain is where the boundaries dissolve between stone and sky, and so it is the place that many of us find such a feeling, a knowing that we are part of the universal whole.

Why does this matter, this experience of connection and belonging that happens within the mountains? Through my own experience and in "conversation" with others (both personally and in literature), I've come to believe that any person or any culture who immerses in the micro-to-macro whole of the Mountain, sensing the unity from cellular to cosmic, material to metaphysical, is forever changed and will forever act with the compassion and grace necessary to protect not just the Mountain but beauty, wonder, life, and the earth our home. Arne Næss articulated why this is so, building on his thoughts included above and expanded in the last chapter of this book.

> Humans do not depend on nature by minding it, trying to dominate more and more and be less dependent; you see the dependence as a plus, because it means an interrelation, whereby you see yourself get to be tremendously greater, reaching from macroworld to microworld and back again. Feeling extremely small in the dimensions of the cosmos, you yourself get somehow widened and deeper, and you accept with joy this thing that others might perceive as a duty: to take care of the planet. The care of the planet becomes something joyful and not something that is done merely to survive.[10]

~~~

My own relationships with mountains have shifted and merged over my life, leading me to an appreciation for the diverse perspectives people and cultures have for the high places. In this, I have also gained a better understanding of the inherent conflicts that arise out of the different ways we think about mountains, the Mountain, and the natural world in general. It seemed there was a story to tell. After years of wrestling with journal entries and ideas, struggling to articulate what you now hold in your hand, the story took shape.

The premise of this book is simply stated, though as the above thoughts and following chapters might indicate, it is far from straightforward. I
~~~

hope to share how the character of mountains shapes our relationship with them, even as the way one relates to mountains is simultaneously shaped by other influences, including mentors, studies, culture, and experience, creating a sort of dialogue between people and mountains. What results are the many ways of "knowing" mountains. Yet it seems no matter how one interacts with the mountain, no matter what general perspective one has of the mountain, if that dialogue is allowed to carry out, then one finds that feeling of simultaneous insignificance and also a sense of belonging within a greater, interconnected "whole." That joyful sense of belonging is significant for today in a world facing numerous planetary crises, for it creates a desire to care for this planet and all that it holds.

It is because of that significance, alongside what I have experienced—moments like the day I stood in the alpine meadow with the peregrine, times where I intuitively and deeply felt what is at stake—that I felt compelled to write this book.

The journeys are not presented in a personal chronology. In the initial stages of developing the book, I realized my own ways of experiencing mountains fit into a sequence that reflected—both personally and culturally—a broader development of knowledge and evolution of understanding. The chapters are ordered based on that idea.

The foundation is set with chapter 1, "Beginnings: Montana." Here, I share the beginnings and evolution of my relationship with mountains, a connection rooted in the mountains surrounding our extended family's Montana property. From my youth spent partly in that place, I lived forward into different ways of perceiving and interacting with mountains.

The actual journeys into high places begin with chapter 2, "The Sacred Mountain," for understanding mountains as sacred is perhaps our most ancient way of knowing them. On a trek around the Māori sacred mountain Ngauruhoe in Tongariro, New Zealand, I immersed in the question of the sacred—how and why the mountain inspires such feelings. There, I encountered cultural tension, and the journey subsequently wrapped around another two questions: What does one culture's understanding of a mountain as sacred mean for someone of another culture? And how does one deal with cultural conflict that arises from different views about a particular mountain?

The rational scientific perspective is a fairly recent way of understanding the world that can (but does not always) exclude or even negate spirituality and the sacred. Chapter 3, "The Scientific Mountain," explores how mountains and their topographic and biological diversity advanced the natural sciences during the nineteenth century. Yet even at that time there were some—including Alexander von Humboldt—who believed science as an exclusive way of seeing may fail to comprehend the greater cosmos. In this chapter, I return to the Teton Range, the mountains where I completed the research for my master's degree, exploring how the mountain nurtures a worldview that merges the rational scientific with subjective, sensory, aesthetic, or even spiritual ways of knowing and why that is important.

Romanticism was a reaction against the purely rational and objective, a response to the Enlightenment and its rise of rationalism. Romantics emphasized the subjective, emotional, and creative, and so the sublime was a significant part of Romantic philosophy; mountains were known as places that inspired that intensity of feeling. Chapter 4, "The Romantic Mountain," finds me backpacking into Yosemite with John Muir's words as my guide. Muir, a man of Romantic persuasion, illustrates how the Romantic naturalist—who included the likes of William Wordsworth—allowed rational scientific inquiry and Romantic subjective perceptions to rest comfortably together in mind and spirit, an integrated worldview particularly apt for the mountain environment. Significantly, the Romantic naturalist celebrated the minuscule as much as the awesome, perhaps unlike many Romantic "tourists."

The Romantic movement opened up the mountains to Euro-American sensibilities, a freedom that nurtured solo mountain wanderings in people like Scottish naturalist Nan Shepherd (1893–1981). Such solo experience is not based on a movement (like Romanticism) or a practice (like science) and is an intimate and individual experience. In chapter 5, "The Solo Mountain," I follow the path of Nan Shepherd into the mountains of her homeland, experiencing how solo time within the mountain's extremes raises awareness and so can take one into a broader sense of being.

Chapter 6, "The Peopled Mountain," turns to a relationship with mountains that contrasts to other ways of being within mountains, for it is communal, the chapter exploring mountains as home as well as the character of mountain communities. Because of the demanding environments and seasons, traditional mountain communities lived closely tied to the cycles and resources of the land around them. Set in the Scottish Highlands where I had tried to make my Home, the chapter follows my yearning to live within a community connected to a mountain landscape, even as I made the decision to move to the high desert of the American Southwest.

All my ways of knowing came together while I walked beside Hallingskarvet Mountain, Norway. This was a journey that shifted my worldview, as related in chapter 7, "The Whole Mountain: Hallingskarvet, Norway." There in the demanding alpine environment, ecophilosopher Arne Næss mentored me with his words and ideas that I'd written into my notebook. As those different ways of knowing intertwined, I came to better understand how the Mountain can inspire a sense of wholeness and belonging, a kind of participation with the earth that nurtures that desire to care for all life and this planet.

~~~

This is a personal story folded around the mountains' stories, showing a bit of what those high places hold, from creation of rock to breath of bird to musings of humanity. In the end, the mountains are themselves, separate from what we make of them or what they make of us: they do not set out to challenge us physically or philosophically. Thus, I can write of mountain meanings, share the thoughts of others about the significance of the peaks, yet still there are many times I simply see the Mountain as something far beyond all that, an entity in and of itself. I've also come to know that much of what I write is merely alluding to what lies within the mountains, skimming over the depths. Peter Matthiessen explained these two connected ideas:
~~~

> The secret of the mountains is that the mountains simply exist, as I do myself: the mountains exist simply, which I do not. The mountains have no "meaning," they are meaning; the mountains are. The sun is round. I ring with life, and the mountains ring, and when I can hear it, there is a ringing that we share. I understand all this, not in my mind but in my heart, knowing how meaningless it is to try to capture what cannot be expressed, knowing that mere words will remain when I read it all again, another day.[11]

Here, I hope, is a sharing of experience that might serve as an invitation to think in different ways, to hold up the mountain and see it from different angles, and in so doing, perhaps to brush against the mountains' "ringing," expanding an understanding of not only mountains but the earth as a whole.

1
BEGINNINGS
Montana

Over 50 million years ago in what is now North America, tectonic motion created upheaval during the Laramide Orogeny, an oceanic plate smashing its way beneath a continental plate in such a way as to create an inland mountain range.

Orogeny is the word used to describe mountain formation, a term derived from the ancient Greek *óros* for mountain and *genesis* for creation. It is a new word, first used in the nineteenth century, a part of the human desire to label and name and so better understand, for one cannot begin to grasp the mountains without contemplating their conception. They are born from the earth and erode back into the earth on time scales we can imagine but not partake in.

In that great Laramide Orogeny, wrinkles and ripples became mountains and ridges forming the Rocky Mountain Range that stretches through the continent's interior from Mexico into Canada. Like mountain ranges across the globe, the intricate topography of this rugged swath is the foundation for diversity, holding life from minuscule to the unimaginable—forests and meadows, bear and wolf, pocket gopher and biting flies, flower and moss. In those high mountains, summers are relatively warm and dry, the winters extreme, the ocean too far away to buffer the weather.

Long before the Laramide Orogeny, shallow seas covered much of the land that is the modern state of Montana so that the uplift of the Rocky Mountains raised what had been an ocean floor toward the sky. Monument Mountain was born, its bedrock a 340-million-year-old fossiliferous limestone that was once a seabed. Myriad marine creatures are entombed in the rock that now underlies that rounded summit where the flowering meadow arcs against the blue of summer skies and a blanket of snow shudders under icy winds in the depths of winter. Monument, like other mountains, thus holds an earthly archive, the rocks and fossils a reminder of a span of time that reaches even beyond what can be deciphered from the mountain record. Yet in contrast to that eonian history, Monument's alpine life shifts swiftly with the seasons, demonstrating the undeniable ephemerality of existence.

The sweep of Monument's fleeting summer meadow is immediate and familiar; I've come to know what edge holds a carpet of alpine forget-me-nots just when the snow melts off, where the lupine grows in the height of the season, which slight swale has gathered enough soil to support a pocket gopher population. This is a mountain I've crossed in sun and in pounding hail, in joy and in sorrow, in intense stillness and in winds strong enough to knock a person over. This is the mountain where I perched with the peregrine.

Standing on Monument's summit, one looks across an ecologically diverse region of forest, subalpine, alpine, and subnival zones, a rich land inhabited by the full suite of precolonial wildlife. An intricately preserved fossil is stashed on that summit, a spiral shell of marine origin I once placed in a protected spot. Now when I reach the alpine meadow, I hold the stone shell, remembering its origins in ancient shallow seas even as I look across that region, playing my eyes over the rise and fall of the surrounding mountains, seeing the evidence of its twitching and upheavals, the slow folding and uplifting. I've traversed most of the valleys, ridges, and mountains within this viewshed, some places many times. I sense that geological story beneath my feet as I wander. The land feels alive.

Monument Mountain lies in the heart of my Montana homeland, rising behind our extended family's property close to Yellowstone National Park. This small ranch came into our family when Grandpa bought the place in the 1950s to raise quarter horses, and though it is no longer a working ranch, we've managed to keep it in the family. Wildlands stretch for many miles around, a rugged region that embraced me from my early years, providing a foundation for my thoughts and wanderings, always teaching, inspiring, provoking, leaving more questions than answers. This is the earth that raised me, the mountains that shaped me from the beginning in ways that mountains can—deeply. The influence of those high places melded into the other factors that are also part of the complexity of my life learnings, the mountains' teachings notably enhanced by what I learned from family.

In my early years, my father worked as an ecologist at Arizona State University, meaning that I grew up spending the school year in Tempe and summers in Montana. As my father's career advanced, the family's time in Montana decreased, even as the contrast between the Phoenix valley and the Montana mountains did its work on me. While in the city, I held the ranch in my mind, feeling the pull of the wildlands around that mountain home. My parents sensed this, and starting sometime in my middle school years, my parents started flying me to Montana soon after school ended to stay with Grandma and Grandpa. From then on into young adulthood, I would always have at least a few summer weeks alone with my grandparents.

Grandma was an artist, working mostly with clay, creating ceramics glazed with colors of the earth—pots, plates, vases, and more. She shared her creativity with her grandkids, taking us into her corner of the workshop to craft what seemed like small wonders to my eye; we threw pots on her pottery wheel, shaped mushrooms out of clay, painted little wooden birds that Grandpa had cut out of plywood. Grandma was a brave woman with a curious spirit and despite her deep fear of horses and heights, she would ride with my grandfather through the backcountry on her little dun mare, Habebah. I still remember her walking slowly from house to barn with hands clasped behind her back, mounting her horse and setting off, hands now wrapped tightly around the saddle horn.

Grandpa was born and raised in Belgium and merged European tastes into Montana ranch life, wearing western shirts with silk cravats, well-worked cowboy boots when he was outside and leather dress shoes indoors. He enjoyed his wine, liqueurs, and good food and fed the dogs at the table with his own fork. Grandpa could be severe and also playful, scolding us one day for something as benign as throwing grass in the pond (he believed it promoted algae growth) and the next day playing along during lunch on a family ride when we replaced his coffee candy with a carefully candy-wrapped moose turd; he would take that turd, unwrap it, and start it toward his mouth... until laughter broke the charade. Grandpa rode horses, ran the ranch, kept a library of books that lined the walls of the ranch house, discussed history and literature, and sat at the head of the table as the patriarch of the family when we were all together. Yet it was during those summertime moments when I was there without the rest of my family or other relatives that I began to know Grandpa on a different level and so know the ranch surrounds in a deeper way.

During those years, I did chores and various jobs for Grandpa, given such tasks as exercising horses, cleaning out the barn, oiling saddles. Grandpa bought only high-quality saddles and dozens of them hung in the barn, smelling sweetly of soft, sweat-stained leather. I would hang them on the corral fence on chilly June days, soap them clean, then work oil into the seat, the pommel, the straps, and the stirrup skirts. Some days Grandpa would send me off to ride the fence, looking for breaks that would be fixed by hired help later in the summer. In truth, I think Grandpa just wanted me out of the house and busy, for the fence seemed to stretch forever and would slowly dissipate into nothingness in the dense forests and steep slopes of the outer regions of the ranch, places a horse could not even go. Riding the fence was essentially impossible, but I always tried: a young teen, alone on a spirited horse, moving across rugged land and fighting through down timber, joyously making my way as best as I could. The world expanded.

The work never took up the whole day, and often Grandpa and I would ride to places he loved, sometimes just to the knoll behind the house to look for calypso orchids or down to the patch of forest where the pipsissewa first bloomed. Some days we set off on adventures, heading to places like the "petrified forest" across the river valley, where we would marvel at the petrified stumps. Other times we wandered through thick forests and fields to explore far past the ruin of a homesteader's chimney that was a shorter and more frequent destination.

Grandpa was no scientist, but he was an intellectual who studied the land and moved through it with awareness. His knowledge was that of the cycles and flows, which flowers bloomed where at what time of year, what birds would arrive in spring and when they would leave. He knew the terrain from exploring it, and as we rode together, he passed on his understanding of the place that was his home. We shared wildlife sightings, witnessed the blossoming of spring into summer, noted the coming and goings of the birds, and developed, I like to think, a mutual respect for each other, a bond strengthened by our love of that place.

Evenings were soft and slow in late spring and early summer, a time when the grass glows green, highlighted by the first buttercups and bright-yellow glacier lilies. It is a time of renewal, when life begins, sometimes ends, and warmth returns with the drip of a frozen bank into a muddy running stream, a time when the high mountains are still snow packed and wildlife stays at lower elevations, frequently around the ranch. On those evenings, I would help Grandma get dinner on the table before we sat together, my grandparents and I, to eat and watch the world outside the window. Elk grazed in the front pasture and a mother moose often appeared with red gangly twins at her side, settling in to nibble on the front lawn. Once, a large grizzly bear came to play in the sprinkler, delighting in the spray that squirted his face and spewed in different directions as he waved a mighty paw through the scattering drops. When we finished our evening meal, Grandpa would get his yellow Cadillac and we would go for a drive to look for other animals. We always saw a variety of happenings in the golden light at the end of day.

After Grandpa and I returned from the drive, I would sit with Grandma on the couch, sipping tea, watching the view, the expanse of mountains and fields that was her home. Grandma also loved that land, writing of it, painting it, taking its colors and glazing them into the pots she formed. By my high school years, physical art was fading from her hands, but it never left her mind. I remember the evenings, when snow still clung in the mountain crevices, when Grandma waved her hands as alpenglow draped pink over the dark cliffs.

"Alpenglow. See it?"

"Yes, Grandma."

"The best time of day," she would say as her hands waved in the air, stroking, painting, creating masterpieces that merged her mind with the mountains.

Out the front windows, the sun would throw its last rays across the offset symmetry of the panorama. I can tell you that one of those mountains consists of 50-million-year-old volcanic mudflows perched over sedimentary rock, that others are Eocene tuffs and breccias, that the last in the array is an igneous intrusive. And I can tell you that the golden evening light of summer plays across those andesitic cliffs, dropping long shadows across the rock to contrast the shimmer of the last glinting rays on the highpoints. I can tell you that it is beautiful, for Grandma's way of seeing wove into my awareness of the land, a lesson in Beauty's depths. It is a way of seeing the mountains not through rational eyes but through the senses and the soul, a way that nurtures deep connections, even as it opened me to an understanding of other peoples' connections and other cultures' bonds with the mountains as I moved forward in life.

I spent much of those summer days in the company of my grandparents, yet there were times when Grandpa did not ride, when Grandma was absorbed in her book, and I finished my chores early. Those were the days I walked into the wildlands of the designated wilderness area behind the ranch, often without a destination. I set off up a trail, off the trail, into the woods, across a ridge. I wandered and journeyed, the world mine to discover during sweet summer days when there seemed no distinct boundary between our lives and the natural world around us. Sometimes I yearn for the innocence of those years, the time before I'd read so much about Nature versus Culture, dichotomies, and disconnects; when I did not have to wrestle with terms such as *wilderness*, which implies a pristine, uninhabited land; when I did not have to face the dispossession of the people who came before or realize how everywhere on this planet is now threatened by our actions. For a few halcyon years, I lived in peace within the embrace of loving family and wild ways. They did not conflict.

It was years later when I was living in Bozeman that Grandpa died. Grandma and Grandpa lived on the ranch in their later years, and I still spent as much time as possible there with them, only an hour's drive from town. On one visit, I arrived to find Grandpa hunched in Grandma's wheelchair, facing the door leading outside as if wanting to leave.

His face was gaunt, his shoulders slouched. He looked up and seemed puzzled to see me.

I talked quietly. I did what I could. The last slide had come suddenly, that day perhaps, when the caretakers had left to visit their families, and I had only just arrived to take their place. I stayed in the guest room of my grandparents' house rather than our own family's separate cabin, wanting to be there for Grandma as much as Grandpa. I slept listening to ghosts and pipes clunking, until my parents arrived from Arizona and took Grandpa and Grandma into a nursing home in Bozeman.

The nursing home called me six weeks later, around 11:00 p.m. A major stroke. I spent the rest of the night in the room with Grandma and Grandpa, curled on a cot in the corner pretending to sleep to give them privacy during that last long quiet meeting of two people who loved each other. I didn't know it at the time, but to be there listening to Grandma's soft voice sharing stories of their life together, sharing love, talking slowly through the long hours of the night, even as Grandpa lay motionless (though I hold to the fact he heard every word), forever shifted how I remember them. They now rest in my mind not just as grandparents but also as strong-willed individuals, a spirited couple, people who gave their time and love to a granddaughter who didn't fit into the mainstream even then. And so they changed my life.

Grandpa waited and did not slip away until the next day when Dad arrived from Arizona to sit at his side. Grandma stayed in the nursing home for the remainder of her life. I visited her frequently. I was there with her the morning of the day she too passed on, leaving this world in the early afternoon hours.

There's a photo of Grandpa hanging on the wall near the breakfast table where the three of us ate so many meals together, taken a few years before he died. Grandpa is sitting on his horse, waving his battered cowboy hat at the camera, the mountains behind him. His face is lined with character and joy, his hand rests on the saddle, and his smile says he is at Home.

~~~
~~~

My parents gave me an understanding of that mountainous land in their own ways. My mother was a true naturalist, a person with a passion for the natural world. She was from the east, marrying into the Patten family in her twenties. Montana was a new land, with new flora, new fauna, and unknown country; she set about getting to know the place, the flowers and wildlife, the way of the earth. As I grew older, we hiked together, and she taught me to see and ask questions, to wander and roam. She gave me freedom, allowing me to set out on my own at an early age, gifting me the ability to be comfortably alone in wild places, even as she made learning a joyful part of exploring the mountains.

I recall one summer day when Mom and I walked side by side amid the alpine bloom of Monument Mountain, counting colors, each hue indicating a species, diversity proclaimed with varied tints and tones.

"Here," Mom said, dropping to her knees. "It's one of those *Pedicularis* flowers."

The blossom was a head of maroon flowers arranged in a whirling pattern, thus the name we'd created for the plant: the pinwheel flower.[1] We poked and prodded the plant that stood only about nine inches high, inspecting its petals, bracts, and leaves in the way shown to us in the local alpine plant identification class we'd just taken together. Sure enough, it was *Pedicularis cystopteridifolia*.

"*Pedicularis cystopterididida*." Mom laughed.

I tried: "*Pedicularis cystopididterida*..."

We chuckled, giggled, tried again until we got it. "*Pedicularis cystopteridifolia*." And again: "*Pedicularis cystopteridifolia*!" We chanted it to remember it, another mountain plant learned together with joy and exuberance, another plant in our vocabulary of understanding.

Dad was the scientist, the ecologist, the one who put bits and pieces of the natural world into datasets that told a story. He came from a line of holistic thinkers, ecologists who saw an organismic whole in natural communities, using the language of science to say what poets and lyrical prose writers have declared to a wider audience, such as Muir's oft-stated fact that "when we try to pick out anything by itself, we find it hitched to everything else in the Universe." My father inspired me to find the connections, see the patterns, think beyond scenery, even as he taught me the names of trees and other species, both common and Latin. Pointing across a valley, he would ask, "Which tree is that?" knowing the habitat and shape of the tree would reveal its species.

"Douglas fir!" I would reply, or "Whitebark pine!" ever so pleased when I got it right and laughing with Dad as he tutored me when I didn't know.

Hearing my father's stories of his summer days of research in the backcountry and his memories of riding horseback through that Montana landscape to collect data, it became obvious: I would be an ecologist, a career where you could get on a horse and take off into the mountains. Years later, this dream found Dad helping me design a college independent study that put me in the midst of Montana wildlands collecting my own data for the first time. It wasn't as glamorous as I imagined, but it suited me just fine; locating my randomly selected sample points marked on the map meant hiking far off the trails, into places that felt as if no other human had walked there before.

Those early summers of my life also held good family times: backpacks, long day hikes, short saunters, horseback rides into distant valleys, evenings on the porch. On a family backpack, I first stood on a high summit completely alone, having moved ahead of the others. The moment remains in memory—the awe, the expanse, the Mountain leaving an indelible mark.

My youth was blessed by experience in that Montana homeland, my connection to that place deepened because of those who guided me into it when I was young, a time when mind, heart, and soul were open to such a gift. Grandpa, Grandma, Mom, Dad: intellectual outdoorsman, artist, energetic amateur naturalist, kind and patient holistic ecologist. They were my grounding in Place, sharing their knowledge and experience, with no borders between their perspectives, a bit of everything contained in each person. Those mentors were my first path of received knowledge, their teachings gently molding my own way of seeing the world as I grew older. They cultivated my constant curiosity and desire to understand the complexity of things and events by weaving together different ways of knowing, from science to art, philosophical to spiritual. I soaked in their teachings and guidance and lived my way into an instilled awareness honed by unbridled wanderings through a wilderness that is wild and free, where the mountainous earth became a teacher in and of itself.

~~~

Yellow mule's ear blossomed along the edge of the meadow, bright amid the spring flush of brilliant green. I walked with the lightness of the season, taking in colors so welcome after the winter months. Looking for flowers, I spotted an elk calf tucked beneath a sagebrush, its small head protruding from under the bush, tiny ears pressed flat against the skull, eyes wide and moist, catching a glint of the sun. I had stumbled on calves before, usually better hidden, tucked away below a juniper bush or in dense grass, away from the questing rays of light. Always they lie motionless, their way of evading passing predators. I skirted the spot where the young ungulate lay, presumably put there by its mother.

This calf was not well concealed, its head, front legs, and still-soft hooves lying visibly in the open. Looking closer, my chest tightened. I stepped back, then forward, approaching the calf that would not mind my presence, for it was only that head and those front legs, plus a few shards of spine and bits of tattered flesh that remained of the once-living creature. It lay still in death. The eyes that held sunlight glinted, as if asking a question.

A long pause. A slow breath. I moved on, passing through a stand of pine to look down into a broad open pass that leads into a valley to the north, a place frequently traversed by wildlife. Within that meadow a grizzly bear browsed, head down, shoulders humped, large paws delicately plowing up the ground with great claws. Moving slowly, the grizzly methodically harvested vast numbers of spring beauty tubers while chomping on glacier lily blossoms and stirring anthills to lick the ants from his paw, adding plant and insect matter to the elk meat settled comfortably in its belly. The sight stirred an adrenaline surge, a small quick gasp. Assessing the situation, I gauged the lengthy distance between us, noted that the bear had no cubs and seemed intent on its foraging. But one does not linger in a grizzly's presence, so I moved off in a different
~~~

direction after one last quick look to absorb the lumbering grace of the large omnivore who is integral to the ecology of the area.

I knew of that ecological significance, but the bear seemed like more than a keystone species, more than just bear-as-part-of-ecosystem, for the grizzly and the shattered remains of the elk calf were now one and the same. Such a meeting with mortality is the land's mentoring, a vivid encounter holding lessons. There is the age-old story of predator-prey, where death for one means life for others: well-fed, the bear walks on, while raven and beetle pick clean the elk calf's head and bits of bone and flesh decompose into the soil where roots take up nutrients, and the calf also moves on, recycled. Yet such experiences illuminate a deeper complexity to the ecosystem beyond the complicated everyday occurrence of eat and be eaten, revealing the yin-yang, harsh-beautiful, ferocious-tender natural world, the agonizingly beautiful rhythms of earth's life with its mystery of existence, of birth, of death, even our own consciousness of *being* as the ancient instinctual fear rises on encountering a grizzly, the scene expanding beyond that moment into something larger. And one intuitively senses the bear and calf were always one.

Such powerful experiences in the wildlands do not fade. One does not lock eyes with a wolf in reciprocal awareness—not once, more than twice—without being changed.

I will not tell of the most potent times. They hold too much that cannot be conveyed. These are things that cannot be fully absorbed from a book, a word, or anything but the raw essence of experience. They might fall within Gary Snyder's thoughts about the sacred, that "*sacred* refers to that which helps take us (not only human beings) out of our little selves into the whole mountains-and-rivers mandala universe."[2] Such experiences are not specific to mountains, but such things shape a person's view and may open up that sense of the sacred, taking one out of the human bubble, so when the mountain lifts your eyes upward, you see something beyond a peak to climb.

It need not be grizzlies or wolf eyes that situate me within the mandala universe. Not all things hold such outward drama; ongoing smaller events, the seemingly lesser things that weave into the world, become part of what one sees through immersion and time in natural places, revealing their stature of importance. My wanderings are replete with the magic of the minuscule, like the day that was so quiet I could hear an ant dragging a dead insect down the dry trail, the audible scuffle of a creature whose presence is integral to its forest habitat, one small bit of a perpetually seething life that supports the charismatic megafauna and the stunning events that indelibly mark one's memories. Mountain landscapes hold their larger drama in full view, there to see in the rise of a peak, even as the intricacy of the mountain terrain makes such places rich with smaller joys and concealed wonders.

I find it easier to perceive that "magic of the minuscule" when traveling solo. My senses open and awareness sharpens when I journey alone and can get out of my head and escape the "surface ways"[3] that so easily envelop us. Walk quietly and solo through wild land and the place will speak to you, not in words we can directly understand—though I've had many a conversation with elk, jay, fox, and raven, to name but a few—but in a language of senses and intuitions, sometimes subtle, often overt, occasionally brutal. The surroundings are often experienced in a different way when one is solitary, the concealed revealed.

~~~

In those early years, as I walked and watched, sat and mused, the land and its life did nothing but carry on with its doings, even as it provided teachings that I absorbed through time. Yet there is no separating that experience from the factual rational knowledge I gathered from my mentors as well as my studies.

I have always had a curiosity about the natural world, craving knowledge and understanding. I book-learned and field-studied so that I knew the facts about the natural world, acquiring familiarity with both species and the processes bound up in geology and ecology, the intricacy of the food web, and the complexity of material and energy flows. Such information contributed to a better understanding of what was happening around me as I moved within the country around the ranch, informing such moments as the sighting of that grizzly bear. That factual learning intertwined with my experience, catalyzing a deep sense
~~~

of wonder—a feeling of amazement approaching awe that such things exist or can happen. This inspired a desire to learn more as the natural world opened its secrets and in so doing opened my mind beyond the rational. This is a beautiful cycle of expanding understanding, where factual knowledge sparks wonder, wonder motivates a desire for more understanding, and one is back to the books or asking questions, and the wonder grows, and so one is enmeshed on a lifetime journey of beautiful discovery.

My desire for understanding led me along my planned ecologist pathway: a master's degree with fieldwork in the Grand Tetons and a PhD with research in Kenya. Eventually, dissertation demands combined with health issues led me away from campus and back to Montana. I finished my dissertation sitting in the ranch cabin, looking at the mountains, leaving time each day to hike, walk, remember who I am. Once a week I felt the curve of Monument Mountain beneath my feet, renewing the ties and reviving the spirit of Place that resides within. Looking into a future beyond the doctoral degree, the realization came: I could not leave this region. Montana would be my permanent home. I sought professional work in nearby Bozeman.

Perhaps if I'd landed a different academic position, one that allowed me to pursue the intricacies of the natural world in ways I believed in, I would still be a research ecologist. As it was, the numbers and data and sheer distance from the actual earth drove me out of the position I held at Montana State. I was hired to contribute to research that modeled potential vegetation changes over time for around twelve million acres of the Greater Yellowstone Ecosystem, the region with Yellowstone Park at its core. None of the research allowed a moment to see, smell, touch, hear the actuality of the world we studied. Computer programs, satellite data, formulas in a spreadsheet: the natural world was nothing but numbers and models, a feeling of wonder best not expressed within those particular academic cloisters.

I believe in science, but something always pulls me out and away from that path or leads me to reach out and pull philosophy, art, history, spirituality into that path. But to *be* a scientist didn't allow for that, requiring a certain way of presenting and dealing with information that left me feeling claustrophobic. I left the university, moved to a ski resort community close to the ranch, and went to work as a naturalist, guide, and Nordic ski instructor.

Still the learning was done, that academic knowledge woven into my understanding. Scientific information continues to enhance the beauty of the world around me, providing insights and inspiring wonder without contradicting other ways of knowing. In fact, I have found that its objectivity and factual grounding complement more subjective and intimate perspectives.

There was a dialogue developing: my experience and life outside of the mountains contributing to my experience within the mountains. The Mountain was there, part of the conversation, always a force behind my shifting perceptions of mountains, life, and being.

~~~

The mountains and the ranch were close by during those years of living in the ski resort town, always alluring, always calling. My walks were long, sometimes with friends, sometimes with Mom, strengthening the human bonds. Yet most often those long wanders were solo, days where distance didn't matter and twenty or more miles would pass underfoot with ease, still with time to absorb the surroundings. Those solitary times were often deep times—like the day I hiked far out beyond the top of Monument Mountain.

Monument Mountain stands not only as a bald face at the head of the watershed but also as the rounded beginnings of an undulating ridge that snakes through the wilderness beyond in a series of waves, peaks, and passes marching across the skyline. From that ridge, there is no obvious sign of human habitation, no mark of civilization, even the vague trail along the rocky crest maintained by mountain goat feet rather than Forest Service employees. One midsummer day I walked that ridge out to one of the low points draped between the peaks. Perhaps it was the angle of the light on the dun-colored rocks, or perhaps I had captured a search image in my brain, but on that particular day, I frequently noted the many fossils under my feet—coin-sized indentations,
~~~

raised spirals, ridged shells, tiny discs—all remnants of another time, preserved bodies of 340-million-year-old creatures that lived their life under the sea. I ran my fingers over the fossils, wondering at the fact that the rock I touched was once the bottom of an ocean, even the rippling of water preserved in some of the stone's structure. And now I stood far above timberline.

Below a low point in the ridge, a hanging valley held a small lake glittering turquoise blue with meltwater. I decided to drop down and make my way to the lake, where grassy shores might provide a pleasant place to rest. The route from ridge to water is not simple: a steep slope of talus and cliff, slippery stones over hard pan where a boot can't grab purchase. I had done it before and set off without trepidation and maybe not as much care as is required in such environments.

Working my way down the steep slope, my foot slipped, and I fell sideways, breaking my fall with an outstretched hand. The jagged limestone bit into the side of my palm and split open the flesh. Blood poured onto the rocks, bright red against beige. I looked at the blood spilling over stone, squeezed the palm tight-closed and raised my arm to slow the bleeding. Carefully, awkwardly, I continued to the lake where the serene surface mirrored the jagged ridge above.

Crouched on the grassy bank, I rinsed the cut in icy water, swishing my hand back and forth, watching the blood tinge the water red. Ripples fanned out across the lake, carrying the blood away, tiny waves that looked like moving images of the petrified ripples in the rocks above. I made myself look at the cut, finding it not terribly deep, revealing what seemed to be fat globules but not bone. Then the blood welled up again, and the inner workings of my hand disappeared in the red pool. Again, I rinsed the cut free of blood so I could observe the strange things that exist inside of me, realizing that I am more familiar with the rocks and ridges of that land than the inside of my own body.

I changed my focus, looking up to the high ridge overhead with its cracked and jumbled layers of rock holding their fossils and sea striations. I stood alone in the heart of that massif, a land of twisted formations and intricate folds, a mountain that was once a sea looming above as my hand, cut by the fragment of an ocean floor, dripped blood onto the dirt, red liquid sinking into brown earth. That ridge rose solid overhead, a tangible object with a history that I could relate from the Paleozoic onward, yet despite all that explicable, concrete matter, there was the sense of sliding into smallness even while expanding outward without bound, a feeling of true awe—wonder on the one side, dread on the other—a feeling inspired by the mountains, by the unknown, by the sublime.

There are times I feel I have left little pieces of myself tucked away in the niches of that mountain land. To visit those places is to feel complete. There are also times when I am left standing in the wild with only the harsh thumping of my heart as an anchor. The natural world is a tangible place of solid stone and identifiable species yet still holds mysteries we haven't solved and inspires spirit in ways we can't explain. It presents, ever so eloquently, the question of our place on this planet. What significance can a person find, standing alone, bloody, at the base of a ridge that holds the seas and sky within its stone, surrounded by flourishing plants and animals, none of which cares a whit about that person's simple being?

I had lived into that moment from youth onward, as experience accumulated and merged with mentoring and studies. In those years after I left the university, what I sensed of intangibles and what I felt of unseen elementals slipped into what I factually learned. The witnessing and awareness threaded inward in strengthening connections, creating hints of understanding and occasional insights, even as it led to deep questioning. I knew the stretch of time needed to create the world around me, could relate the geologic processes and the ecological complexities, but the rational, objective knowledge of the concrete world didn't stop there, for it sparked an intuited sense of the mysteries we cannot fully know. The Mountain was integral to that sense, the Mountain on whose highest sweeps of grand expanse something shifted to create a sense of unity and belonging, both within the natural community and also within a larger whole. I could not quite grasp what that fully meant, but standing within an expansive alpine meadow that resonates with the energy of life, standing at the base of that Mountain that day of the cut hand, I felt closer to that *whole* than anywhere else—a personal but far from unique response.

~~~

The years I spent in the resort town were rich, yet something seemed missing from life, something Grandma had shown me in her own way when she was alive, something I found in her journals after her passing: a need for community to share ideas, art, life. My good friends and my mother provided some of that, but still I did not thrive in the resort environment. I spent most of my time living on the ranch before deciding to go back to graduate school in the Environmental Studies writing program at the University of Montana (UM). It would provide an education in the humanities as well as a writing community. It would mean living in the relatively large city of Missoula. I am not a city person.

The day I started my application, I took a break to hike the hill that rises above the ranch. Gray, wet skies hung low over the valley, and the bright new grass of early spring contrasted with bare red earth yet to blossom with growth, moisture heightening the colors. A newly dropped elk antler lay on the crest of the hill. I draped it over my shoulders to bring back to the cabin. Elk grazed on the hilltop meadow, thundering off as I turned the corner, the hollow beating of their hooves echoing in the stillness of the overcast day. The smell of musk and blood from the antler under my hand mixed with the scent of earth. Below, I could see the valley with our small cabins nestled at the base of the slope. Place and wild merged into a knowing of Home, a deep comfort of belonging, so different from that sense of greater belonging felt in the alpine.

I finished the application. But before I found the courage to mail it, knowing it would take me away from that Home, I went back and read Grandma's journals,[4] seeking guidance, finding the wisdom I needed in her words. It was as if she were giving me her blessing.

I'd like to talk to Grandma, to ask her about this life lesson: that I can't live in isolation, wander the ridges alone with the wind, listen to the elk bugle, feel the rhythm of the seasons, and pull the quilt of wildlands over my head and call my life complete. The ranch was Home in almost every sense of the word except community, for it was fairly isolated at the time.
~~~

Home. I'd like to talk to Grandma about Home as more than a residence and how that valley and surrounding mountains become embedded in your being, forever to *be* Home, something I would hold throughout my life, even as I moved temporarily to Missoula, and later in life as I moved away from the mountains altogether and planted myself in the desert.

She'd probably chuckle, point her long bony finger at me, and say, "That's very nice, dear. But what does that have to do with my life?"

~~~

Living within a culture is a bit like living within the atmosphere—we are often not aware of the air we breathe unless it blows by and knocks on our skin. There are cultural influences all around that shape how we experience things, what we are taught, what questions we ask, what beauty we see, what we value in the land, and what the Mountain means to us. Culture shapes values, which in turn shape action, including how we treat the earth we dwell within. This is not to say culture is an inescapable dictator, for its sway only goes as far as we allow—which is why travel and immersions in other cultures can be an awakening, teaching the traveler as much about their home culture as the new land they are in.

Going back to grad school increased my awareness of cultural influences on our thought in ways that a science degree never could. It wasn't just the formal course work but interacting with faculty and fellow students who had different backgrounds, different experiences, different mentors that showed me things, lifting veils and drawing back the curtain on the stage of human complexity. Inspired by good years at UM, I continued at Montana State University for a second PhD in environmental history, with minors in American West history and cultural geography. I passed my comprehensive exams and ended the degree with an ABD (all but dissertation); I'd started adjunct teaching at UM shortly after passing comps and didn't need to sweat all the way through another degree to pursue a teaching career. The 2008 recession ended that dream and essentially ended my academic career. Out of a job, I
~~~

moved to the ranch, which became my permanent address and my residence most of the time for well over a decade. Home.

But again, the learning was done, and those years of intense study in the humanities shifted my view of the world. I had learned facts and concepts from Marxist theory to the history of national parks, added words like *cultural construction*, *problematize*, and *dialectic* to my common vocabulary. More significantly, I learned about the unfolding of human interactions with the environment, what shapes our thinking, what can drive people's actions. I discovered that even the wildest-seeming lands around me are cultural landscapes, altered and influenced by a mélange of humanity, the designation of such landscapes as "wilderness areas" a human act built on values that shape those places on the earth. I became *consciously* aware of the deep influence of culture; we may learn through experience, mentors, and study, yet it is all filtered through culture.

I stand on the top of Monument Mountain as a United States citizen who has spent a vast majority of my life in the American West, a quirky conglomerate culture of subcultures and subcultures of subcultures, people with disparate views and relationships to the earth. I stand on that summit and look across the outcome of the American West culture and its ideologies, across a region with vast amounts of federal land "owned" by the public, across private land where landowners decide the fate of their "own" slice of earth. All of it is managed, modified, and used by people of diverse perspectives—preservationists, conservationists, recreationists, walkers, trail bikers, skiers, developers, spiritualists, wanderers, moneymakers, philanthropists, hunters, poachers—all carrying their beliefs and values as they encounter the land. The diversity of knowledge and experience refracts into a rainbow of beliefs, many of which clash.

It must be noted there is a void in this array of humanity: beneath that modern overlay is a deep history of the Indigenous people brutally decimated and removed by incoming Euro-Americans. Their culture haunts this particular landscape, those native people pushed out of the area into distant reservations.

Euro-Americans now dominate the region viewed from that mountaintop, and for the most part this populace looks to the mountains as beneficial, even glorious, some venturing into the high places to experience magnificent moments and ecstatic freedoms, find a sense of spirituality, even encounter something akin to the divine. While in grad school, I learned this was not always so, that mountains were once denigrated, even loathed by European societies, seen as products of the Flood, warts, evil. Things changed, mountains becoming revered as the eighteenth- to nineteenth-century Romantic movement unfolded. Romantics found the sublime in the land, in the earth itself. They went to those places that made you feel small, the places where time stretched, space expanded; they went to the uncomfortable places, far from the pastoral easy domesticated controlled places. There they faced an infinity beyond human control, beyond human existence, and so approached the divine. A cultural movement—the Romantic movement—had changed the way Europeans experienced the mountains: culture affecting perception, swaying experience, shaping actions.[5]

There is a thread of thought in the academic world of environmental history that our Euro-American appreciation and emotional response to expansive,[6] wild places is therefore a cultural construction, that we are "taught" to value landscapes that evoke awe, even terror, tutored by the likes of poets Wordsworth, Shelley, and Keats and painters Bierstadt, Church, and more.[7] I followed that thread, listening to the historians and grad students within the department, examining my own connections to wildlands, wildlife, the nonhuman, the earth. I learned from it and could see that, yes, we are a product of our culture. I scowled as I learned, for in those discussions there seemed a neglect of other cultures who revered mountains for millennia—Asian cultures, Indigenous cultures—and a complete oversight in terms of the ultimate mentor: experience. This is not true across all of academia or with all those who think about these things, and perhaps it was simply that it was never part of our discussions, but it seemed that it certainly should have been.[8]

One of my graduate seminars on Nature and the sublime took up this idea of the influence of culture, the role of the Romantics in "teaching" a certain view of mountains. As the conversation ebbed and flowed around me, memories and images came to mind: my first time solo on a high peak; standing by a turquoise lake, dripping blood; the eye of a wolf; the scent of an alpine meadow. These experiences and all the feelings they wrought might be viewed in the Romantic terms of standing before the face of God, or more simply, encountering the divine; it all fit neatly into the Romantic sublime, awe threaded with a ripple of fear. Yet my "sublime" moments were not taught: I went seeking nothing of the sort, had originally gone into the mountains without any knowledge of Romantic sublimity. The Mountain and its life rose up to meet me and showed me various angles of its mystique, showed me the depth of time, providing a gateway to the expansive cosmos that stretches out and out. I am not alone in this: mountaineers bent on conquest have had their perspective shifted by similar *experience*, not so much by culture.

I came away from all that schooling thinking that no philosophy or cultural construction, no poet, or painter, or academic treatise could provide the depth of connection and deep understanding of mountains I found in my Montana homeland and developed in other places over time. Those all contribute to learning but cannot and never have conveyed anything like what I found through experience. To walk in the wilds by choice rather than confront it by necessity may be a luxury allowed by modern life and enjoyed by modern cultures, but the entirety of what the Mountain holds cannot be *taught* by Western society; it is more than a cultural construction.[9]

I know what I've seen, and I know what I've felt long before I set foot on a university campus.

The Mountain is a powerful mentor.

~~~

The mountains had shown me their different facets—sacred, scientific, Romantic, home—even as their physical and existential qualities filtered into my way of knowing on a broader level. Still, I was left with
~~~

the feeling there was something more that I wanted—needed—to better understand. What I'd felt in the heights, I wanted to explore; what I intuited there on the lakeshore with blood dripping, I wanted to hold in my hand, unwrap my fingers and find it in my palm, not an unknown but a *known* unknown. It had to do with more than the mountains, perhaps a hope to understand the significance of a deep connection to the earth. Perhaps. As Matthiessen said, "I admitted that I did not know. How could I say that I wished to penetrate the secrets of the mountains in search of something still unknown?"[10]

I set off exploring, heading to New Zealand, to Scotland, traveling beyond the States and into a larger planet, carrying thoughts about our human relations with the natural world, holding a yearning to know how we as humans might belong within the natural world and the greater community of life, how we might participate in the wonder, the beauty, the mystery that we can only intuit. Within those queries were deeply personal questions about my own life: how I might find a sense of belonging as a member of a species who has become increasingly disconnected, disengaged, removed, and even destructive in its relationship to the earth. And why is that so important? To hold a sense of belonging, not just to community but to a larger world beyond humanity? So many of us feel this yearning, as if it flows through what it means to be human. It seems this sense of belonging can grow out of connection to a particular Place that shapes one's worldview. In my case, it was a mountain Place—and so my travels took me to the mountains.

Exploring these questions, I started to follow in the path of naturalists who were deeply connected to a distinct landscape, people like John Muir in Yosemite, Nan Shepherd in the Cairngorms, Arne Næss on Hallingskarvet. Before trekking into their Places, I read, learned, recorded, and transcribed the thoughts of those I followed into a notebook that went into my pack, staying with me for the ten nights, eleven days I spent in the Place of their belonging. To have their ideas with me was to have a wise person speak to me of the surrounds, revealing a riddle of truth while I engaged with the unfamiliar place that was always somehow familiar through features of earth, plants, and animals. I was compelled to contemplate—pushed, pulled, till thought dissolved into deeper understanding. And then I glimpsed that known unknown, an intuited perception of something beyond what we can actually know.

During every such trek, as I felt a slow shifting that brought deeper intimacy with the earth's community, there came insights into why connection to a Place is significant on a much larger scale than just enriching the lives of us wanderers out communing with the wilds. I came to see that many different perspectives—mountain paths, if you will—lead toward a sense of belonging within a greater whole and how that matters.

This I found in my journeys in high places. This is what I share in the following chapters. Of course, I can only narrate through my own worldview, shaped and molded by received knowledge and my own mountain experience, especially the Montana region. I am forever grateful to have lived in that place where I had the chance to perch with a peregrine on an ancient seabed in a glorious alpine meadow and look into a hunter's eye.

2

THE SACRED MOUNTAIN

Tongariro, New Zealand

Ngauruhoe looms overhead, its summit cloaked in cloud. Dark streaks of solidified lava run down the volcano's flanks, holding the memory of motion in their rumpled, twisted surfaces. Below the mountain, the land bears the mark of heated upheaval: knotted black-rock sculptures strewn across lumpy foothills, cliffs of igneous columns, ramparts of lava old enough to hold a bit of soil. Vegetation is sparse, with small islands of scrubby growth where the thin soil allows, woolly fringe moss carpeting the space between grass tussocks and introduced Scottish heather. The moss is bleached gray, its mats holding decaying alpine daisies whose season has passed. Examined closely, the moss reveals dense fibers, squiggly thick like a sea plant, with only a hint of green below their thicket of wool, a surreal plant that oddly fits in this lean, rocky land of little hue. There are no trees around Ngauruhoe. There is no shade except for that made by rock and cloud.

A clear stream runs through the valley below the volcano, grass clumps and a few white flowers dappling its rocky edges. A different moss, brilliant green, clings to the stones that litter the streambed. The water is cool when cupped in my hands and washed across my face, refreshing to my bare feet immersed in the flow, boots and sweaty socks set aside. A pipit, or pīhoihoi in the native language, perches and bounces on a midsize boulder amid the moist oasis. The bird has captured my attention, my view narrowed to that immediate life so vibrant in the spare land. The pipit flits off upstream, and I am left with plant, rock, the purity of water flowing over my toes, and a volcano above. The cone of Ngauruhoe is not far from where I sit, clouds embracing its heights. I have yet to learn it breathes steam like a living being.

I've come to New Zealand for a few months, to walk, to travel, to be within another land and listen to its heartbeat. This walk in Tongariro National Park is the first trek of my journey, a four-day walk around the volcano Ngauruhoe, with three nights in comfortable Department of Conservation (DOC) backcountry huts: Mangatepopo Hut, Oturere Hut, and Waihohonu Hut. *Hut* is a misleading term on the New Zealand Great Trails, as the well-maintained buildings provide gas stoves and bunks; you need only bring your food, pots, and bedding.

On this first day of my trek, I walked about nine kilometers from Whakapapa Village, following a rutted and eroded trail through tussock plains to Mangatepopo Hut. The walk in was quiet, peaceful, contemplative, with only a few hikers passing me on their way out and one energetic young woman bouncing by on her way in. Reaching the hut midday, I picked a bunk, laid out my sleeping bag, and left my pack to explore the trail I will follow tomorrow, walking slowly out toward Ngauruhoe, who towers at the edge of the hot, flat land. Such meanderings are integral to my New Zealand journey. One could easily walk the forty-three-kilometer circuit in fewer days, but I came to engage with this terrain, to saunter and sit, watch the birds, examine the plants, consider the volcanic landscape. I came to immerse.

What I immerse in is sacred land. Only after deciding to walk this circuit did I learn this. Only recently did I come to understand how deeply the people of this region are connected to the land around me.

I look up toward Ngauruhoe, knowing the mountain is *tapu*, sacred, and consider this holy nature, and wonder, *What does this mean? To be sacred? What does it mean for me, a traveling, trekking Euro-American visitor?* The dark mountain rises above.

This is not an old peak in geologic terms; only around 100 million years ago the Tongariro volcanoes were born—like the Rockies of my homeland—out of the earth's wandering plates. A chunk of continental crust broke away from the supercontinent Gondwana, birthing the new continent of "Zealandia," which drifted, stretched, and thinned, the plate becoming less buoyant, slowly sinking to leave only a portion above the ocean. The mostly submerged Zealandia eventually came to lie across two tectonic plates, the Pacific and Australian plates. Earth's forces pushed those plates around, sending the Pacific plate beneath the Australian plate and melting it into magma that exploded upward, building land anew through volcanism. The moving plates not only fueled the belly of the earth to create volcanoes but also tore Zealandia apart, leaving two islands. The heart of New Zealand's North Island is now a volcanic hub, dominated by the three active volcanoes of Ruapehu, Tongariro, and Ngauruhoe; the South Island is renowned for its Southern Alps, jagged young peaks pushed skyward by the elemental forces of the planet. Mountains are integral to this country.

That is the story as told by modern science. The Māori know the creation of Aotearoa, the Land of the Long White Cloud (the country that Europeans labeled New Zealand), in ways far different from that of scientists' account of plate tectonics, their narrative told through other concepts and terms. The Māori relate how the islands came to be prior to humankind when the demigod Māui brought a great fish up from the sea that became Aotearoa, its mountains home to the *atua*, the gods and guardians. Humankind eventually evolved, and there came a time when the Māori ancestors set out from their mystical homeland island of Hawaiki to cross the Great Ocean of Kiwa (the Pacific Ocean), reaching Te Ika ā Māui, the Great Fish of Māui, the island of Aotearoa.[1]

I've arrived at these islands of Aotearoa, reached the foot of Ngauruhoe, with the volcanoes Ruapehu and Tongariro not far away, and find the surroundings compelling in ways I cannot decipher. Pulling my feet from cool water to mossy bank, I dry them slowly with the top of my socks. I do not know the waters too are *tapu*, though I should have surmised that, for I have learned about the *tapu* of Tongariro's volcanoes. What I have not learned was that the volcanoes and waters, being *tapu*, are not to be climbed or swum in.

I sit in the midst of sacred mountains, mountains that are ancestors, lands that are *tapu*. I do not fully understand, for I have bathed my feet in the water of this country.

Evening approaches. I put my boots on and head back toward the hut, following the trail that seems overly constructed, built of planks, cement, and gravel, as if protecting against heavy use, something I've not seen on this afternoon excursion. Only two hikers passed during my lengthy musing by the stream. They spoke in soft voices, looking down toward the burbling stream. "I remember this place," she said. "This is a wonderful spot," he replied. They passed by without noticing my presence.

The walk back is peaceful, slow, and solitary. Arriving at the hut, I find it now occupied by other walkers, all of whom speak in quiet voices as they go through the end-of-day activities of setting up bunks and preparing food. Gentle camaraderie settles in.

The sun is low in the sky when our hut-hiking clan of about fifteen people gather on the benches and planks of Mangatepopo Hut's large deck, Ngauruhoe standing to the east, always in our consciousness, his summit now in view under clear skies. We sprawl, eat, chat, repair boots, poke at blisters. As the last food is scraped out of bowls, the hut warden arrives to give the orientation talk, a middle-aged woman dressed in DOC uniform, with clipboard and registration numbers to check us in. For the most part, the hut lecture is routine: pack out all your trash, clean up after yourself, nothing but toilet paper and human waste down the outhouse hole, respect your fellow hut hiker.

"And if you want to use the loo in the morning, do it before 7:30. That's about when the day hikers come, and there'll be a *lo-o-ong* line for about two hours after that."

Raised eyebrows and questioning looks prompt her to explain.

"The next stretch of the circuit overlaps with the Alpine Crossing—that's one of the most popular day hikes in New Zealand. People start at a car park about half an hour from here, walk the trail below Ngauruhoe, then drop down to come out at Ketetahi. So the day walkers won't be on the whole stretch between here and the next hut, but you'll be walking with the crowds for most of the day if you leave too late. They say five thousand people walked it last Sunday. But tomorrow's Wednesday... maybe there won't be as many."

A pause. *Five thousand?* There is a long silence.

"So, does anyone want to learn some of the plants? I could do a little botanical tour if anyone wants." A handful of us join her to learn a bit more about this place where we walk.

Later, I ask the warden, "How do you pronounce it, the volcano? *Inga-u*..."

Her face breaks into a smile, and she thanks me, saying, "Break it down. *Ng-ar-oh-hoi-ee*. Ngauruhoe."

I repeat the word as best I can but don't think I ever get it right. Still, the warden nods, "That's great." She pauses, then adds, "Thank you for trying. If I hear one more person call it Mount Doom, I..." She shakes her head, her smile gone. "I... I... I'll scream," and she goes off on a rant.

Mount Doom, the pyramid-shaped volcano where Sauron forged the One Ring, where Frodo and Sam dragged themselves up steaming slopes to destroy that all-powerful evil. Mount Doom, at the heart of the black land of Mordor within Middle Earth, where heroic elves, hobbits, dwarves, and humans save their world from destruction in J. R. R. Tolkien's legendary but very fictional *Lord of the Rings*. Mount Doom resides within the story, within the pages, and more recently, within the movies. Mount Doom is a mythical mountain that only exists within that lore; it is a symbol, an icon, a powerful legend that has carried through generations in a story that holds meaning for many. It is a fantasy mountain that people want to experience in reality.

The moviemakers used the very real Ngauruhoe as their Mount Doom. The elegantly shaped pyramidal volcano, a sacred mountain within sacred lands within the intricate Aotearoa landscape, a mountain that is an ancestor, of kin to *atua* and Māori alike—this Mountain became to many people the virtual-reality Mount Doom. The region has gained popularity, overwhelmed by thousands of visitors.

Where might these visitors have learned of the Māori cultural beliefs, of the *tapu* of Ngauruhoe? I had turned to academic texts for most of my pretrip learning, but I'm probably in the minority on that. And I had to ask to find out anything in the Whakapapa Visitor Centre, where I was just yesterday.

~~~

Whakapapa Village is a jumble of buildings set in the shadow of the Ruapehu volcano within Tongariro National Park. It serves as a ski resort in winter, a hiking destination in summer, and a sightseer's attraction year-round. Chateau Tongariro Hotel dominates the setting, standing
~~~

tall since 1929 in all its colonial grandeur. Another hotel of more modern, mundane design sits on one edge of the town, and a holiday park with tiny cabins, campsites, and caravans (trailers), on the other, the latter where I stayed before my walk. A few small houses for employees, a café, public toilets, and the bar round out the mix. Somewhere in the middle of it all lies the Tongariro National Park Visitor Centre. I planned a day in Whakapapa to organize gear, see the visitor center, walk the nature trails, and begin learning about the area.

The usual visitor center gestalt enveloped me when I entered the building: items for sale up front and forward—postcards, maps, sunglasses, water bottles—and display boards and panels all around. The interpretive material was good, interesting, informative—and all about the region's geology and natural history. I could find no cultural history.

I approached the young woman behind the counter who looked like a seasonal employee freed from university for a summer, wanting to be helpful but afraid of her own naivete. Her eyebrows were permanently raised, a smile frozen on her pale face.

"I understand this land is sacred to the Māori?"

She looked at me, offering nothing but that unmoving smile.

"Do you have . . . um . . . anything on that?"

"We have a film," she said. "I could put it on for you."

"Thank you, yes, if it's no problem. That would be good."

Alone in the expansive theater, I watched the Tongariro story unfold on film, much of what I remember presented as an animation, a way to capture the legendary history and sacred stories in images. I had done my homework before leaving the United States, read environmental histories of the land, and delved into Māori relationships to their ancestral home. I meshed what I saw in the displays and video into what I had already learned.

The Māori recount how before all things there was the original void, the world of potential, out of which came the original darkness, the realm of becoming. From darkness unfolded the world of light, the realm of being. *Ranginui* (Father Sky) and *Papatūānuku* (Mother Earth) came to be, their union the beginning of the *whakapapa*, the great genealogy.

In a grand embrace, *Ranginui* and *Papatūānuku* held their children between them in darkness. Some tell that it was the child Tāne, god of the forest, that split apart *Ranginui* and *Papatūānuku*, creating a burst of light, a great primal energy spreading out with the unfolding of the cosmos. With this creation, all things were imbued with the life force *mauri* and the cosmic sacred power, *tapu*.

Mauri, the life force, is within all that exists, uniting spirit and body, weaving together the spiritual and the physical, binding humanity to Mother Earth. All things have *mauri*—mountains, rivers, trees, stones, people, thoughts. Disruption of *mauri* has catastrophic consequences, thus a reciprocal and respectful relationship between people and land is a necessity.[2]

Tapu is a complex concept holding a complexity of meanings. *Tapu* is the cosmic power that infuses all things at creation, a power that holds sacredness and awe. It is the power of potentiality and commands respect, and so *tapu* can also mean a restriction; it is a means of controlling behavior toward the sacred. All life holds *tapu*. All lands hold *tapu*. All things are originally created with *tapu* within them. Anything *tapu* is not to be violated or profaned, not to be put to common use. It is to be respected for what it holds. This complex meaning was reduced down to just the aspect of restriction by early Euro-American observers, carrying forward as "taboo," as brought to the English language by Captain James Cook.

The children of *Ranginui* and *Papatūānuku* became the *atua*, personifications of natural phenomena, the gods and guardians who look over earthly domains of forests, oceans, rivers, wind, and the earth's great motions. Significantly for Tongariro, it is Rūaumoko who is the god of earthquakes, volcanic activity, and the cycling of the seasons. The *atua*, earth, mountains, living things, people, are all of the same unfolding. The great genealogy, the *whakapapa*, shows the lineage, the connections going back to a shared creation, a unity of animate and element, of breathing beings and cosmic phenomena. The Māori thus view themselves as belonging within the cosmos, related to and part of the natural world and their environment, in both spiritual and utilitarian ways, the land both sacred and a sustaining resource. There is kinship between all things, and so Māori know the mountains as their literal ancestors; they came to be before humans in the *whakapapa*. Thus, the traditional Māori culture is one of shared community across all beings rather than of human dominion or control over the earth and its life.

These ancestral mountains run through Māori lore and ancient history, their slopes and peaks replete with legends and gods. In a culture where people and *iwi* (tribes) identify themselves through significant features of the land, mountains may be part of a Māori's identity, "self" grounded in "place." Such it is with the Ngāti Tūwharetoa *iwi*, who have their cultural and spiritual center in the Tongariro lands, where the *hapū* (subtribe) Ngāti Hikairo ki Tongariro, the "true people of the homeland," serve as guardians; these people connect their identity to the land itself, lands of reverence and spirit. They maintain the ancient accounts of these volcanoes, telling of the high priest Ngātoroirangi, who climbed Mount Tongariro during freezing weather, calling for his sisters to send fire. After warming himself, he threw the basket of flames onto the mountain, creating the Ketetahi ("one basket") hot springs. Ngātoroirangi's slave Uruhoe suffered a harsher fate, dying on the volcano now known as Ngauruhoe. The mountains' love quarrels are remembered, how Mount Taranaki was sent to the west to end his love affair with the volcano Pīhanga, who was engaged to Tongariro. Taranaki now stands as "the guardian of the setting sun."[3]

These tales were shown to me as I sat in the empty amphitheater. Then the film spun forward, moving on to colonization when Europeans came and settled, cleared, and exploited the Māori lands with extensive grazing and logging. Land that was communal and sacred became private and commodity. In the common story of colonization, there was a cultural schism with conflicting perceptions of human relationships to land, a desire for control and power by the colonizing culture, and so a taking. I do not remember the film explaining that Māori traditionally do not own land, believing they are part of the land in a shared inhabitation with the greater community of life, don't recall the film informing the viewer how that life is filled with *mauri*, the original life spark that can be disrupted and destroyed through negligence or attack. There is much that remained hidden behind the old photos and brief history presented.

In 1887, at a time Europeans were seeking to purchase lands to graze sheep on Tongariro's slopes, Chief Horonuku of the Ngāti Tūwharetoa *iwi* enacted a *tuku* (an offering) with the British Crown to protect the sacred mountains, keeping the sacrosanct lands whole and preserving the volcanic peaks for all Māori Tribes and all New Zealanders. The *tuku* was meant as a partnership with the Crown, "an arrangement of shared responsibility"[4] with the purpose of keeping the sacred *tapu* lands and mountains from passing through the Land Court to be dispersed and developed. The film solemnly stated Chief Horonuku's reason for establishing the *tuku*: "There burns my fire, kindled by my ancestor. If they [the volcanoes] are sold, the *tapu* will be gone."

The film reached its end, the lights came up in the deserted room.

I later learned the arrangement of shared responsibility apparently didn't last. As the DOC describes it, "In 1894, Tongariro National Park was established—the first for Aotearoa (New Zealand), and fourth in the world. Legal ownership of the sacred mountain peaks increased significantly from the original 2,640 hectare *tuku* into a 25,000 hectare land block vested solely in the Crown."[5] Yet that too evolved, and the designation of Tongariro as a UNESCO World Heritage Site in 1993 served to strengthen the Ngāti Tūwharetoa involvement in park management.[6]

As stated in the New Zealand Parliamentary Debates, the Crown desired to establish a national park because the land was not worth developing, being "almost useless as far as grazing was concerned," and would generate far more income as a tourist attraction.[7] It seems the British entered into the *tuku* not to protect the sacred but to commodify the land and its natural beauty.

Unproductive land yet potentially lucrative land as a site for visitors: something that could and desirably should be set aside as a national park. Build the railroads, build the lodge. Tap into the visitor's desire to visit sublime landscapes, to see great mountains, to test oneself against them. Such wild, challenging places became part of the country's character, the natural world replacing deeper cultural history as a marker of greatness in a young nation. Reflecting on my Montana homeland, I see the same history as that of Yellowstone National Park in the American West, apparently not a unique history, as a similar trajectory took place there and in New Zealand. The result is that the lands, the national parks, were and *are* protected: places with wild remain in the States and in New Zealand. But this is associated with tragic dispossession and loss that cannot be swept away by whitewashed history.[8]

The visitor center was bright and noisy when I emerged from the theater. I made for the door, brought to a halt by a sculpture in memory of Horonuku's offering, something I'd overlooked on first entering. Carved into the gray stone were the words "The Sacred Tuku. Horonuku passed, under the mantle of *tuku*, the mountain peaks to the people of New Zealand." Like the history hidden behind the old black-and-white photos in the film I'd just watched, there is a poignant and complex story lying within those seemingly simple words.

The next morning, this morning, I walked into those mountain peaks for my four-day circuit, reaching Mangatepopo Hut, within sight of Ngauruhoe. Now standing on the deck in the dusky light, I set Ngauruhoe and Mount Doom side by side in my mind, one woven into a peoples' cosmology, the other a setting within a modern fictional fantasy. I make no sense of it, coming up with no answers.

The hut is quiet now, people speaking in low tones, organizing for the next day, or simply watching the evening. The sun has departed, leaving the far-off volcano Taranaki—he who was sent to the west—silhouetted black within a copper horizon, a sky that fades upward into ocher that pales in soft transition to the indigo of the darkening day. I watch sacred Taranaki, the mountain who is a Māori ancestor, until all light leaves the sky and the volcano disappears into the night.

~~~

The understanding of mountains as sacred has filtered through my life for as long as I can remember, but it was in my early thirties that the Sacred Mountain unexpectedly revealed itself in a very conscious way,
~~~

sometime after Grandma and Grandpa had passed away, when I often lived solo at the ranch. Though I believe a form of spiritual connection shaped my initial bond with the mountains—with the earth itself—that day decades ago was a tangible sense of the sacred not so explicitly felt before.

It was on a sunny summer day, the kind of day when the alpine takes on intensified clarity of color, a heightened definition of each rock and petal. I had gone to the summit of Koch Peak, the mountain where I first stood alone at such a height, and then lingered long in the alpine basin below. There, the green of new growth, the warmth of the sun after the gasping chill of a dip in a small lake, the sparkle off the snowbanks that clung into July, the blaze of a flower, the call of a bird—this was the world, elemental being. I was just there, my mind and self nowhere else.

The day progressed, and I eventually dropped down out of the basin to a subalpine meadow, with its array of wildflowers and islands of fir, turning back to muse on the peak—the same that had stunned me in my youth. Though Koch was now a familiar, it still pushed me into humbled awe. There stood the peak, towering over that land.

I raised my hands, together at the wrist, fingers spread to form a cup around the view of the mountain, Koch Peak now settled into my palms.

There is Something More.

Such a feeling—strong, flowing, undeniable, the thought seeming to arrive from outside rather than within. Me so small, the Mountain solid and weighty in my palms, a sense that *it* cupped *me*.

Somewhere I have a poem written about that moment, choosing poetry for its ability to distill thought and emotion. That moment was a distillation, an embrace of the Sacred that comes at such times like a soft singing, a warm breath against a cheek. The Mountain's energy eternally sings that song, breathes that breath, though it is not always heard or felt.

I ramble on about the Sacred and know it has nothing to do with words. It has to do with that Mountain cupped in my hands, holding me in its essence. About *Something More*. I return to Gary Snyder's idea: "*Sacred* refers to that which helps take us (not only human beings) out of our little selves into the whole mountains-and-rivers mandala universe."[9] I stood within that, for it was within me, cupped in my hands, cupping me.

That feeling was not inspired by religious teachings—our family did not follow a formal religion. This was not something taught to me. It was purely an individual response to the Mountain. In this I am not alone. There are those who have encountered the sacred on a mountain's summit, some without seeking it—at least consciously. There are individuals like myself who have found the sacred standing at the foot of the Mountain that rises into higher realms even as its roots sink into the foundation of the earth. Either way, it is the potent qualities of mountains that stir that response, that make one see the essence of existence, even for a fleeting moment. The power of mountains to inspire such feelings resonates out into cultures in different ways, where the mountains become symbolic of purity, morality, and our most valued beliefs, even as they provide a conduit to connect with something far beyond our own aspirations.[10] The Mountain's powerful effect is such that the understanding of mountains as sacred is an ancient way of knowing, long preceding more empirical views, a way of knowing that comes from somewhere beyond rational analysis. And so sacred mountains rise across the planet, found in most if not all cultures.

What drives this response? Simultaneously earthly and unfathomable, mountains present the hungry human mind and the sensing human body with parallax—a shift in perspective. Their verticality and sheer immensity press up against the cosmos, against that which cannot be fully known, and so there exists a long mythic tradition of mountains connecting earth with the heavens above. So it is with the Māori, who view Mount Ruapehu, the larger volcano next to Ngauruhoe, as "touching the heavens."[11] The mountains thus unite the infinite with the ground at our feet, write the eonian into our everyday lives.

The mountain is utilitarian and tangible, providing resources and reserves; the Mountain is Other, the Mystery embodied. We can make sense of the mountain in one way, but in another, it stands beyond us, haunting our spiritual longings. Mountains link the ecological and metaphysical, bridge the material moment with the infinite eternal.

Humanity brings to the mountain encounter the universal hunger for deeper understanding of metaphysical and existential truths: the interaction of mountain and human psyche stirs the soul across the spectrum of humanity, transforming mountain into deeper meaning than rock and stone, cliff and crag. The Mountain is sanctified.

The Sacred Mountain cannot be defined through any one way of knowing.[12] With variegated brilliance, cultural diversity creates a mosaic of traditions and beliefs around holy mountains, the Māori way of knowing just one culture's expression of the sanctity of the peaks, of mountain gods and epiphanies, of the divine, of the mystery encountered in the heights. Some cultures know sacred mountains as cosmic centers, or home to the gods, even gods themselves; others revere sacred mountains as the origin of their people or look to the holy peaks as boundary points for the territory of a peoples' creation. There are mountains that hold sacred sites, sacred mountains that do not exist except in myth, and those little-known mountains a single person may humbly hold as sacred to their existence, for the personal meaning they have found there. And there are mountains of power, such as the Tongariro volcanoes, where "in the past Maori warriors crossing the plateau beneath Mount Tongariro would avert their eyes."[13]

The Mountain is unlike many other sacred geographies, those places with an existential atmosphere, such as deserts and oceans; the Mountain has a defined shape, a singular point of ultimate height, a mappable definable loci where you can plant your foot and make your mark, possibly find your epiphany. Across the sacred beliefs, that summit too is not one thing. There are those cultures who have their stories of monks who found enlightenment on the summit. There are cultures like the Māori who hold the mountain as sacred in a different way; they are not to be climbed. The summit, the apex, that point where one cannot move any higher, where perceptions are shaped and experience distilled—that elevated site, viewed with such different perspectives by diverse peoples and cultures, is often the focus of conflict, where cultures clash in a collision of beliefs, whether that be through an observatory planted on an Indigenous holy place[14] or a hiker reaching the top to violate (possibly unknowingly) another culture's sacred space.

Māori view the mountains as sacred, but their beliefs go beyond symbolism, for they know the mountains as true ancestors, within the same *whakapapa*: we are all of one creation. Those who reach Ngauruhoe's summit will, in the Māori perspective, trample on a Māori ancestor, stand on the ancestor's head. They will break the *tapu* in a conflict of cultures.

~~~

I try to leave Mangatepopo Hut before 7:30 but miss the mark. At 7:40, just as the first of the day walkers appeared, I set off. The sun is low in the sky, silvery-gold rays reaching into the valley, highlighting the walkers who fill that well-constructed trail below Ngauruhoe. The people are diverse in size and shape and gear, some lightly clad carrying tiny packs that could hardly hold a water bottle, wearing skimpy running shoes or treadless sneakers, others shouldering backpacks, outfitted with hiking boots, sun shirts, and trousers as protection against the rising blaze of rays. No clouds break the blue of the sky, the volcano's summit clearly in view.

The mountain stands above the stream of people I have joined. Many walk ahead of me, but most are behind; on looking back, I see a wave of advancing hikers, lines and lines strewn along the trail. My stride lengthens in an effort to stay ahead of the throngs despite my heavy backpack. Now I understand the planks-and-cement trail so well constructed to protect the earth against the many passing feet.

The track climbs to the base of Ngauruhoe, where several hikers have paused to rest and take photos. Looking down at the many people coming up, I keep walking. There below the volcano, the broad path levels out, now a hard-packed track crossing a dark igneous plain. Patches of woolly fringe moss, grass tussocks, and brilliant white alpine gentians grow amid the stones. The white flowers catch the morning light, shining within the lead-gray moonscape. The walkers ahead are spaced apart, dark silhouetted figures with shadows streaming behind. Surreality swamps the scene—the barren scape, the black shadowed bodies moving step by step over stony ground. For a moment, it has the sense of a pilgrimage, a path toward the holy. Maybe for some of
~~~

those who walk before me, an essence of that feeling lies in their gentler stride, a sense of what the mountain holds—this I cannot know. They are not headed up Ngauruhoe but walk in his shadow, not intent on reaching the summit.

Not far past the cutoff for the route to the summit, a small side path takes me to a secluded spot a distance off the trail. I unshoulder my pack and settle onto a rock to sit with the volcano's presence. I am alone, though not removed from the sound of voices nor the sight of people scrambling up the mountain's rocky slope. The noise emanating from the lines of those headed toward Ngauruhoe's crest rattles through the clear air, similar to what one might hear from a roller coaster ride—shouts and squeals, loud guffaws and yells. Added to that is the crack of falling rock, tumbling talus, stones dislodged by people's feet.

Ngauruhoe watches. This is what I feel.

I often have this sense of a mountain as a watchful presence, not like a person or being or god, but something that emanates an energy. Usually it is reassuring, like the earth's watchful guardian is there. Sometimes it can be ominous, and I know to take a different route or turn back altogether. It is the feeling that there is something more than the mineral mountain, a sense of the mountain's life energy infused with all the life that it holds: the breathing beings, the moving creatures, the rooted plants. It is an intuited connection with the storied Mountain that holds the experience of those animate beings who have known it, be they human, wolf, hare, or sparrow, each blossom, blade, bug, and snake. Conservationist Aldo Leopold called it "Thinking like a Mountain," the Mountain "knowing" in its own way the threads that weave us together into unity. It is a Thinking beyond the quotidian, a way of knowing that one can dip into like a spring of clear water. The Mountain thus feels animated and so watchful.

Sitting within the alien igneous landscape, I sense that about this land. Ngauruhoe carries weight, holds a presence. Perhaps the energy I feel is something akin to the Māori *mauri*, life energy flowing through everything, for what stands before me is far from inert matter to those first peoples of this land. Would I feel that powerful essence without my factual knowing of its sanctity? Am I predisposed to this sense? Would

I feel differently if I hadn't done my reading, made my inquiries, and learned a bit of the ways of this place, and come to know the volcanoes are *tapu*? And again I ask myself, *What does this sacred mountain mean to a visiting Euro-American? What does this sacred land hold for someone like me, a foreigner, whose feelings flow along a similar current?* Pulling up that word *sacred*, holding it. Wondering where the boundary is crossed into some form of cultural appropriation.

I look up toward the summits around me, but I do not avert my eyes from the heads of Mount Tongariro or Ngauruhoe, for I am of a different culture living in this modern age.

We come to a foreign landscape with our perceptions and our cultural inculcations, our desires and our determinations, our baggage and our learnings. We come with what we have seen, learned, experienced. Today, modern Western culture is often shaped and swayed by media, movies, television, commercialism, and so many visitors came with the received knowledge that "Mount Doom" exists within Tongariro National Park. They may never have encountered the Māori's truth of the mountain.

I sit and watch a portion of the hundreds of people who will summit Ngauruhoe on this day and the thousands of people who will walk this trail today—myself among the latter. We carry our preconceptions, be that of a sacred mountain or a fantasy land, while the Mountain looks on.

~~~

It is time to move. Balancing my camera on a rock, I set the timer and take a picture of myself with Ngauruhoe in the background before shouldering the pack and setting off toward the second hut, Oturere Hut, moving through an otherworldly landscape. Barren slopes and ridges of beige, brick, and lead-gray rock surround the path, lakes turned turquoise by silt dot the low points. At a high point on the trail, a sign with lights and solar panels states, "WARNING! VOLCANIC RISK. IF LIGHT IS FLASHING, TRACK IS CLOSED. Turn around and go back." The surroundings are constructed by active volcanoes, by sacred mountains of power that could erupt and end the lives of us all. Western scientists
~~~

will explain the eruptions in their words. The Māori may describe it differently, though there is no conflict in the contrasting viewpoints.

I descend from the pass with its WARNING! sign, walking by the cutoff for the Alpine Crossing and so moving down and away from numerous people, past the shimmering turquoise lakes, through rough, rocky ridges, and steep, scree-covered slopes. There is time to stop for a bit next to one of the lakes, to watch a pipit hop around on a rock beside the water, catching insects, a spritely bit of life in the stillness. Not too much farther on is Oturere Hut, small, quiet, the second hut of my circuit. I am the first to arrive. A conversation with the hut warden results in the loan of a plant book, a treasure that I take back up the trail in hopes of identifying the species I've seen on my walk in. Learning the names and a bit of the natural history brings a gentle familiarity to the plants, which filters out into the land.

Even with eyes and heart wide open, even *trying* to build connections to the land, the transformation from experiencing somewhere as a visited-landscape versus a Place-of-bonding is difficult, takes time. I stepped into the natural world of New Zealand to meet the mysterious—plants, insects, birds found only here and nowhere else in the world. I was delighted. I was stunned. Learning species is one thing. Understanding the natural communities yet another. Connecting to a place moves to another level all together. Knowing it as sacred is beyond all of that.

But I have to begin my understanding of this place at some level. I take pictures of pages in the borrowed book, then a picture of the plant. Click. *Gentiana bellidifolia*. Click. Gentian flower. The growing things start to gain character, a twist of the leaf, the way the bark covers a stem, how the petals circle the bloom. I feel a bit more learned yet not much more connected. Click. This time a picture of a rock, a weirdly shaped black lava structure, striated, bent, rippled, mushrooming out at the top, looking like something rejected from a devil's smelter or the work of a modern artist gone mad. *Hmmm... no...* This particular landscape may never be a place of connection, far too alien for someone from the Montana mountains to embrace in a few days. That does not mean, though, that I do not appreciate the place for what it is, both ecologically and spiritually.

Back at the hut, the sun is slipping behind Ngauruhoe's flank, the gold orb blazing, the mountain black, the air so dry the sky holds only faded remnants of blue, a hint of lemon—no coppery red—and then the sun is gone. Sitting in the fading light, my journal lies open in my lap, but the pen in hand is still, no words coming, struck by what I've witnessed and walked through: a world of stark beauty that strikes into all senses, the living plant and bird community that thrives in the stony land, the people, the Mountain. Rather than write, I take out the clipping from the DOC Tongariro Northern Circuit brochure carefully tucked into the journal to read once again the Ngāti Tūwharetoa (the local Māori *iwi*) statement about this land. The paragraph resonates now as it did when I cut out the blue page to carry with me: "It is a world of reciprocity and respect, of guardianship and devotion, of stunning landscapes and epic stories, of deep reverence and spirituality. May the guardians of our mountains keep you safe, may the memory of this experience lie warm in your hearts forever."[15]

Voices and chatter flow out the hut door. An older couple discusses the surrounding vegetation, making me smile—perhaps I will go in and join them soon. Young people are having a loud conversation about drinking and alcohol, then change their topic to Ngauruhoe. One voice carries above all the others: "Those poor Māori! It's like, 'Whoa... that's our sacred mountain!'"

I sit stunned by the remark. The young man's statement is planted in my mind, to return again two days later when a Māori woman tells me, her dark eyes flashing, "Rūaumoko will rise up, then we will all be underground."

I will meet this woman in a store in Whakapapa, and she will explain her anger over the number of people trampling the sacred lands, climbing the *tapu* mountains: "People have no respect for the land. The caravans just dump their rubbish, their human waste.... We will get it back someday."

Standing before her, my gut will twist as an ache grows in my chest, even as I try to express my understanding and accord, knowing full well I am one among the thousands of white tourists who descend on this place every day of the summer.

"We will take it back someday. You won't be able to come and walk here. We will take it back. Someday."

Her dark eyes will meet mine, despair as clear as anger.

"That is how it should be," I respond without thinking.

She still scowls, but perhaps there is a softening in her face.

"And it is sacred land?"

"Yes."

"So many people."

"Too many people! They have no respect for the land.... Rūaumoko will rise up, then we will all be underground," she will again declare.

I think she said Rūaumoko, the *atua* responsible for the earth's stirrings, for earthquakes and volcanic eruptions.

I will hear this woman's thoughts days after that evening at Oturere Hut, but something similar is within me now and rose up there along the trail as I looked at the WARNING! sign on the pass. What is happening seems unsustainable, the waste dumped, the unknowing violation of *tapu*. But what is happening stretches to a larger scale. Will there be a planetary reaction to this loss of awareness? Will the gods rise up against this—a *this* that stretches far beyond Tongariro? It seems the warning signs are already flashing, but we continue on this path—and the volcano will blow and we will all be underground.

Raucous laughter follows the young man's remark. I look up from my journal, out across the land, and wonder if he understands what he is saying.

~~~

Next morning, a pool of mist fills the valley below Oturere Hut, fog slipping upward with fingering tendrils, reaching toward my breakfast spot on the rim. Golden rays explode from the far horizon as the sun lifts, turning the mist copper and bronze. Looking behind me, I see Ngauruhoe's upper slopes shining bloodred, his flanks still inky black. All the elemental forces have gathered—water, fire, air, and the dark earth beneath me tangibly alive. The presence of the Mountain is strong. Godlike.
~~~

The sun rises, the light becoming day, and with it I am back within Tongariro National Park, sitting beneath a gray volcano. Yet on the mountain's edge, a drift of steam appears. Now I know that Ngauruhoe breathes steam like a living being.

With not far to walk on this day, I pack slowly and set off after my hut-mates, many who are skipping Waihohonu Hut, the third hut, and heading out to Whakapapa Village. The traverse between the huts crosses the barren expanse of the volcano's foothills where scrubby pockets of shrubs, grass, and woolly fringe moss grow in a land of gravel and sand. I see no one, as if I'd trekked into another time where Ngauruhoe presides over all things, the volcano always there, moving across the land with me.

Descending, the trail leaves the moonscape, dropping through lichen-draped trees into a shallow valley coursed by a clear running stream with grass tussocks curling off the banks, then up and down again to reach Waihohonu Hut. The building is spacious and newly constructed—the floor gleams, the wood walls are unmarked, a woodstove sits within its clean stone cubby, and the stainless-steel countertop sparkles in the cooking area. A large picture window frames the surrounding hills and Ngauruhoe, who on this day again ascends into cloudless skies.

The day is young, and I am eager to walk under that deep-blue sky, but the dining area tables catch my interest; interpretive signs are varnished into the tabletops, snapshots of the region's history. Some of these signs tell of the first Māori settlers and the coming of European colonizers. There is a description of early colonial farming and the attempts to secure land for agriculture, with Chief Te Heuheu's (the father of Horonuku) response: "Let your people keep the sea-coast, but leave the interior to us, and our mountain, whose name is sacred, to the bones of my father."

And there is the story of J. C. Bidwell.

In 1839, J. C. Bidwill marked his place in history as the first European to climb Ngauruhoe, reaching the crater's summit to find "the most terrific abyss [he] ever looked into or imagined." In doing so, Bidwill also became the first European to break the mountain's *tapu*. Chief Te Heuheu heard of Bidwill's ascent and "was furious that his sacred mountain had been violated, and was no doubt enraged by Bidwill's response that he was greater than the mountain (god) for climbing to the top of it."[16]

Mountain climbing is embedded in Euro-American history, evolving in the nineteenth century out of Romantic tourism aided by the early glaciologists and geologists who sent out their reports of the mighty environs they encountered in the heights. Reasons to climb mountains and reach peaks grew out of cultural shifts and trends of that time: as the Romantic movement blossomed, some went to mountains seeking the sublime; as explorations of unknown landscapes proliferated, the explorer mentality took climbers to new peaks. There was also the growing idea of the positive aspects of the mountain's challenge: in 1900, New Zealander Leonard Cockayne, an early believer in the benefits of mountain recreation, stated, "Mountains are the noblest recreation ground, the finest school for physical and moral training,"[17] a sentiment echoed in the United States and Europe. Thus, colonizing Europeans of that time looked at the mountains with a very different eye than the first peoples of both New Zealand and the United States.

And so one might say that Bidwill conquered Ngauruhoe in the way of his culture. But in conflating the summit with the first people, Bidwell's conquering was not just mountain climbing. Bidwell knowingly and literally stomped upon the Māori and their worldview—their very essence of being—by declaring that in standing on that summit, he became superior to a foreign god; he believed that he had dominated the land, its people, and their deities simply by reaching the top of Ngauruhoe.

Almost half a century after Bidwell stood on Ngauruhoe's head, Horonuku understood he could not stop this European force with their desire to dominate, could not put an end to those who would overrun his country, and so offered the *tuku* of shared responsibility of the Tongariro lands. He hoped for a different form of protection than the Māori *tapu*, creating what his son-in-law called a "*tapu* place of the Crown."[18] The Crown took the land, making it a place protected by Euro-American ideals wrapped in boundary lines and tied up in law and economics: a national park.

But this is not 1839. Those who climb Ngauruhoe are not climbing in the same mindset as J. C. Bidwell. What I am witnessing is not Bidwell's knowing domination, not a perceived conquest of a people or a worldview. All those I walk with—we are visitors, tourists, travelers, there for different reasons. Many may have no idea they are summiting a sacred mountain. But many may know full well they are climbing Mount Doom and find that truly an adventure.

Landscape is a recent word, dating back only to the seventeenth century when Dutch artists started painting rural or natural scenes to please a rising merchant class.[19] By the eighteenth century, English landowners embraced the aesthetics of these "landscape" paintings, transferring the word and the concept to an actual view of the land, especially wild nature. So entrenched was this idea of landscape as painting that the Claude glass was created, named for Claude Lorraine, a seventeenth-century painter who laid out the rubric for landscape painting. A convex, blackened pocket mirror, the Claude glass altered hues and perspective, transforming whatever view it was pointed at into something like a Claude painting. The European culture thus became a culture that looked *at* the land, seeing it as an inanimate display, a pretty picture, a landscape painting rather than a rich community humming with life, wondrous interactions, and cultural connections. Vibrant, living *place* turned to static scene.

Perhaps the Claude glass of today is media, carried in our head, shaping our view of the landscape, fostering ideas of "mountain as stage" and "summit as challenge," even turning Tongariro into Middle Earth, Ngauruhoe into Mount Doom. As I sit within my culture, I wonder, *In their mind, what mountain do those who summit Ngauruhoe climb?* I don't believe visitors call the volcano Mount Doom simply because it is easier to pronounce than Ngauruhoe. How many returned home to say they'd summited *Mount Doom*, reaching the top of a fantasy world, rather than embracing the wonder and sanctity of that very real place?

But an intimate union with the mountain may develop in an individual outside of cultural perceptions; it may happen in a moment or mature over a lifetime. Did some who clambered up the slopes to reach Ngauruhoe's summit and look into "the most terrific abyss" feel a shift? Perhaps the Mountain's presence forever changed how they know the world. Experience is a strong mentor.

Looking up from the table that holds Bidwell's story, I see Ngauruhoe outside the window. The volcano tells his own story, one carried down through the Māori generations, a narrative that entwines the people and the place—the real actual place of rock, bird, mist, plant. When media-made stories are the tales that are told, when ancient ways of knowing and a sense of the sacred slip into obscurity, we lose an awareness of the holy that permeates the natural world.

Ngauruhoe stands watching.

~~~

Across the planet, there is a growing recognition of the need to honor the Indigenous peoples' sacred relationship to the land, and so it is in New Zealand. In 2017, a few years after my visit, the DOC put out a visitor advisory that the Tongariro mountains should not be climbed and Ngauruhoe should not be listed as a side trip nor referred to as Mount Doom. With a growing understanding of the Māori beliefs, the number of people climbing to the volcanoes' summits has been reduced.[20] I have also heard the Whakapapa Visitor Centre now has displays on Māori culture. Perhaps a video plays regularly too.

Yet different perspectives carry forward. A 2020 *Wilderness* article entitled "To Summit or Not to Summit?" included thoughts from New Zealand Mountain Guides Association (NZMGA) president Jane Morris.

> The "wider issue" according to Morris, is cultural differences—notably, many Pākehā climbers and trampers see getting to "the summit" as part of their cultural experience.
>
> "We [all] engage differently with the mountains," Morris says. "They are sacred places to Pākehā also. This is, for many people, their church on Sunday."[21]
~~~

It is a tension between cultures, reaching the summit part of European mountaineering history and, for some of those who summit, a spiritual experience.

A few paragraphs down, the article makes the point that Māori, their beliefs, and their relationship to the mountains as stewards and guardians "existed long before European settlers and other cultures established themselves in New Zealand."[22]

And so the Māori perspective now receives more respect. Changes have been made.

As for me, the wandering Euro-American, I cannot know these lands as sacred in the framework of Māori spirituality—I have no Māori heritage or connection. I am simply another visitor in a land overwhelmed by visitors. But I can learn from their perspective and respect their traditions as best I know them.

~~~

I'm done reading the tables. It is my last afternoon of the circuit, and so I put aside study and thought. There is plenty of time to wander before the sun sets, time to do as I had hoped and immerse in this land so new to me, that very newness working to heighten my own awareness. I head to Ohinepango Spring not too far from the hut.

A sign marks the path leading off the main trail, telling me "Ohinepango Springs, 10 min return." Following a crystalline creek filled with runners of green algae, I reach a sheltering stand of shrubs and trees that grow around a pool of water freshly emerged from the earth. So clear is the water, it would almost be invisible without the wind's gentle motion that ripples the surface so that it catches the sun's rays, setting the light to dancing. Birds flock in the trees, flitting from shadow to sun, glinting like the sparkles on the water as they pick bugs from the twigs and snatch insects from the air. The quiet is not silence or stillness; it is the gentle hum of water-endowed life thriving in an oasis in the heated land. I sit beside the spring, the outside world lost to view, not even Ngauruhoe visible above the thicket of trees foresting the banks.
~~~

The small birds dip and dance in nearby branches, coming closer to examine me, their black eyes ringed with white in an olive-green head. I know them now as silvereyes, the name learned a few days ago. More important than the label, their way of being has become a bit understood—flitting, flocking, moving in a group, curious. The wee birds are no longer strangers but acquaintances. *Pshh . . . shh . . . Pshh-shh?* I query. They flood me with twittering notes.

A dragonfly approaches, transparent wings glittering in blurred motion, moving in a swerving trajectory that brings it closer, brings it in front of my face, onto my head, where the insect lands. For a long moment I sit, joined by singing silvereyes, a dragonfly nestled in my hair, murmuring water, and lush plants gathering sunlight and turning gold to green.

On the banks of Ohinepango Springs, distance fades, boundaries break down, the land around gaining familiarity, losing its label of Tongariro National Park, becoming the natural world of *itself*. Birds and water invite me into a belonging, a kinship of being. These waters at my feet are not removed from the unseen Ngauruhoe, for the high places are the collectors and wellspring of moisture; the Māori respect the volcanoes for providing water to a land where the waters and peaks, birds and gods, people and plants are all kin, all part of the sacred geography.[23] I sit within it.

When the bright-winged dragonfly lifts to return to its aerial home and the singing silvereyes resume their feeding, I slip out of my clothes and into the cold water with a gasp, submerging into clearness, emerging wet and sparked, aware. I go back to my seat on the bank to dry, thinking my skin must have absorbed some of the water, the liquid of the place now part of me.

With that immersion into Ohinepango Springs, I have unknowingly violated the spring's *tapu*.

I've submerged in the earth's clear water in many lands, including my homeland of Montana. This often feels a true "merging," a connection with the earthly elements, part of sensing the whole of the place. That thought that ran through me, that the water of the spring was now absorbed into my skin, even as birdsong resonated within my ears, light soaked into my eyes, air sank into my lungs, was a conscious feeling of uniting ever so briefly with that place so far from home, a sense of becoming part of its wholeness. Such deeply felt sensations make such watery immersions a holy act in a way, for the early, pre-Christian definition of holy is thought to be derived from "whole," a whole that "must be preserved whole or intact, that cannot be transgressed or violated."[24] It is a word that seems the distilled essence of sacred. It is a word that expresses the unity of the infinitesimal within the infinite, the eyeblink within eternity. The cosmos is a whole, holy. Sacred. As is the Mountain. As is the silvereye and dragonfly and the drop of water soaking into my skin. I sat with the Mountain, Ngauruhoe, and now sit with the pool in his shadow, and can feel the stretch between, connecting the mountain that reaches toward heaven with the ephemeral sparkles skipping across the water and the silvereye dancing in the tree.

That swim held the spirit of "holy," a connection with the earth and its greater-than-human community. At the same time, that swim was a violation of the sacred *tapu*, a violation of *tapu* in its restrictive sense that protects the sacred from transgression, a violation of the local iwi's request that sacred "waterways are not touched and lakes are not entered."[25]

I brought my experience, my culture into that land, and my way of knowing led me into actions conflicting with Māori way of knowing simply due to my ignorance. I would not have broken the *tapu* if I'd known, for my own worldview is in concordance with the Māori.

While in Aotearoa/New Zealand, I listened for what I could learn, from both the people and the land. Reflecting back, I remember learning step by step, through words and museums and visitor centers, how the Māori view humanity as part of the earth and all its life, everything not just connected but also *related*, everything holding *tapu* at creation, and so everything initially sacred. *Everything.* I learned of the history, of how Māori arrived on Aotearoa only 750 to 800 years ago and how after centuries of occupation with impacts on the country, regulatory mechanisms were put into place to preserve species and lands. These practices and ideas developed and carried forward, contributing to contemporary

Māori ideas of environmental management.[26] And so I learned of kaitiakitanga, which means guardianship, the management and stewardship of land, life, and resources, a practice that continues into today.

The concept of kaitiakitanga is complex, based on the Māori understanding of humans as part of the natural world in a deep connection to the earth and its life.[27] Kaitiakitanga goes beyond protecting and managing the material "thing" such as the forest and its trees or the lake and its water; it includes guarding the *mauri*, the life force of the forest or lake, thus allowing the *mana*, the spiritual power, to flow, running through all things. Kaitiakitanga embraces the utilitarian and the sacred, providing for conservation of both resource and spirit through prohibitions such as *rāhui*, a restriction on resource use, hunting, or harvesting when a species' numbers are low or a habitat damaged. *Tapu* is the spiritual restriction I would come to better understand while in Aotearoa, controlling the interaction of people with a sacred place or thing.

To begin to understand the concept of kaitiakitanga is to envision what might be if similar concepts as "life force" and "spiritual power" were regularly incorporated into environmental regulations, conservation efforts, climate change actions, and more—not in the sense of any specific canon, but in the sacred *or* secular sense of respect, reciprocity, and all that holds meaning and spirit.

Indeed, there is nothing inherently contradictory between spirituality and the science behind land management or environmental regulations nor between ancient traditional knowledge and recent scientific theories that would exclude such an alliance of thought processes. In my studies, I came across information on a program carried out by Natalia Pardo and colleagues out of New Zealand's Massey University.[28] Their project combined scientific knowledge with Māori traditional knowledge and beliefs to develop volcanic risk mitigation strategies for areas around the Tongariro volcanoes. The academic article published on the project acknowledged that their approach was not the norm, that "traditionally, spirituality is not included in science."[29] The program not only created a risk mitigation strategy but also showed how ancient stories can roughly correlate with geologic events; Māori cosmology from the original void to humanity of today is analogous with big bang and evolution theories.[30] I believe this intertwining of different ways of knowing does more than recognize the validity of Indigenous cosmologies and epistemologies as well as traditional knowledge: it also opens the mind and senses, nurturing a deeper awareness of a world that is not separate from humanity.

Many field ecologists will tell you that study long enough in the natural world and that awareness will happen, with something like a sense of the spiritual and the sacred filtering into those days spent unraveling nature's mysteries.[31] This I found pursuing my master's degree in the Tetons in another journey in a high place, a world where the mountains felt more than material mass, somehow a part of a greater animacy. The scientific facts hold true, but the Mountain implores one to imagine beyond the material. Therein lies the foundation for the fact that Sacred Mountains rise across the world, across cultures, throughout our human visions, hopes, and longings.

To tell of "spiritual epiphany" on the Mountain is so common it slips into cliché, but it is a truth that it happens, an opening to something greater that reduces one even as it plants one in this wonderful mysterious cosmos. Once experienced, that feeling carries forward into one's life. It doesn't have to happen on the Mountain, it doesn't have to be a mountaintop or a mountain setting. It can just be the natural world, it can be sitting with a loved one, it can be anywhere or any time that the sense of the sacred overwhelms. The accompanying sense that we are part of this richly physical, spiritual, material, and metaphysical cosmos, connected and participating, reaches outside of any religion. It provides a sanctity of peace and belonging, a sense of the holy. Though it may take different forms, it engenders compassion for all beings and for the earth and so a desire to preserve, protect, and care for the earth, for we are part of it, kith and kin.[32] This suggests the potential of incorporating concepts similar to that of spirit and the sacred into a larger arena of thought and action. It allows me to better understand the power of kaitiakitanga.

The volcanic mountains of Ngauruhoe are foreign to me, the Māori people unfamiliar before this visit. My own culture is very different from the Māori's. Obviously, I do not have the ecological knowledge of Aotearoa learned through generation upon generation of living with it. My sense of the sacred has grown out of my own experience. I had hoped to share time with some of the Māori, to listen and so learn about their beliefs, their cosmology, their creation stories, learn this directly from the people themselves. I did not have that opportunity, for I had not come for a project, did not arrive with ideas to interview, write, produce, and so did not work to create such an interaction. It seemed invasive, because yes, the fact is, I am a white visitor of the Euro-American culture, of the culture that forever changed the land the Māori originally settled.

Yet to be in a new country is to see again, to remember while learning, to gain a broader perspective on the complexity of existence. To be for a time in Aotearoa, the land of another culture, is a reminder of our planet's cultural diversity and also of our unity. It is to hold and see the importance of knowing humanity as part of the whole, that all things have *mauri* and *tapu*, in whatever language you might want to express it.

The query still rests within me: What does the sacred mountain of another culture mean to a visiting Euro-American? What does the sacred land of Aotearoa hold for someone like me, a foreigner? Perhaps it is just this: to walk in the lands that are sacred to other people, to be aware of that, open to that, and respectful of that, is to walk into the sacred that is part of all things.

The dragonfly has departed, carrying on with its day. The birds have slowed and quieted as the afternoon advances. The pool is unchanged, as if it has been here through all eternity, connecting mountain to lowland, bird to tree, breath to blood—but it too is ephemeral. I am hesitant to leave, so stand on the bank for another long moment before starting back. The oasis has a gentle feel, the spring, its pool, the animate and elemental, all part of a sacred geography that extends out across the earth, beyond any one culture.

~~~

Unbroken blue skies spread across the land on the fourth and last day of my circuit. It is a mellow, thoughtful walk out to Whakapapa, with Ngauruhoe in view, and Mount Ruapehu now visible to the south. Grass
~~~

and shrubs increase as I walk, as if I am returning to a known world, leaving behind the place that has touched me yet holding what it has gifted. There are few people on the trail, and I walk light of step. The Mountain is there, watching.

3

THE SCIENTIFIC MOUNTAIN

The Tetons, Wyoming

A deer walked through the meadow last night, not far from my tent. She pressed her hooves into the dust, leaving small heart-shaped tracks along the granite ledge where I too have walked, so that her passing imprinted on mine. I have hoped a deer would come through this peaceful glade while I was here, and so she has.

In the five days that I've camped in the meadow, the fireweed has blossomed from bottom to top on their inflorescent stalks while the purple asters have completely lost their petals, their seed heads now producing the next generation of flowers even as they generate abundant food for birds, rodents, and insects. Monkeyflowers have dropped most of their blossoms into the damp streambed near the small pool where I rinse my body. The season is turning. If I'd sat just here in this lush meadow over the last five days without leaving for my wanderings, would I have actually seen the change? Witnessed the fireweed unfurl that last flower, the aster drop its last petal?

There's the robin! I have heard him calling but not seen the bird. He just hopped across the soft-polished granite slab near where I have hung my food to thwart hungry bears. Each night I lay on that slab and watched the sky where swallows from the nearby cliffs swooped and soared as they gathered insects from the air, regularly disappearing back to their haunts around 8:30, so orderly are the patterns creatures hold.

So much life in this meadow and so much peace, tucked only a quarter mile or so off the main route that runs along the crest of the Teton mountain range. I'm near where the trail leads into Alaska Basin, a bowl of lakes and whitebark pine where I'd thought to camp—but the

Tetons are crowded, Alaska Basin busy. I've set my tent in this meadow instead and have stayed five nights.

Almost four decades have passed since I last spent time in this mountain range. All those years ago, I clambered and crawled on nearby slopes, measuring, recording, working on my master's degree. Now I've returned to the Tetons for this extended backcountry trip, a bit more learned and a lot more questioning, no longer entertaining any thought of being a research ecologist and no longer bound by boxes or Cartesian attitudes that disallow mystery and negate sensuous learnings. Yet in those decades, I've gained a deeper appreciation of science. Now I carry my past scientific learning with me, part of my way of knowing this world so that the meadow and its surrounds gain depth and meaning in my seeking awareness.

In a sense, I carry ecology with me in another form on this Teton trek, having brought with me the words of a mentoring scientist, though someone I never knew—wildlife biologist Olaus Murie, a man who'd done extensive elk research in the lands east of the Tetons. Before setting out, I reread *Wapiti Wilderness*, in which Olaus and his wife, Margaret Murie, recount their thirty-plus years of life at the base of the Tetons in the Jackson Hole area, where they moved in 1927. The book relates experiences of town life, field research, and raising children in backcountry camps while Olaus collected his data. Bits and pieces of that story are written into the first pages of the journal I carry with me into these mountains, inspiration lying in the Muries' words. I also carry a tiny book, *A Short Biography of Margaret and Olaus Murie* by Christen Girard, to read during my Teton time.[1]

Any contemplation of Murie's thoughts was set aside for the first four days of this Teton sojourn as I worked my way into this meadow below Alaska Basin. It was a hot and strange start, in the midst of the COVID pandemic, mask and gloves part of my kit during a heated summer that sapped the mountain's limited water, baking the earth with unusual temperatures. The water situation was of more concern than COVID once the trek was underway; potential campsites that I'd picked out on the map before starting—places located next to small streams away from the trail—had no water. Alternative sites were found, away from people. I could put the mask away.

On my first night, I pitched the tent amid willows next to a large creek that still ran, finally reached after a grueling uphill climb miles beyond where I'd hoped to camp, every step looking for water, looking to refill my water bottle, to replace the sweat that flowed until it stopped; I had become desiccated like the land. My hands shook as I drank from that stream, the mountain water sweet beyond taste.

My second camp was higher, in a rocky meadow not far from a trickling stream. In the evening and morning, I sat in a garden of paintbrush plants blooming near my tent, a mix of the familiar brilliant red and also a greenish-cream species unfamiliar to me. Despite the lack of summer rain, the flowers appeared at their peak, blossoms rich and full. In the morning, the sun's rising rays lit the land, backlighting the paintbrush so they glowed with color. Hummingbirds buzzed from one flower to the next, stopping only at the paintbrush. A bee worked its way across the opening, visiting just the blue flax that grew amid the paintbrush, extracting the nectar, carrying the pollen. The intricate relationships of sun-plant-insect, cycles and flows, unfolded before me. That rocky meadow entranced; I would have stayed but regrettably had to move on, my days controlled by permits and regulations—a necessary thing in these crowded times.

The third night, I sat with the evening. Having scoured the area where I'd hoped to camp, I again failed to find water. Mountains are a source of the life-giving liquid, the top of the watershed gathering moisture that nourishes lands below... but not this year. I'd had to drop quite far down a side creek before finding water, knowing I would have to haul myself and a heavy pack back up the next day. I made camp next to a trickle in the mostly dry stream channel and sat in the end-of-day stillness, writing in my journal:

My chamomile-lavender tea brews in my big old metal backpack cup. A small bird flies over. Another chirps in the distance. A slight breeze rustles plant and tree. Now a flock of small birds plays over the meadow, perhaps having found an insect hatch. Then gone.

Maybe I should be considering the Muries, or Daoism, or life.

Right now I will just sit and be and drink my chamomile-lavender tea.

I was tired, the tea was good, the water used to make it precious.

The fourth night, I arrived here, in this meadow, removed from the busyness of the main trails. On the meadow's edge is the rock shelf where the deer walked last night, a bench ground by glaciers, smooth with clear striations across its bronze surface. Within the meadow are more polished rocks, patches of trees, a few small, mostly dry water channels lined with pink-blooming monkeyflower, grass-of-Parnassus, senecio, saxifrage, and countless other blossoming plants. The streams are reduced to rivulets connecting tiny pools, enough for drinking and moistening a cloth to wipe the crusted salt off my sweat-stained skin.

The evening that I arrived, the Clark's nutcrackers raucously called, swooping nearby to examine me, their wings catching the air with stiff feathers, a soft *whooph-whoo-whoo* marking their passing even as a marmot chirped repeatedly, a squirrel set up a chatter, and a red-tailed hawk alighted on the top of a subalpine fir and stared down toward camp. These residents seemed surprised by my presence, though over the course of the days, they apparently have accepted me as benign—alarm calls ceased, and now the marmot simply splays on his rock until night falls, when he lumbers into his burrow.

Five nights have passed since I arrived, and now I have reached my last morning within this place. I look southward to take in the massive rise of the Grand Teton, with its streak of icy snow slipping down one face, miles away but seeming close now that the skies have cleared of the heavy pall of wildfire smoke that has permeated this time. Toward the east, an equally impressive Buck Mountain shoots upward, blockier than the Grand, at least from this perspective. I have camped here with these mountains that stand like guardians overlooking the land below. I've watched the peaks dance in and out of smoke-filled skies, knowing they are there even when they are lost to sight. But mostly, nearly always, my attention has been on the life that dwells below the rock and ice.

~~~

The Grand Teton. Buck Mountain. These are but a few of the peaks of the Tetons, a young mountain range uplifted millions of years after most of the Rockies arched toward the sky.

Around nine or ten million years ago, there was a plain where now there are mountains. Rising from the flats, the Tetons thrust rapidly upward, a massive fault sending the nascent peaks skyward as the eastern plain dropped down in a hinge-like motion, the rock rising an average of a millimeter per year, a foot in 300 years. They are still rising, growing in jerks and bouts, the earth working spontaneously with slow, uniform motion cracked by sudden faulting, lifting, and also downfall. Gravity works against height, pulling off rocks, tearing at slopes. But the core of the Tetons is composed of some of the earth's hardest rock, ancient Precambrian granites and gneiss that resist the tearing of time.

The great peaks of the range, the Grand, Middle, and South Tetons, as well as Buck Mountain, are composed of that hard granite, an igneous rock formed underground from slow-cooling magma about 2.5 billion years ago. No creatures walked the surface of the earth as that magma pushed up from below, its upward rise stopping before it broke the surface—life was just beginning. As the molten rock filled in cracks around and within even older rock, it broke apart the metamorphic gneiss lying far beneath the earth's surface. Eons later, while still there was a plain, shallow seas came to the land, surging and ebbing, depositing sediments filled with remnants of marine life over the granite below, layers that in turn became stone over the millennia. When the fault cracked and the Tetons shot upward, those layers of sedimentary rock were pushed up and aside as the granite rose into the sky.

The final sculpting started about 200,000 years ago, when Ice Age glaciations swept over the mountains, ice carving out cirques and U-shaped valleys, leaving high arêtes and sheared ridges, a mountain range of drama and awe. These peaks are young and tough—they remain dramatic against the sky, the rising sun shedding light on abrupt cliffs and spires of the east face, evening rays illuminating more gentle slopes on the west. The result is a geologically and ecologically complex geography
~~~

holding abundance and diversity, a place of discovery for scientists, naturalists, and the open-eyed wanderer.

Much of this geological story is there to see in the present-day structure and composition of the Teton Range, for the mountains open the book of deep time, lifting up the past and laying out the pages for the scientists to analyze, the earth's history made visible. Geologists find blocks of gneiss amid the granite, evidence of that subterranean impact when the magma flowed in. Marine fossils of crinoids and shells lie within the sedimentary layers, a picture of the seas' life petrified in time. The creeping of glaciers dragging rock across rock writes the motion of ice in gouges and striations in hard bedrock. With study, the narrative becomes legible. But there are swaths that lie hidden, vast periods of erosion that sweep away the geologic record. We cannot know the whole story.

The rocks hold this ancient narrative, the mountain a bard of creation. Yet more lies in the mountain terrain than stone stories, for the heights and rugged topography, the lowland to slope to summit traverse, reveal more recent patterns and immediate processes. Physical and biological gradients play out across mountains, climatic factors and available habitats varying with altitude.

Look to the Grand Teton, which stands at 13,770′ above sea level, around 6,770′ above the plain below, that plain that dropped as the mountains lifted. As the raven flies, there are only four horizontal miles from those lowlands to the summit. As the hiker walks, the distance is much farther. The mountain unites all the diversity existing between the dry sagebrush flats at the foot of the range and the rocky windblown point of the peak, holding an abundance of life within its realm. Characteristic communities exist within distinct elevation zones as plants and animals shift in sync with altitude so that an entire Rocky Mountain biota exists in that short stretch from low to high: sagebrush spread in the bottom lands transitions to lodgepole pine that takes hold on the mountain foothills; spruce-fir forests wrap around meadows lush with flowers and green in higher regions; whitebark pine begins to dominate in the uppermost forests, giving way to alpine meadows of stunted hardy plants and tough critters like the pika; then it's into stony fell-fields where mat plants cling on surfaces left barren by winter's blasting winds, roots reaching into soil and moisture in the depths. Above it all is rock and ice, the summit, the peak.

The avian populations move between the zones, lingering in their seasonally preferred habitats: hummingbirds dip beaks into meadow bouquets of paintbrush and fireweed; nutcrackers crack open whitebark pine cones to dine on fatty nuts; vireos and flycatchers, sparrows and hawks wing their way through the ridges and valleys. Mammals from minute to massive fill the niches on mountain slopes, relocating or simply hibernating as seasons dictate. That mix of living beings eats, sleeps, hunts, hides, mates, buds, blossoms, raises young, sets seed, migrates out, returns back, is born and dies within flows of energy, water, and nutrients, all the while immersed in currents of events and time. It is all there on the mountain, from plain to peak.

There is more to be learned. The distribution of that life is related to physical changes over elevation. Temperatures drop with altitude gain, in what science calls the adiabatic lapse rate, cooling about 6.5 degrees Celsius per 1,000 meters, or about 3.5 degrees Fahrenheit per 1,000′. As the air grows chill up high, the water vapor it holds condenses, the peaks gathering their clouds, the clouds dropping their moisture, the rivulets gathering into streams, providing water for the lowlands, making the hydrology of mountains a life source. Atmospheric properties morph across altitude, pressure dropping, UV rising, gradients of physical properties there to be witnessed.

All of this exists within a raven flight of a few miles, a relatively short span, where one can see the earth's workings, view that great stretch of natural diversity, and grasp the unity within the diversity, unlike what can be observed in the endless ocean, the sand-bleak desert, the ice-plain of the Arctic, where the gaze is swept into the unknown. But the significance of what the mountain shows stretches beyond the singular mountain out to earthly importance, for the mountain is a synopsis of planetary properties and patterns, the altitudinal shifts corresponding to latitudinal changes, the peaks reflecting island biogeography. The mountain condenses the earth, its life, its processes, and so presents a laboratory; mountains have been sites for scientific study since studies of nature began.

Over the ages, myths and sacred stories along with utilitarian knowledge explained mountain origins and ecology. As modern science evolved during the age of reason, inquisitive minds turned the developing rational way of knowing toward the mountains. Where mountains reveal the planet's rocky skeleton, theories on mountain creation developed; where ice gouged and glaciers carved, glaciologists and glacial geologists arrived, the first studying the ice itself, the latter analyzing its effects; where mountain species and their diversity hinted at patterns and processes, natural historians found order. The Enlightenment rationale sought that order, classifying and documenting, some seeking to understand, others pursuing that knowledge so as to control the natural world under man's dominion. A barrier grew between objective and subjective, between rational thought and feelings: sacred split from secular in European cultures.

Studies of natural history and the environment flourished in the nineteenth century with two primary ways of exploring nature: a reductionist, taxonomic approach growing out of Linnaeus's work based on classifying the parts, and an integrative, explorative approach of living communities and geographic distributions of life. The mountain satisfied both, its diversity providing a reductionist herbarium of delights as well as a holistic view of relationships and patterns that knit together environment and biota.[2]

Geographer and explorer Alexander von Humboldt (1769–1859) was one of the holistic thinkers. Humboldt studied the world with an eye for connections, synthesizing the parts, weaving together what he witnessed, seeing beyond objects into relationships. On the mountain, he could see the expanse of the world before him and in that, a glimpse of a greater universe: a microcosm of the cosmos. It was the Andean mountain Chimborazo that showed Humboldt the ways of the planet, the environment and life of its slopes providing insight. During his exploration of South America, Humboldt attempted to climb Chimborazo, and though the summit wasn't reached, the mountain revealed the interconnections of nature and the concept of vegetation zones still used today. Later, the data and experience provided the basis for the *Naturgemälde*, "the painting of nature," a depiction of Chimborazo showing in exquisite detail the connected vegetation zones.

The Chimborazo painting is as much a work of art as a synthesis of data, the mountain looming in the center, script filling the sides explaining the relationships, the factors that change with altitude and also with latitude. Humboldt stretched his *Naturgemälde* to correlate the mountain zones to the entire earth, taking what he'd seen on Chimborazo into interrelationships north and south, pole to pole. This painting was, in Humboldt's words, a "microcosm on one page,"[3] for Chimborazo showed him more than the earth; Humboldt saw the cosmos mirrored in the mountain, the interconnected oneness of it all. And in turn, Humboldt showed it to the rational world.

Humboldt was certainly not the first to see the interwoven, interrelated whole of nature, for Indigenous peoples and other cultures had recognized and honored that fact for thousands of years. What Humboldt uniquely did was bring that concept of interrelated nature—all is one—into a scientific world, seeing it through the rational mind of the European Enlightenment, juxtaposing holistic thinking against the reductionist line of thought that dominated during his time. Humboldt could not reduce nature to simple parts; he did not see nature as a machine. The Mountain showed him other truths.

Mountains hold these lessons of connections, relationships, processes, and also "something more," as I have thought, looking upward to the peaks. And within these high places, I too learned far more from the Mountain than simply objective machinations—a learning that took place in part within the Teton Range.

Enduring as they might seem, mountains also teach of change in a natural world where nothing is static. Rocks and crags reveal the earth's motions and modifications on an intermediate scale within the cosmos's eternal flux, even as the mountain's extreme topography and environment drive more immediate and graspable change, like the rapid, chaotic disturbances of tumbling rock, debris flows, and billowing snow avalanches ripping down steep slopes. That last is what brought a young scientist to the Tetons to study and learn, a hopeful ecologist in training.

The Tetons provided an intriguing site, for in the deep valleys between the rising peaks, avalanches careen down the steep slopes in winter, impacting all in their path. Those avalanche paths became the topic for my master's degree in the ecological sciences.

Cascade Canyon was my research site, a narrow valley running into the heart of the Tetons, surrounded by towering peaks and unforgiving cliffs. There, I plunged into a study of the relationship between vegetation patterns and the region's frequent avalanches. Almost every day for two summers, I scrambled up and down those steep slopes, analyzing the plants and vegetation communities found within and aside the avalanche tracks, coring into the heart of countless trees to determine their age, stretching my tape measure to quantify vegetative diversity, marking number after number on my data sheets. Every day around noon, I unpacked lunch and a small notebook and wrote prose and poetry, noting the creatures and marvels that had crossed my path, my words and thoughts meandering far from quantitative assessment of the ecosystem. Often before returning to the fieldwork, I stood under icy waterfalls or dipped breathlessly into bubbling creeks to rejuvenate. The sun rose and set over the peaks while I worked, gold light splashing across steel-gray rock at the beginning and end of my days—except those days when rain settled in, laying a quiet hand over the valley and sending misty ribbons through the pinnacles.

From those field days, I learned that avalanches in Cascade Canyon are so frequent, they can hardly be called a disturbance: they are part of the ecosystem's function. I learned that avalanches snap trees and send them hurtling down the slope when the trunks reach ten centimeters in diameter; smaller trees bend under the crashing snow and survive. I learned that trees in avalanche tracks grow at extremely slow rates, either due to the annual winter stress of being hit by tons of snow or because the only trees that survive for any length of time in avalanche tracks are the stunted ones, and so only the slow-growing trees reproduce: some of the oldest trees I found in all my measuring and recording were in the middle of avalanche paths, small conifers that I could easily wrap my hands around. I learned that the avalanche tracks, with their stubby trees and thick bushes, provide habitat and forage for bears, moose, and other creatures, many of whom I saw in my days in Cascade Canyon.

The research came together, data and conclusions duly published in an academic, peer-reviewed journal.[4] But that article skimmed the surface of what I came to know in the Tetons. Within my growing understanding of the cycles and connections, the shifting patterns, the ebb and flow of life, a deeper relationship with nature developed, growing out of a conversation with the mountain during the dialogue of the days, a glimmer of something beyond the how and what, beyond the physical measurements. I came to know that science contributes to understanding even as my mountain experience, past and present, Montana and Teton, led to a comprehension of the environment that was far more than physical.

~~~

This Teton journey took on a new tempo when I reached the camp below Alaska Basin, only a few miles from Cascade Canyon but many years away from the time of my master's research. Camp made, settled in for a few days—now there was time for contemplation of Olaus Murie's thoughts. On the first evening in this meadow, I turned to my journal, considering Murie's words copied into the front cover: "When we attain a new understanding of something in the field of science, the thoughtful scientist is filled with wonder and a degree of reverence for what we only partially understand. A poetic appreciation of life, combined with a knowledge of nature, creates humility, which in turn becomes the greatness of man."[5]

That was the evening I first sat on the stone bench, that long ledge of burnished stone where I rested, cooked, wrote, sipped whisky, mused on the immediate and pondered the unknown, all the while supported by the silky smoothness of ancient rock polished by glacial ice. Technically, I believe the rock under my campsite was quartz monzonite, an intrusive igneous rock that cooled slowly underground in the Precambrian, a rock like the Teton granite but with different mineralogy. The scientist in me fascinates in such things; the person sitting on the
~~~

bench, lying on the stone slabs watching swallows, wasn't too concerned about technicalities. In my journal it is granite. Mostly it was beautiful.

The next morning, I again sat on the stone bench trying to focus on Murie's thoughts; it seemed that in a few sentences, Murie had captured the essence of a worldview or way of knowing that could be significant to this Earth we live on. Smoke warped my focus, smoke that had rolled in during the night, now so dense the sun's morning light sifted dully through the gray, that sun having risen coppery-bronze into a rusty sky. As the morning progressed, the muted light remained orange-gray, Grand Teton and Buck Mountain only ethereal silhouettes in a haze. It had been a smoky summer, with wildfire across the west, but things were getting worrisome.

The world around me carried on. Two ravens flew over, and I called to them, *Crawack! Raven!* They circled, then flapped off, my presence only a momentary curiosity. Small birds called and chattered; swallows came off the cliffs, soaring overhead for a time. Six more ravens circled and called from above. I called back, but they were heedless. Were they at play or in hunt?

I gave up on Murie's words, jotting down, *Do the birds, squirrels, other beings feel the apprehension like I do? Where does the smoke come from? Need I worry?*

My mind wandered, my pen slowed. The flowers around burst with color, though some were getting a bit faded in their autumnal slump. Bumblebees harvested nectar and pollen from the younger blossoms. I sat watching the bees... Then—

The smoke is thicker... I need to do something about it. Find a cell phone signal or something.

In the margin, I jotted a note to remind myself that I wanted to write about the color preference of pollinators:

Bees ▸ *Blue, Flies* ▸ *White*

Lunch, water, raingear, first aid kit, journal—the necessities packed,

I hurried back up the trail, headed to the Teton Crest, the highline of the uplifted rock, hoping to stand on that edge and catch a signal. Hiking upward, out of the valley that ends in Alaska Basin, I moved up through time, out of Precambrian igneous rock into Cambrian limestone, a sedimentary rock that was once a seabed under those shallow seas that came and went. Did I notice? No. Maslow's hierarchy of needs, I suppose, safety and security more important than musing about deep time.

A solo woman appeared headed the other direction, white hair, dressed in shorts and T-shirt, carrying a light pack, moving quickly along the trail though she did not appear too athletic. We greeted, and I asked,

"Are you day hiking?"

"Yes..."

"Do you know where the smoke is coming from?"

"No. Maybe Colorado. I talked to someone from Colorado, and there are fires there."

She was cheerful, friendly.

"I've been in for four nights... a bit worried."

"Oh, nothing to worry about. I came from down there..." She pointed west toward Idaho. "No fires there." She described her hiking route to me, a *long* route, and then said, "I have a baby shower to get to."

"You'd best be on your way then!"

And off she went, an impressive person, and one who had alleviated my fears.

Still I pursued contacting my parents, though my pace slowed, my awareness focused more on the surrounds, as I simultaneously envied that woman for all the terrain she'd cover in one day, even as I relished my slowness. *Saunter*, Thoreau advocated. Saunter so as to see, sense, immerse.

Headed up the crest, I crossed a strange landscape of bare, gray rock and faded dispersed yellow plants spreading out in a flat plane under smoke-filled skies. It had a surreal feel, such a rocky contrast to the lushness of nearby places, though it was far from lifeless, with scattered plants, birds, and the numerous burrows and scat piles of pocket gophers and marmots. The smoke hung low, the sky pressing down, gray against that stoney grayness. The only sign of the Grand Teton was the pale streak of snow running down its side, hardly visible in the murk.

I walked higher, moving above that bleak-feeling landscape into a moist drainage filled with color, where lupine, bluebell, groundsel, and an unidentified plant with a white umbel flower grew in abundance. Bees buzzed on the blue and yellow, flies fed from the white. *All in "cooperation,"* I thought, remembering Olaus Murie's word for the pollinator-flower relationship. The buzz was soft and soothing, the colors rich. An impressive buck mule deer appeared above, followed shortly by three more, all with antlers so big that for a moment, I thought they were elk. They watched me watching them, then moved away nonchalantly. A bluebird appeared, an unexpected avian familiar. For a moment I was just there and nowhere else. For a moment, the outside world slipped away, the desire for a signal diminished.

I met the cliff edge of the Teton Crest just above the glacially carved Death Valley, the view down the valley barely reaching to Phelps Lake at its base, everything beyond nonexistent to the eye, awash in smoke. My trek had started near that lake, at the Death Valley trailhead, that first hot afternoon in the midst of the pandemic, wearing a mask half the time, walking through dust and tourists and COVID to Open Canyon, where there was no accessible water for such a long way. Now I'd come to the crest to connect with that crazy world below, and yes, there was a signal—and a disturbed sense filled me, tension and concern returned. I sent the text. It failed. The text message did not go through. I moved along the crest for a better signal. Tried and failed again. And again. It felt manic. There was a signal. The text did not go. I did not want to be sending a text, did not want to connect with that world of phones and media and materialism, but I did want to connect with my family. *There's a signal, damn it. Send.* The text just sat there, going nowhere. Smoke thickened, and the Grand Teton disappeared from sight.

I walked farther along the crest. My juniper-bead sunglass strap broke, the one I bought from a friend of a friend in Arizona. "They will protect you," the Navajo woman told me of the wooden berries strung along the eyeglass retainer, handing it to me with her merry eyes that held more than humor.

I stopped, sat where a few of the beads had dropped to the ground. The juniper berry string—strung through with meaning—had suddenly broken for no apparent reason.

I picked up the beads, tied the broken strand together, put it back on. Carried on. Tried to send again. Carried on, carried on...

And eventually a text reached my mother.

The fires were in California.

I turned my back on the pandemic world of pandemonium, retreating to my camp in the meadow below Alaska Basin, where the bees were sipping at the blue flowers and the flies were tasting the white flowers and the marmot sprawled and the nutcrackers called. As evening fell, I sipped my whisky, read Murie's words—*wonder and a degree of reverence*—and noticed a tree on the ledge across the glade, an old whitebark pine that looked a bit elfin, possibly a good home for gnomes. When the sun had set on my campsite, the Elfin Tree held the last rays, shining gold-green for a long time after my slick granite bench was in shade, though it was only a stone's throw away.

~~~

After that first smoky day at this camp, I've headed out each day to immerse in notable meetings and memorable sights: a pika's haystack beneath a massive boulder, the pile of leaves and stalks stored for winter decorated with a cream-colored paintbrush flower laid across the top like a bouquet; an ouzel—the American dipper—bathing in a trickling stream, its wings splashing the water in a glittering array of drops; a black marmot, a color I've never seen on that animal, lounging on a rock amid a wildflower garden; a vireo, the slightest of birds, bouncing down a branch to stand an arm's length from my face, chipping in apparent curiosity. There were the towering peaks, the sweep of the ridges, the alpine meadows awash in color—these I remember too. There were many people along the trails, some good conversations, the two men with their backpacks, moving slowly: "We came to saunter through the Tetons," they told me, referencing Thoreau, I believe. There were also some discouraging sights—campfires built in fragile areas where fires are
~~~

not allowed, horse hoof tracks gouged into delicate soils where horses are not allowed. There was a group of young women, scantily clad, jogging along the trail, their leader obviously coaching them on how to run through the Tetons: "You have to pace it, run where it's flat, jog on gentle places, walk for a rest..." I was sitting not far off the trail on a natural stone bench composed of a rock that had piqued my curiosity. They were not aware of my presence, did not see my wave, leaving me to wonder what else they did not see outside the trail beneath their feet.

On one of those days of wandering, I headed toward Hurricane Pass, which lies due south of Grand Teton, Middle Teton, and South Teton. Stand on that pass and the three peaks rise before you, a panorama of granitic grandeur, rock and ice, where lichen clings to stone and other bits of life tuck into protected crannies. I went as far as the slopes above the pass, hiking through the smoke that lay thick over the entire western United States, though at the time, I only knew that it enveloped my immediate surrounds. The three high peaks of the Tetons towered dark gray against the lighter pall of leaden skies. Two backpackers stood on the pass below, tiny bits of red and blue amid a vast sea of rock and smoke, talus and crag. People probably stood on the high point of the Grand Teton that day, the day of their precious permit to reach the summit. What was it like to stand there on the peak, in the haze, to see nothingness? Did the power of the Mountain, the immensity of the cosmos overwhelm at that point, without any perspective of solid earth to ground them in immediate reality?

Beyond the peaks, the head of Cascade Canyon opened, haze cloaking the extent of the valley. I could make out a few avalanche tracks, strips of rock and shrubby vegetation running down the very slopes where my master's degree research took place. I could see the span of diversity from the Grand Teton's summit rock to the lodgepole forests below, but no farther.

It was an odd feeling to look into that canyon on that surreal day of smoke and peaks, thinking of my cynical rejection of science for so many years, how I would later come to embrace the rational scientific as significant, even a foundation, for deeper understanding. I'm not alone in that by any means: as the decades have passed, there seems to be a growing amount of transdisciplinary thought, collaborations that combine the objective rational with subjective, even spiritual, ideas, both ways of knowing making legitimate contributions to our understanding of the cosmos. This includes an embrace of the traditional ecological knowledge of people who have lived within their lands for generation after generation, people who often gracefully unite sacred and secular, holy and utilitarian.[6]

But that was not the case at the time (1980s) and in the department where I earned my master's degree.

At the end of nearly three years of study, I endured my thesis defense, a ritual demonstrating knowledge while proving (so I was told) that you, as a graduating graduate student, could stand in front of a room of senior scientists and hold your own as they interrogate and examine and follow a line of questioning until you are ground to a standstill at the extent of your factual knowledge. The questions I faced delved into every aspect of relevant ecology, from predator-prey interactions to nutrient cycles to landscape dynamics to chaos theory. My answers came from textbooks and lecture notes, crunched numbers and literature review.

And then came the question, "Do you believe there is order in nature?"

Standing in front of five senior scientists, I unthinkingly responded from a different realm of learning. "Not as much as we would like to think," I said and went on to explain in stumbling words that I believe scientists put nature into boxes and connect those boxes with arrows and equations because humans need to think like that. Although there is a truth to our equations and our models, there is another element beyond the box.

Eyebrows raised. "Hmmm…" my committee responded and left the exchange hanging heavy in the air.

Later, reviewing my examination results, my advisor looked at me with a seemingly sorrowful expression and told me that my response to that question had almost led to my failure. The committee felt strongly that a person could not be a scientist unless they firmly believed in the order of nature—atoms and systems and cycles that are predictable and systematic. The message seemed clear: Do not think outside of the box that fits into the model. Not if you want to be a scientist.

In those young years, Humboldt was known only to me through the names of the Humboldt Current and Humboldt's life zones. Perhaps if I'd known of Humboldt's "order and adornment," I could have answered the question more eloquently and completely, for Humboldt was not a man to stick purely to objective science: his approach to exploring the natural world combined a sense of wonder with detailed observation, a merging of spirit and matter, emotion and fact. This he poured into *Cosmos: A Sketch of a Physical Description of the Universe*, a five-volume[7] exploration of "the whole material world—all that we know to-day of celestial bodies and of life upon the earth—from the nebular stars to the mosses on the granite rocks."[8] Volume 1 was the order of the cosmos, the physical, objective, "external phenomena"; volume 2 was the "adornment," the interaction of that material world with "man's inner being, his ideas and feelings." Adornment is humanity's depth of spirit and sense of beauty integrated into the universe.

Though the physical aspects and orderly composition of the material world include but are not dependent on humanity, adornment according to Humboldt is contingent on the "reflexivity" between human and the universe, the universe taking on the qualities of beauty and wonder through our perceptions and creative spirit; it is the Beauty that rises from order like the music of the spheres, a symphony playing across the universe. "There is geometry in the humming of the strings, there is music in the spacing of the spheres," said Pythagoras. Entwined with order is Beauty—perhaps not literal notes, but music that grows out of our human awareness, our aesthetic, creative beholding of the order.

"Order and adornment" combine in composing the cosmos, Humboldt believed. There can be a material universe without art, creativity, intuition, spirit, emotion, but there cannot be a cosmos, cannot be "one great whole... animated by the breath of life." Humanity's and all life's creative endeavors and sensuous relationship with the world are part of the greater ecosystem, part of the interacting whole.[9]

Humboldt's thinking broke away from the Cartesian dualism of the time, planting wonder and beauty, our senses and feelings, in the midst of facts and rational ideology. Still, he felt that scientific knowledge was critical, for the particulars and the factual sat at the heart of things. The mountains, with their material complexity combined with their capacity to spark wonder and inspire awe, provided the prime environment for a man who comprehended the universe in this way. The Mountain sat within Humboldt's thinking, its influence shaping his perspective, tutoring him in the ways of the cosmos. As one environmental historian stated, Humboldt's "Goethean ideal of total knowledge, rich with the combined virtues of art and science, and whose scientific dimension included not only knowledge of the natural facts but also human experience of them, was best implemented in mountain landscapes."[10]

Olaus Murie was a man not so different from Humboldt, and I carried his words and ideas with me in my pack and in my mind during those Teton days. Perhaps this is why that master's degree defense question rose so clearly to the surface on the day I went to Hurricane Pass and looked into Cascade Canyon. On that day, I again began the morning reading Murie's thoughts, those I'd copied into my journal, a passage where he described the "small adventures" of the natural world he'd seen in the wilds: the moose walking out of the fog, the pure white weasel "hopping up, carrying a field mouse," the eagle overhead. "These are the adventures of the wilderness, the scenes and the music which make up Nature's great mosaic. Why do we so delight in the wild creatures of the forest, some of us so passionately that it colors our whole life? Why do we love music, Art? Are not all akin, a part of beauty which we really do not understand."[11]

Murie was a wildlife biologist with years of field experience in Alaska and Wyoming, time spent in intimate relationship with the natural world. His scientific knowledge made legible the material environment, enriching his holistic understanding of the natural world as a complex, integrated community. Within this tangled web, across the relationships that included the bloody deaths and killed creatures who become food for others, he saw an interrelated whole, each participant, each living being, a part of the community. He understood the animals were not devoid of awareness, even holding a glimmering sense of aesthetics, expanding Humboldt's idea of reflexivity beyond the human; we are all kin.

Murie's cosmos was also not limited to the material; his sense of the world was a meshing of nature and culture, science and spirit, holding a beauty we cannot fully know but can feel. His was an embrace of Humboldt's "order and adornment," extended out to include the sentience of other life.

I should have answered that defense question differently, for as Murie and Humboldt before him knew, yes, there is order in nature: a beautiful order of celestial orbits and migratory movements and seasonal change, of birth and death and nutrients that move in an orderly fashion through an ecosystem, of vegetation zones that shift in a predictable manner as one moves up the mountain slope. The order is exquisite. I find nothing wrong with quantifying and modeling, finding order, learning more, and so having a better understanding. But call it adornment, call it what you will—there is simply more. I can't stop at the border of the box.

The wide eyes of the dead elk calf, the contentedly grazing grizzly bear, the piercing stare of the peregrine, the light in the wolf's eyes guarding its young, the scream of the first hawk of spring, the coil of a crinoid entombed on a ridge-top seabed, the solitary raven so black he is silver flying overhead on a bright summer day when I stand in a field of alpine flowers and the blood runs sweet through my veins—the visceral existence of those moments drove my answer that day of my defense. I can't put those moments, those beings, those places—that *life*—in a box.

I passed my master's degree defense, went on for a PhD, then a research position. But I didn't have the disposition of an academic scientist and it didn't last. Yet I will always be an ecologist; it is a discipline that can fertilize wonder and nurture joy in the natural world, a foundation for that leap beyond the box. That's what the Mountain taught me.

Looking into the smoky depths of Cascade Canyon, I considered all of that, understanding how that mentoring continues every time I immerse within the stretch of the mountainscape.

~~~
~~~

After each of my wandering days here in the heights of the Tetons, I have returned to this meadow where my tent is tucked into the trees along the edge, where the inviting stone benches provide my place to sit and eat and write and the slabs of polished granite provide a place to stretch and lie and watch the sky. I have come back to this place with its islands of subalpine fir, where my food hangs in its bear-proof sack, where the squirrel lives and the little black bear wandered through, where the hawk watches and the marmot lounges. Returning to this meadow is to enter a world of exquisite peace, and I've wanted nothing more.

In the later evening, after rinsing my body in mountain water, writing in the leather journal, and dining on quinoa and lentils, it became my habit to take steaming ginger tea across the glade to sit at the base of the Elfin Tree and watch the sun set—again, for it already had dropped below the horizon from the perspective of my cooking site along the rock bench. The craggy old tree is a whitebark pine bent in a gentle curve like an elderly woman, its feet wrapped around stones, a long scar running down one side revealing bare wood amid the bark. Whitebark pine is a high-elevation species, a mountain lover, and this particular tree had been sitting here not far below timberline for quite some time—old yet prospering, a healthy crop of cones resting in its upper branches, plump full of seeds as thick and fatty as any pine nut you might purchase at a grocery store. Every evening, I sat with the tree and watched the world turn until it hid the last of the sun.

On those short evening strolls to the Elfin Tree, I've walked past a patch of mountain bog gentian in full bloom, each flower an exquisitely shaped vase of deep-blue petals, sometimes bordering on indigo. Watching this particular cluster over the days, I've learned the gentians close at night and open during the day when the big *Bombus* bumblebees plunge into the vase, leaving only their fuzzy, orange-striped behinds visible. This is visually a beautiful sight—the complementary colors, the grace of the flower cupping the softness of the bee. Yet the wonder of that beauty is deeper than what I see, built on the intimate relationship between insect and plant developed over the eons: as the bee sips nectar, it both gathers and drops pollen grains, spreading pollen plant to plant, fertilizing, carrying the cycle forward. And marvelously, the bees specifically choose that blue flower, for bees best see blue and don't see red at all. They also see a color beyond human sight: we see yellow, they see "bee's purple," a combination of yellow and ultraviolet light.

So bees most often go to blue and violet and are well rewarded, for apparently those are the flowers that produce the highest volume of nectar; the plants have "learned" how to attract their pollinator through color and nectar. Coevolution. "Cooperation," Murie might add. Pollination takes place.

Bees ▸ Blue...

The bees' relationship to the gentian might be called the *order* of nature, something humans have come to know through rigorous research on such relationships and properties. The understanding of the bees attraction to blue flowers and the resulting pollination involves different disciplines—phenology: the changes and movements happening with the regular cycling of the seasons, including when and why plants flower at certain times; evolutionary ecology: coevolution of species, some so specific, one pollinator species is required for one plant species; plant physiology: how and why a plant looks blue; entomology: how a bee sees blue and why not red. This is science uncovering the processes of the natural order of things.

Yet there is more than the order, if one agrees with the likes of Humboldt and Murie. Woven into that order is the wonder and beauty that grows out of our human spirit interacting with the natural world: my emotional reaction in witnessing the bee-plant relationship was wonder, sprung from watching the exquisite beauty of the bee at work in the gentian. Yet perhaps in departure from Humboldt's "reflexivity," I do not believe that beauty existed because of my presence but rather is an innate quality of nature, just as creativity and aesthetic sensibilities are not limited to human beings. I may have animated the beauty through my sense of it, brought expression to it by recording it, sharing it, spreading its strength to others, but it seems to me it is always there, a current beneath the order, flowing throughout the cosmos, there to be seen—especially in the mountains that inspire and stun us with all that they hold, from foothill to peak, valley to ridge, a microcosm of the cosmos.

On the evening after I'd been to Hurricane Pass, on that day that began with those words of Murie about beauty, I contemplated the idea of Beauty. And like the other evenings, a *knock-knock tap-tap* above me heralded the arrival of a couple of Clark's nutcrackers. The bird is a corvid, an intelligent creature in the jay family, sleek and handsome with gray head and breast, black wings and flashing white tail feathers when in flight. Above me, the nutcrackers would diligently, delicately peck the seeds from the cones with their long sharp beaks. There is purpose in this—sustenance and survival—but there is the arc of the bird's beak, the grace of the motion, the end-of-day light accentuating the colors; there is something more. *There is*, I thought, *Beauty*.

A long-standing relationship exists between the Clark's nutcracker and the whitebark pine. The bird takes the fat seeds, stashing them in the earth in scattered piles for future consumption. Not all these stashed pine nuts are exhumed and eaten; some establish and grow into trees, meaning the nutcracker serves to disperse the pine. The whitebark pine is also critical food for grizzly bears in the fall, the bruins ripping cones from trees, raiding squirrel stashes, and presumably gobbling up any discovered nutcracker hordes as well.

It's all connected, coevolved into a dance, order adorned. From the beginning of life, the steps have changed, the climate shifts, and species adapt or disappear. Yet now the speed of climate change and habitat destruction is often too fast for adaptations and evolutionary catch-up; high rates of extinction result. The smoke knocks on this meadow with a pall that reaches beyond my week in this place, for it rises from unprecedented fires in the west during a brutally dry summer, "unprecedented" a constantly changing baseline as the world moves into a new norm. The seasons temporally shift as the climate warms. Bees to blue, flies to white—until the blue and white flowers blossom at a different time, blowing away the synchronicity, the pollinators missing their sustenance, the plants losing their procreative force. Seasonal temperatures also change. A majority of the whitebark pine around our family ranch have died off due to milder winters that created conditions ripe for pine bark beetle infestations at high altitudes: the beetles girdled the whitebark, leaving ghost forests no longer visited by nutcracker or grizzly. Order disrupted, the music off-key, the rhythm lost, the dancers no longer knowing when or where to step.

Climate change. The scientists have done their work and the science is there, the facts blazing across the planet, the species dying off on a world where habitat dwindles even as temperatures rise. The public holds that science in their hand. And?

The cosmos is a community, and we are part of it, alongside all of the other beings and matter. Beauty is as integral to that vast community as all of its tangibles, for Beauty arises out of the intricacies and order of the material universe, sometimes raw and terrifying, sometimes as soft as a bumblebee on a flower. And Beauty is a quality of the cosmos that inspires wonder, love, and compassion; the great naturalists of our time who made headway into public consciousness thus did not stop at objective facts, for to experience that Beauty means one cannot stand aside and let it be destroyed.

Aldo Leopold, a wildlife biologist, wrote in the *Sand County Almanac*, "That land is a community is the basic concept of ecology, but that land is to be loved and respected is an extension of ethics."[12] *Love* is not a word found in academic articles.

Rachel Carson, a marine biologist whose *Silent Spring* changed the world by catalyzing the environmental movement, embraced wonder within her science, writing in her book *A Sense of Wonder*, "If I had influence with the good fairy who is supposed to preside over the christening of all children, I should ask that her gift to each child in the world be a sense of wonder so indestructible that it would last throughout life."[13]

Olaus Murie wrote of beauty, wonder, and reverence. He and Margaret contributed greatly to protecting the environment and natural world.

Humans are not simply creatures of factual knowledge; our ancestors created exquisite paintings and flute music well over 30,000 years ago. Who we are as humans is planted in that aesthetic with its spiritual undercurrents; tucked into our genetic makeup is an understanding that nature is not simply a machine, and the cosmos is not simply matter. This is remembered, keenly felt, with intimate time on a mountain, where the awe and sublimity rise up in grand perspective, where the smallest of creatures carries on, where vireos sing and gentians bloom, and where a "whole" is sensed, intuited if not grasped. For within all the tangible, material, explainable properties of the mountains, what most tantalizes many of us is that which cannot be seen, what is felt outside of the data, what cannot be fully articulated. Humboldt, whose greatest insights were nurtured on Mount Chimborazo, felt that "what speaks to the soul, what causes such profound and various emotions, escapes our measurements, as it does the forms of language."[14]

And so the Beauty of the Bumblebee. The Charisma of Elfin Tree.

Science is necessary but apparently insufficient to address the global environmental-cultural crises we face now. Humanity must recognize what is being lost, and that seems best achieved by truly seeing the beauty, feeling the wonder, sensing in all ways what nature holds. We are here to witness this moment on Earth, an Earth where science provides facts and experience offers opportunities to be in a natural world where beauty and wonder are intrinsic. But so many on this planet are caught up in surface ways and run through it seeing only the trail beneath their feet, and perhaps more are facing Maslow's hierarchy, survival and security trumping all things.

I thought about Murie's words and the smoke and the beauty the evening after I went to Hurricane Pass, my last evening in the meadow—then set it aside, to sit by Elfin Tree, listening to the end-of-day hush, the familiar meadow taking on a golden hue. Soon I would go lie on the granite slab polished by ice and watch the swallows fly until—in their orderly fashion—they soared and swooped back into their cliff.

But for the moment, I thought, *I will just sit and* **be** *and drink my chamomile-lavender tea.*

~~~

And so I come to my last morning in the meadow. The robin has now landed on a rock about fifteen feet away. He hops off, pecks a few bugs from a plant, and is away. Smaller birds near the willow-lined streamlet peck at the umbels that look like hefty Queen Anne's lace—perhaps
~~~

warblers gathering insects or sparrows gathering seeds? The birds and plants are backlit in an intricate entwining of light and movement. A hummingbird flew through this morning, paused at the last of the fireweed flowers, sipped and drank, then flew on—a calliope, I think, migrating. A nuthatch has been beeping all morning, after calling off and on all the days—I have not seen him, but he holds a presence—and the squirrel just loped past with another cone.

It is clear this morning, the sky blue, the smoke gone. The mountains stand tall, holding their teachings, inspiring awe, harboring life in their slopes and hope in their heights.

When I finish my coffee, when I put away the journal…

…a huge flock of birds just flew in, sounding like a chirping wind gust, landing in the spruce behind. Finches? Red polls? A *Bombus*—a BIG *Bombus*—just buzzed me…

…when I put away the journal, I will pack, and I will leave. But not before I walk over to the Elfin Tree and lay a hand on the old Being, lie on the cool polished slab, and look at the sky…

…then walk out, and up the trail, and away.

The life will carry forward, the season will cycle, and the aster seeds will drop to nurture the next generation. And it will be beautiful, though I will not be here to see it.

4
THE ROMANTIC MOUNTAIN

Yosemite, California

It began underground, as is the way of granite, magma pushing up from below, amassing in vast amounts before cooling into hard rock beneath the surface. Once again, it was the traveling plates of earth's outermost layer driving this orogenic event, one plate sinking beneath another along the west coast of what is now North America. The submerged plate heated as it descended, melted, then rose in a hot flow, cooling as it neared the surface, where it solidified into granite some 70 million years ago; a mountain embryo rested within the earth. Erosion ate at the land over the granite, exposing the resistant rock. Millions of years later, faulting drove the granite and neighboring strata upward. The Sierra Nevada range was born.

Released from the pressure of the earth, the granite expanded, causing layers of rock to explode off in an erosion aided by the elements, the exfoliation of stony sheets sculpting stone into massive domes and high curvatures. But not even granite is hard enough to withstand ice. Over two million years ago, as temperatures dropped, ice scoured the Sierra Nevada—hard ice, fluid ice, ice that polished rock, carved stone, shaped the earth, ice that flowed in rivers as glacial ice, the same form of ice that shaped the Montana mountains and burnished the granite slabs of the Tetons. The ice in the Sierra Nevada cut into mountains, carrying away the rock, leaving knife-edge ridges, high arêtes, and half domes. A dramatic landscape. A sublime landscape.

The ice scooped out a basin in the heart of the region we now call Yosemite National Park, its floor uneven with dips large enough to hold water, creating Ten Lakes Basin, a glacial bowl where granite cliffs and rugged mountains rise over a cluster of lakes. Fish swim in the modern-day lakes, one caught by a preying osprey on an early August day. On the surface of that same lake, on that same summer day, a duck paddled, followed by a handful of fluffball chicks. On the edge of that lake, I sat watching Mama Duck and her children floating over a reflection of forest and cliff while the osprey ate its catch, all of us settled within the granite that cupped the lake in its palm.

I found the way of that rock unfamiliar—its habit of layering itself, of splitting off in sheets, the freshness of its pearly color where it seemed so recently polished, its granite smoothness contrasting to tumbled talus. The rock rounded into humps, heaved into heights, snapped off into cliffs, curved into bowls, and slid into valleys in ways that didn't fit within my knowing of mountains. Yet even so, I recognized the mark of the glaciers across the range, from the least striation scratched into a boulder to the U-shape of the vast valleys.

I'd already encountered the unfamiliar as I walked in, for the mature forest around the trail to Ten Lakes Basin also held the unknown, a woodland composed mostly of tall trees with stately trunks of a species I hoped to later identify. In the decaying wood of a long-dead conifer, a seedling sprouted, so new to the world that its cotyledon leaves still converged at the tips, like a hand with the fingertips touching. Only a few centimeters high, the tiny tree represented the possibility of the next generation of forest, a significant bit of life within the immensity of the mountains.

Climbing upward toward Ten Lakes Pass, I walked out of the forest and through a lush meadow where white and purple patches revealed an abundance of bistort and shooting stars, the same flower species that grace my mountain homeland—welcome familiars. Rock came to dominate at the higher elevation, trees reduced to pockets at the high point of the pass. Before me rose peaks and arching ridges, the splendor of Yosemite. Below, lakes shimmered amid the woodland of Ten Lakes Basin, my home for the next ten days.

Yosemite had never been on my radar screen outside of a momentary discussion with my sister-in-law about sharing our fiftieth birthday celebrations there; it was never a place I'd yearned to see. For many of the same reasons, Yosemite's patron saint, John Muir, was not a man I'd chosen as a focus for any of my studies. Both mountains and man hold their exceptional qualities, making them icons in many ways for many things, but that very popularity and renown pushed me away—and honestly, something didn't sit right about Muir. So ironically, on a warm August day, I walked into Ten Lakes Basin to share paths with Muir, perhaps slip into Muir's essence by wading into his Yosemite. He had been in Ten Lakes Basin, calling it "a glacier basin with ten glassy lakes set all near together like eggs in a nest."[1] I walked into the basin in the footsteps of a man I did not understand.

Alaska

It was Alaska that connected me to Muir, when my naturalist work planted me on a ship that took tours between Juneau and Sitka through the Inside Passage, a coastal waterway of intertwined fjords. Over a century before, Muir had traveled those same waters, exploring their shores, interacting with the region's native Tlingit people.[2] It was the ice that drew him, the glaciers that flowed and scoured, shaping the Alaskan terrain. Muir went to where glacial processes were still visibly happening, hoping to demonstrate that glaciers were a driving force in Yosemite's creation.

Muir knew glaciers were at work in Yosemite; his university studies combined with his intimate knowledge of the Sierra Nevada range to make this obvious. He could see the working of ice in the land's curves and cliffs, its sweeps and sliding rock faces. The sculpting of the glaciers was written in the terrain, the mountain shapes and contours telling the story of the past. Muir knew it to be true, proclaiming it in his writings: "Half Dome was probably the first of the Yosemite rocks to emerge from the ice.... Its flinty surface, scarcely at all wasted, is covered with glacial inscriptions from base to crown, and the meaning of these is the reward of all who devoutly study them."[3]

Now he set out to prove it, heading to Alaska to confirm his theory of glaciation, a concept that contradicted other ideas of the time. It was a journey both of study and of adventure for this man whose wanderlust was driven by his bond with nature.

In Alaska, Muir saw the mountains emerging from ice, walked over the glaciers themselves, took in the freshly carved stone. He wrote articles and books and became the first to truly "understand the physical processes in motion" in that wild land.[4] Alaska provided Muir with a view of creation, and Muir provided the American public with a view of Alaska.

With my own Alaska departure imminent, Muir became a topic of my studies, his words adding to my understanding of the Inside Passage where I would be a tour guide and naturalist. I came to better understand how Alaska marked Muir, how the wildness and primal essence of the land sank into his soul to shape his view of wild nature through Kim Heacox's book, *John Muir and the Ice That Started a Fire*.[5] I arranged to meet Kim in his hometown of Gustavus, Alaska, before joining the small cruise ship I would be working on.

Our conversation took place at the festive Gustavus Fourth of July celebration. We shared ideas about Muir and wildlands surrounded by laughter and happy shouts, three-legged races, horseshoes, music, booths, and other elements of such small-town events. Within that conversation, one singular idea struck me more than anything else: Heacox's idea that "John Muir saw primal America in Alaska. He realized what was at stake."

What Muir encountered in Alaska was a land newly revealed, largely uninhabited, as close to "pristine" wilderness as may happen on Earth in modern history, for when Muir and his Tlingit guides first paddled into Glacier Bay in 1879, they entered waters so recently covered with ice that the 1794 charts showed only a great glacier swathing the land. With each paddle stroke, Muir moved farther into the newborn country surrounding the bay's water, land that appeared clean and unsullied by human activity. Muir absorbed this untouched land, this "primal America," even as mines gouged and logging ripped across the American frontier and into the California wilds he had come to know. Heacox led me to understand that Muir realized what was at stake: wild nature. All that is good.

I carried Heacox's ideas with me alongside Muir's *Travels in Alaska*[6] as I sailed with other naturalists and about 140 guests on the tour through the channels and narrow fjords of the Inside Passage. As we ventured along the same path as he had traveled, I delved into Muir's thoughts, intrigued by the complexity of the man and the significance of his Alaska journeys. As the ship moved up Tracy Arm in the Tracy Arm-Fords Terror Wilderness, I read Muir's observations, his belief that this was a "wild, unfinished Yosemite" where "domes swell against the sky in fine lines as lofty and as perfect in form as those of the California Valley."[7]

Battling ice as his group ventured up Tracy Arm, Muir reached Sawyer Glacier, where "berg after berg was being born with thundering uproar."[8]

I watched calving bergs fall from that same glacier, though Sawyer Glacier has receded far up the valley since Muir was there. I watched from a motorized inflatable boat lined with visitors. We all gazed upon the glacier with awe before returning to the ship for hot showers, clean clothes, and fine dining. My forays on shore were short, and I yearned to journey into the "majestic peaks" and feel the mountains' presence. We watched from afar, unlike Muir, who camped, paddled, and took long trips inland—to the surprise of his Tlingit guides.

Muir saw what he came to find; he had found the evidence for Yosemite's creation: "Standing here, with facts so fresh and telling and held up so vividly before us, every seeing observer, not to say geologist, must readily apprehend the earth-sculpturing, landscape-making action of flowing ice. And here, too, one learns that the world, though made, is yet being made; that this is still the morning of creation."[9]

~~~

Muir's time in Tracy Arm provided "two of the brightest and best of all [his] Alaska days." Looking back on my own journal and my observations of that land with its brown bears and mountain goats, I remember I felt much the same about Tracy Arm, recording,

The dramatic scenery, the obvious glacial carving, the land feels dynamic and is the place I best appreciate on this voyage. This is not a land for humans to dwell.
~~~

It seems curious that I wrote that last, for that region had been inhabited prior to the Little Ice Age, and I am sensitive to the historical presence of Indigenous people. But I know what I was thinking in terms of "human": postindustrial humans, people desiring resources or comforts that require development that destroys habitat. Tracy Arm Wilderness is not a place for that. I wrote those words because of wildlands crushed by development and overuse, the impact of visiting people on wildlife, on the earth itself.

I had a conversation about such visitation while in Alaska, an exchange that also turned Muir from a historical figure lurking in book pages to a human who shifted the trajectory of conservation. A Tlingit woman came on the ship while we were in Glacier Bay. Her lower jaw stuck out when she talked about her homeland, especially when she paused to gather her thoughts. She spoke with passion about her people's relationship to the land, how the Tlingit people lived connected to the earth, meshing culture and nature, knitting together sacred and secular. When she spoke of the warming climate, of the land dying, tears streamed down her cheeks.

Her people once inhabited the land of Glacier Bay, including lands now underwater. During the Little Ice Age, the glaciers flowed over that land, coming down "as fast as a dog can run," and the Tlingit were pushed out, moving to nearby Hoonah. Before the Tlingit could return to the lands now adjacent to the bay's water, Muir arrived, finding uninhabited land.

"What," I asked this woman, for I trusted her view, "did your people think of John Muir?"

She narrowed her eyes, tilted her head, and stared at me for a bit. "We should never have let him in."

I believe her hesitation was because she felt that I, as an American on a small cruise ship, would want a positive spin on John Muir, but apparently that was not how the Glacier Bay Tlingit viewed him then or now. At the time that Muir was in the area, "Glacier Bay was 'the Hoonah breadbasket,' or 'the main place of the Hoonah people.'"[10] Muir was the beginning of the end of that life.

Waving her hand toward the ship filled with travelers and tourists, she told me, "He brought this. We called it the Second Ice Age. It pushed us out again."

Muir came into the Tlingit land; the tourists followed. They probably would have come anyway, washing upward on the tide of nineteenth-century Romantic tourism, when travelers set out to visit places of majestic beauty, seeking the sublime. And although the Romantic movement is historical, its ideology and beliefs do not sit simply in the past; the Romantics had an impact—good and bad—that did not end in the nineteenth century.

Turn back a few centuries to Edmund Burke's 1757 treatise on aesthetics, *A Philosophical Enquiry into the Origin of Our Ideas of the Sublime and Beautiful.* The sublime was not simply beauty, Burke asserted. He declared that anything of "any sort terrible, or is conversant about terrible objects, or operates in a manner analogous to terror, is a source of the *sublime*; that is, it is productive of the strongest emotion which the mind is capable of feeling."[11] This is not beauty. This is a threatening awe-full experience that can invoke a terrifying, transformative sensation, a collapse of rational mind into astonishment, when all else is suspended. The sublime is the darkness, the infinite, the unknown. It is death, it is life, it is horrifying. It is the mystery. To encounter the sublime is to look into the abyss, is to be pushed into seeing the world through a different lens, one that acknowledges our human frailty and insignificance.

Romantic philosophy incorporated the sublime encounter as part of a larger philosophy of existence. Rejecting the objective machine view of nature, Romanticism embraced the sublime's emotive, experiential force that counteracted the rationalism of the Scientific Revolution.

The Romantic movement sparked a desire in many to feel that strong emotion, encounter the sublime, have transcendent experiences. Those who could afford to travel went to dark and wild places, especially craggy, towering mountains. And they went to Alaska, many having heard of the region through the writings of John Muir.

Muir had no malice nor greed, and he respected the Tlingit people he worked with. Yet in a colonization of their native home and sacred space, he reimagined the Alaskan landscape as an uninhabited wilderness of beauty. He brought in visitors wanting to see that wilderness, people who did not stay. Perhaps Muir felt it was "not a land for humans to dwell"; it was pristine and wild, not to be sullied by the human hand.

~~~

Throughout my Alaska voyage, Muir intrigued me, even as he remained an enigma. *Travels in Alaska* was replete with descriptive, celebratory writing, glory and wonder and magnificent detail, yet something felt lacking, something not put into words. What did he *really* feel? Confronted with such a wild landscape, did that expanse reduce him? Did he contemplate a human role in the cosmos, contemplate his place amid infinity and eternity like other Romantics? I wanted to see the humbling effect of that vast landscape, to read how it led Muir into a sense of belonging to a greater whole that rises from the humbleness. I wanted to know if Muir felt the stretch of the mountain, from the awe of the immensity to the wonder of the diminutive. Perhaps I did not read closely enough.

There on the Alaska ship, I felt separated from John Muir by decades and ways of thinking. Standing on the deck, I looked past the impenetrable forested slopes below the peaks and felt the same disconnect with the mountains. Maybe in Yosemite, immersed in the mountains, Muir would resonate. Or not.

Glaciers took Muir to Alaska. Alaska brought me to Muir and so to Yosemite, the national park finally a destination as I continued the Muir exploration, walking into the mountains that shaped him as surely as the ice shaped the mountains—to find myself on Ten Lakes Pass, looking over a region unlike any mountain range I'd seen, thinking of Muir exploring so much of that place that it became part of him, who he was. Then down I went, from the subalpine pass into the basin, to find a camp.
~~~

Yosemite

The biggest lake within Ten Lakes Basin was a hubbub of activity, with tents and loud voices, people in bright swimsuits and an uncontrolled German shepherd running in wild circles, barking madly, though only service dogs are allowed in the backcountry of national parks. I found a smaller, quieter lake away from the trail and a flat spot in the woods for my tent. It seemed a good campsite, until I discovered the nearby barely covered poo piles and used toilet paper, remnants of messy campers' latrine. I moved my tent a distance away but still near the lake.

I stayed three nights by that small lake, with time to explore the basin during the day and linger on the shore morning and evening. In the soft light of day's end, the lake shimmered as if alive, its water caught by zephyrs, the air itself animate, the elementals in a dance. Beyond rose the cliffs, the granite streaked black with stains like that of desert canyonland rock, with either algae or minerals, I do not know. On the second evening, the osprey arrived to perch on a craggy pine across the way, dark wings arcing across white breast. The bird sat in stillness, even as trout rose in splashing ripples across the lake below. Then from stillness to plunge, the osprey dropped, hitting the water to rise with a small trout. Returned to the perch, the raptor rhythmically devoured the fish, gracefully bowing time and again as the hooked beak tore flesh from bone, uniting feather and fin in the cycle of life.

In the evenings when the small lake was still, even as the osprey hunted and fed, Mama Duck and her six chicks would float serenely across the water, their wake turning the reflected forest and cliffs into a rippling of trees and stone. She was a plain duck that I took to be a female mallard, her chicks fluffy brown and yellow, following her as if all were threaded together. As day dimmed, she would gather her chicks and swim off toward the far shore, disappearing around a bend. She swam with deliberation, a destination in mind? I wondered where she went.

The basin spread above my camp, an intricate mosaic of water and tree, meadow and rock. Walking within that bowl, the life of the place made itself known. A red-tailed hawk soared above the cliffs. A chipmunk watched me, peering over a rock, only its head visible. Steller's jays scolded, chickadees called, and at one of the upper lakes, an ouzel took flight, chittering as it circled over the water—all familiars. Alpine laurel and monkeyflower blossomed, flowers I knew. Then there was Labrador tea to consider, a plant I'd only seen in Alaska and Greenland.[12] I met a pika, a feisty little lagomorph with a loud, bleating cry. The pika's call caught my attention, and at first I wondered whose voice echoed from the talus slope, for it was a different inflection—a different dialect?—than that of the Montana pikas I've heard. But there sat a pika, rounded ears and rabbit face, the fur so closely matching the granite that only the call and the motion gave the creature away.

It was a different feel from the Rockies, known mixed with unknown, the first grounding my senses, the latter expanding my awareness.

Yet even though mountains and peaks lifted around me, with cliffs rising in sheer verticality and lakes shimmering below, by most standards, Ten Lakes Basin is not the most dramatic section of Yosemite—probably the reason I managed to get a backpacking permit for that trailhead. Consequently, the basin might not have satisfied the nineteenth-century Romantic traveler seeking the sublime and the divine encounter, the kind of traveler who would venture up to the glaciers of Alaska to stand in awe at the crashing "bergs." It might never have drawn Romantic painters like Albert Bierstadt, who set up his easel in Yosemite Valley to render the landscape into Romantic splendor.

Unlike Ten Lakes Basin, Yosemite Valley fit the sublime ideal, enhanced in Bierstadt's painting; the artist took the existing topography and stretched it, exaggerated its topography, bathed it in a heavenly light. Such Romantic paintings reimagined the landscape to create a feeling, sometimes shifting or combining elements so no singular viewpoint on the actual landscape could hold what such a painting portrays. Bierstadt often included small figures in the foreground of his works, wildlife or people shrunk to insignificance by the looming mountains beyond. I've heard these paintings called garish, unreal, unnatural portrayals of the natural world—even Mark Twain considered Bierstadt's *The Domes of the Yosemite* "altogether too gorgeous... more the atmosphere of Kingdom Come than of California."[13]

What Bierstadt attempted to capture was the Romantic sublime—the sublime that provides a path toward transcending the ordinary. I've looked at those paintings, heard the criticisms, yet immersed in the mountains, is this not what one can feel? Standing alone for the first time on Koch Peak, was that not what I felt? How often does one return from a mountain trip to look at their photographs—accurate portrayals for the most part—and say, "That just doesn't capture it." Mountains can take one into encounters that create a feeling so strong that Bierstadt's paintings pale in comparison. They provide a physical conduit to that sublime experience by shifting perspective, opening new ways of seeing, both outward and inward. It was on the mountain that the early Romantic poets—William Wordsworth, Percy Shelley, John Keats—found a mentor, believing the high places an "ideal classroom for a poet's education."[14] One might associate Wordsworth more with daffodils than craggy cliffs, but he was a man of the mountains and considered himself a mountaineer. In such poems as "Simplon Pass," he wrote of the essence of the sublime, the stretch of infinity and eternity, the smallness of humanity in the face of the cosmos.

But the sublime is subjective and, just like mountains, is not one thing to all people. The sublime encounter might be felt as an engagement with the divine in a meeting with one's God. It may be a more secular transcendent experience, felt as a dissolution of the ego-self, a union of a greater self with the cosmos. In contrast, the sublime encounter can be an all-out ego experience, a sense of superiority found in reaching sublime heights, either physically on the mountain or perhaps by perceiving a greater level of the soul.[15] Romantic philosophers like Burke teased apart the meaning of sublime, Romantic tourists like those who visited Glacier Bay sought the epiphanic uplift of experiencing the sublime, while some—like Muir—brought their naturalist wonder into their interactions with the sublime, noticing the flower growing within the crack of the towering cliff.

Yet though nature shares only truth, no matter how one encounters it or what one calls it, what is felt and taken away from any sublime encounter in the natural world is infused with all that is human, with all one's cultural and experiential learnings, both good and bad.

But what is brought into that encounter can shift when faced with the sublime, ego slipping to humility, hubris sliding into humbleness, domination disappearing into belonging.

Muir did not live within the height of the Romantic period, but he was a descendant of Romantic thought, influenced by the Romantic poets and their view of nature. He sought sublime encounters consciously or not, be it on a remote Alaskan glacier, in the mountain heights, or clinging to the top of a storm-tossed tree. Like the Romantic painter who attempted to portray the feeling of the sublime, Muir wrote to share the essence of what he found in the mountains, his words often gushing, sometimes judgmental against those who did not experience the awe. Magnificent or minute, he knew none of it could be fully captured by paint or pen. It cannot be done. One has to *be* there to feel it.[16] The only way to truly experience nature in all its glory, to truly experience the sublime, is to be within the truth that nature has to share.

Within that sublime floats Mama Duck and her chicks, peacefully paddling around a mountain lake.

~~~

I *was* there, in Muir's Yosemite, within that place for ten nights and eleven days with Muir's writings as a guide. This was a journey like others I've done in the path of respected naturalists and environmentalists, following them into their place of belonging, always learning much through this melding of place and person. But in my first days in Ten Lakes Basin, I was distracted from that learning, was not reading Muir, was writing very little. Honestly, I was disgruntled by the behavior of some of my fellow human beings.

There I was, within the beauty of Ten Lakes Basin. Yet despite the presence of osprey and duck, despite the inherent peace of the place, that first camp was a constant barrage of noise—yelling and barking—and more disgustingly, a constant encounter with poo. Human waste. Used toilet paper. Shit.

On my second full day in the basin, while exploring away from the trail, I crossed paths with, as I described it in my journal, "three young,
~~~

scuzzy-looking men." They carried bear spray, which I'd been told was not allowed in the Yosemite backcountry because it is a weapon. They scowled and were hairy and dirty. I am a single female; I felt distinctly uncomfortable. Passing them, I soon came on a fresh pile of shit and stained toilet paper, a single rock plopped on top of the waste. It was disgusting. It was appalling. I wanted to leave Yosemite altogether.

I'd had enough. That evening, I watched the osprey sweep across the lake, smiled at Mama Duck and the bobbing chicks. Wrote in my journal, "It is glorious here. If I can look beyond the human impact."

And decided to move camp a day earlier than planned.

~~~

The next morning, I hiked just a few miles deeper into the mountains, then cut a quarter mile or so off the trail, looking to escape people. I wanted wildlands devoid of humanity. I wanted purity. I wanted unsullied nature. I guess you could say I was looking for pristine wilderness.

A broad ledge above a lake provided a site, with scattered trees for shade and shelter, smooth granite slabs for sitting with views across the mountains. A cheerful stream ran from the slopes above, chuckling its way down toward the lake below. Sun bathed me as I filtered water from that stream, its banks abundant with blossoms, the water crystal clear, looking pure enough to simply drink without purifying. I tucked my tent into a protected spot on the edge of the shelf, backed by thick trees, with a view out to a multipeaked mountain I came to know as Temple Mountain. Each morning I stretched, ending with a bow to the Temple.

There was an entire world on that granite shelf, from ants and dragonflies to the chipmunk who sat and nibbled cones on her rock each morning near my breakfast spot to the tall western hemlock and pine that dominated the place. Chickadees called from the surrounding trees, clustering around my camp and cook space for most of the first morning. I talked to them, *pssh-psshed* to them, wondering if they were discussing my human presence, my tent and bear-resistant food container and various paraphernalia. I could sit within the quiet voices of the place,
~~~

listen to bird call, wind whisper, stream song. Abundant life filled that nook, and I looked out across a landscape filled with similar nooks. A quarter mile from the trail felt like a leap away from modern humanity.

My five nights at the ledge camp slowed time, opened thoughts, the days soft and slow, the weather dry and warm. I had time to study the plants, intrigued by the ones new to me. Pussy paws grew scattered across the rocky terrain, bundles of cottony pink balls on stems shooting from a central circle of leaves. At my Montana home, pussytoes[17] grow small, fuzzy flowers, but there in Yosemite, it was not just *toes* but whole *paws*—pussy paws. The plant lies flat on the ground, as if stepped on or wilted, but that is how they grow, with the flower stems reaching out from basal leaves. Apparently, the plant does lift its stem in the morning, raising the flower bundles off the ground, but rarely did I see the little paw flowers anywhere but flat on the ground, lying alongside their leaves, gentle and soft within their rocky habitat.

Pussy paws and chickadees, dragonflies and chipmunks, all seeming small and delicate, feeling of purity and innocence, all hardy and well adapted to thrive in that mountain terrain.

I had time to study the trees, using my recently purchased laminated sheet: "Trees of the Sierra Nevada: 20 of the most commonly seen Sierran species." Lodgepole pine, Douglas fir: these were easy, known since youth. But the rest? Though it's a tree I don't know well, I could easily figure the hemlock with its drooping tips, every tree flopped at the top, looking like they were crowned with an evergreen elf hat. Intrigued, I started gathering photos for a portfolio of drooping tips: craggy dead hemlocks with their gray droop against the blue sky, vibrant young hemlocks with green droop against white cloud, a droop with many cones against blue sky, a droop silhouetted black against orange sunset. Later I learned the lore of the Northwest Coast First Nations people, which says the hemlock was given small cones and so droops its head in shame.

One species of pine baffled me, its needles bundled in fives, its cone looking like five-needled limber pine—but that was not on my laminated list. The cones were not "enormous," as was noted for the sugar pine, the only five-needled pine listed on that same short list of arboreal possibilities. I puzzled, then wrote in my journal,

Why does it matter that I know what trees grow here?

Knowledge ~~> Wonder. And knowledge leads to connection. To know the species is to see the creature as something beyond an object—not an IT; is to see the living being as an individual evolved into a unique entity—as a "plant-person" in Muir's words; is to see a glacially carved landscape or know a rock as granite and be aware of the eternal processes that shaped this earth—leading to the broader consideration of the cosmos.

Awareness, learned knowledge, wonder—and Beauty blossoms, the Mystery deepens.

In pursuit of knowledge, I discover something more—like other Romantic naturalists? Like Muir?

Attending the University of Wisconsin in his early twenties, Muir found himself in an academic world that entranced him. Science meshed with poetry as he learned of glaciology and geology, studying the details of botany even as he delved into the writings of Wordsworth, Thoreau, and Emerson. His Romantic sensibility developed, then blossomed when he left the university to enter "the University of the Wilderness," taking his formal learning out into the world where a different kind of learning developed from his experience in natural realms. There are no papers or articles, no prose or poetry that can compete with nature's training, no words that can stir emotions nor show the elementals like the ways of the wild.

From his initial wanderings onward, Muir studied nature, combining the rational-factual with the intuitive-emotional to grasp the world around. The Mountain reached into Muir's thoughts, the same mentor Wordsworth and Thoreau encountered, the complexity of mountains tutoring the Romantic in more ways than revealing the sublime. Within the mountains, the walker also encountered smaller aspects of nature, just as wonderful, just as awe inspiring in their simple existence within the rough terrain. Muir reveled in each detail, felt a kinship with all the mountain life. The smallest creatures, the delicate flowers, the subdued elements of the mountains—all danced through his writings: "Nowhere will you see the majestic operations of nature more clearly revealed beside the frailest, most gentle and peaceful things. Nearly all the park is a profound solitude. Yet it is full of charming company, full of God's thoughts, a place of peace and safety amid the most exalted grandeur and eager enthusiastic action, a new song, a place of beginnings abounding in first lessons on life, mountain-building, eternal, invincible, unbreakable order; with sermons in stones, storms, trees, flowers, and animals brimful humanity."[18]

Muir was as much a botanist and geologist as a bard and celebrant of nature, seeing the order while gathering more from the "sermons" and "lessons" that arose from petals as much as peaks. In this awareness of the mountain's micro-to-macro stretch in all regards, the study of material nature was the path toward something far greater.

~~~

There at that second camp, I turned to Muir's ideas and reflections in the small book *The Meditations of John Muir: Nature's Temple* by Chris Highland.[19] The thin volume held a distilled selection of Muir's voluminous writings, some of his more thoughtful pieces that moved beyond description into various musings. Each morning, I would read from this, then write my own musings before wandering into the surrounds.

One morning as I sat with book and journal at hand, a deer came to graze in the small clearing above camp. Tucked into the rocky slope, she watched me writing, reading, sipping coffee. She gazed my way, flicking her ears, yet seemed unafraid and gradually grazed her way out of sight. Finished with my coffee and my thoughts, I packed up for the day. The doe appeared again, just as I was leaving camp, with two fawns at her side. The twins were young, still spotted with long, gawky legs and a bit of clumsiness as they meandered near their mama, then came to her for milk. The doe tenderly nuzzled her young as they suckled, occasionally looking up to analyze my actions. Quietly, I walked upward, out of camp, leaving her in peace, whispering, *Go well, Mama Deer.*

My plan that day was to take the trail into the South Fork of Cathedral Creek and make my way toward Tuolumne Peak. Walking the trail, I met people, three backpackers who were coming up the South Fork.
~~~

We shared good conversation, a moment of camaraderie, united by our joy in the place around us. They went up as I dropped down.

The view opened as the trail descended into the South Fork's deep valley. The landscape plunged, lifted, rumpled, fell, soared, with high cliff-walled ramparts rising in all directions. *God's creation in motion!* I could imagine Muir declaring, seeing the ongoing processes of the earth displayed with such splendor before him. In the distance I could make out a small half dome (not *the* Half Dome), a marker and reminder of those very processes.

Down I went, into the forest. The views disappeared. I stopped for a time on a polished granite slab by a stream that caroused down the rock, the water running in sheets, resting in pools, singing the elemental song of rock polishing just as the glacial stream once did. Then up up! I turned around, taking the trail back up, for I did not want to spend the day in the deep valley following a trail. Up, up, climbing high, leaving the trail to make my way out a thin ridge, out to a point with a steep drop-off on three sides. High peaks spread across the close horizon, cliff-edged mountains over 10,000′ all around, dominated by Tuolumne Peak, sublime in the old sense of the term. This was not a view visible from my comfortable campsite. Exposure and the dramatic landscape worked their spell; I shrank, vulnerable in the face of the elemental forces around me, diminished and elated. The sky arched above, the rock flexed its muscles, and I raised my arms—mountains, rock, trees, deer, life, all of this here on this day! And me so small, and me *here*!

I suppose I am a hopeless Romantic, but those gushing words are nothing to what I felt at that moment. Think of Bierstadt's paintings, Muir's writings; these cannot capture such moments. And within that sublime, part of that sublime, stands Mama Deer and her fawns, peacefully grazing in a mountain meadow below.

Headed back toward camp, I passed two boulders, glacially polished and striated with numerous small grooves. The glacial markings wrote a story that folded me into Muir's fascination, an inner glimpse into his glacial query that was as much about creation as geology, a curiosity beyond the shape of Yosemite's mountains.

Never was I closer to Muir than when standing by those striations, on a day when the elements of the land came together, when a meeting with fellow hikers melded in with grace. In the way of the Romantic naturalist, science paled before the beauty of that day, even as the known facts enhanced what I encountered. My rational knowledge of the boulder's creation from magma plume to striated rock helped me see that boulder for what it was: a marker of time and process, of ongoing creation and erosion. That rock told its story, illustrating Muir's sentiments and showing me "beauty beyond thought everywhere, beneath, above, made and being made forever,"[20] echoing Wordsworth's understanding of such things, expressed in "Simplon Pass" as "The types and symbols of Eternity, Of first and last, and midst, and without end."[21]

Muir stands alongside others who demonstrate that the Romantic naturalist did not discard scientific inquiry. Reductionist science that grinds nature down into cogs and gears was rejected by the Romantics, but holistic exploration of nature was embraced by people such as Wordsworth, Thoreau, and Muir, all of whom did not denigrate or avoid the scientific study of nature. Romanticism may have emphasized feeling and emotions, but it was not a wholesale rejection of rational fact. The mountains played their role in this scientific exploration, providing an environment that entranced these nineteenth-century Romantic naturalists as much as geographers like Alexander von Humboldt at work during that time, "order and adornment" flowing through the cosmos,[22] witnessed and wondered at by those who embraced both science and the sublime.

The facts found by the Romantic naturalist open the world, stretching space and time, the material world leading to metaphysical musings. Within that is the humbling knowledge that the material natural world is not about the human race, not about me or Muir or anyone having a transcendent experience or meeting the divine—though yes, that might happen. But the biocentric view looks beyond that, finding a place within and not superior to nature. This belief is reflected in Muir's writing: he wrote of the natural world without always inserting his "self" into the picture.[23] In his biocentric view, nature was not about John Muir, the sublime encounter not about ego-self enhanced.

The Romantic concept of Nature has been criticized as an

anthropocentric search for the divine, an idea based on a culturally constructed concept of nature's morality and purity. Yet again, there is no escaping the diversity of human experience. The Romantic tourist who goes to the grandest of peaks to elevate the soul in an anthropocentric venture is not the same as the equally anthropocentric Romantic philosopher who asserts Nature is for human purposes of transcendence, nor are either comparable to the biocentric Romantic naturalist. Ralph Waldo Emerson exemplified the Romantic natural philosopher. He was a man whose actual time within the natural world was limited; he pondered Nature more than experiencing it, focusing on the human meaning found therein. Emerson and Muir, philosopher versus naturalist, both men of Romantic persuasion, one intellectualizing the natural world, one immersed in it, resulting in different relations to the greater-than-human community of life.[24]

The naturalist felt kinship, not superiority.

~~~

Despite the day of the deer and the sheer wonder of the place, Muir did not totally captivate me; I struggled with the man—with my culture, for that matter. Especially on the day of the obsidian flake.

That day, I went for a wander, crossing two passes, dipping into two watersheds beyond my camp, returning at midafternoon to the highest of the ten lakes. I'd visited this gem of a lake before, nestled against a snowbank and a steep slope of polished, tumbled rock. Pikas bounced and chattered on the boulders across the way while I dipped in the icy water, then sat naked in warm sunshine on smooth granite within grassy meadows plush with mountain laurel and mountain heath.

But it was not the lake nor the wander, not the swim nor even the pikas that I called the "notable event of the day" in my journal. It was the obsidian flake.

The glassy black chip lay in the granitic sand on the pass just above the lake where I swam. One side was knapped to create a serrated edge, obviously worked by skilled human hands, the Indigenous people who had lived here, people who had deep connections to the land. Why had
~~~

I not thought of them? They had not been part of my journey until that moment. The pass where I walked—was it a well-used traverse through these mountains? Or was the flake from a hunting party or singular hunter? Either way, I was walking in the footsteps of the people who once knew this place as home.

And I had come to walk in the footsteps of John Muir?

The Tlingit woman's words came to me: "We should not have let him in." An American who'd heard the Tlingit woman speak called her "toxic" for openly expressing her views on the Tlingit peoples' history and modern situation. It seems some don't want to remember the harsh history.

~~~

A vast majority of Yosemite National Park is classified as wilderness area, 94 percent protected and preserved under the California Wilderness Act in 1984.

The concept of "wilderness" has been scrutinized and debated: it is a land classification that regulates human presence, eliminating motorized traffic and development and so protecting "an area where the earth and its community of life are untrammeled by man, where man himself is a visitor who does not remain."[25] It is also an idea, a way of thinking about wildlands that reaches back to nineteenth-century ideology and Romantic notions. The debate surrounds the question of whether the idea of "wilderness" is simply a cultural construction carved out of a belief in the purity of pristine lands unmarked by human occupation. Such lands hardly exist on the planet, past peoples having roamed much of the earth. Muir's travels in Alaska provided him a unique view of land recently exposed to human eyes in Glacier Bay's wildlands; it was a basis for believing wilderness that is uninhabited and untouched by humanity is pure.

With the negative impact of modern Euro-Americans on habitat and biodiversity in the United States, the protection provided by wilderness designation seems a good and necessary thing for many wildlands. Yet the foundation of the *idea* of wilderness is a different thing and is
~~~

woven through with dark threads. History is now being brought into the open: more and more of us begin to understand the tragic removal of Indigenous peoples that created what are now uninhabited lands. Look to Yosemite: what is now designated wilderness in Yosemite was once home to the Miwoks.

During the 1849–51 gold rush, before Muir arrived in the area, miners descended on the Sierra Nevada. After years of varied forms of violence against the people, the Miwok Indians were attacked and forcibly removed from Yosemite Valley in 1851 by the Mariposa Battalion. The Euro-American settlers moved in; the Miwok claim to the land was gone, though some did return. As Muir pushed for preservation and extolled Yosemite's virtues, tourism increased in the 1880s, intensifying the pressure on those Miwoks who persisted in the area. The tribe unsuccessfully petitioned Congress for aid, stating the "destruction of every means of support for ourselves and our families by the rapacious acts of whites will shortly result in the total exclusion of the remaining remnants of our tribes from this beloved valley."[26] When Yosemite became a national park in 1890, the Miwok were allowed to stay within the valley, but their lives were dependent on tourism and laboring for the park; traditional ways of existence were no longer possible. In a series of events, the National Park Service eventually removed the last of the Miwok in 1996.[27]

Did Muir want the Miwok gone long before that? Did he want to ensure the pristine, uninhabited quality of the mountains he wandered? Perhaps it is out there, but I have yet to find a reference in which Muir specifically calls for the removal of remaining Indigenous people to create uninhabited land. But it seems he felt anyone dirty or beggarly did not have a place in the wild, for the wild was clean, and such people were not of wild nature. Ugly. Hideous. Dirty. This is how Muir described the California natives, denigrating words, lacking compassion, his apparent ignorance of the circumstances faced by the Indigenous people appalling.

Muir has been reproached as racist, his derogatory remarks against Black people and American Indians oft repeated. Yet it seems it was dirty or destructive people in general—not just Indians—that Muir felt were the antithesis of the wild nature that inspired him and nurtured his soul. A *Sierra Club Magazine* article notes he "carried the prejudices of most white people in his time and place,"[28] pointing to such quotes as his description of an elderly Miwok woman: "In every way she seemed sadly unlike Nature's neat well-dressed animals, though living like them on the bounty of the wilderness. Strange that mankind alone is dirty." Interesting that it is "mankind," not just Indians, that Muir points at. And that passage continues: "Had she been clad in fur, or cloth woven of grass or shreddy bark, like the juniper and libocedrus mats, she might then have seemed a rightful part of the wilderness; like a good wolf at least, or bear. But from no point of view that I have found are such debased fellow beings a whit more natural than the glaring tailored tourists we saw that frightened the birds and squirrels."

It seems Muir wanted to find the Noble Savage living in the American West, the Romantic ideal of the native person, at one with nature, wild, honorable, pure, and clean like the animals of the wild, dressed to reflect the union with nature, handsome through *European* eyes—a concept and literary trope that flowed through the Romantic period. Instead, Muir found the reality of a cruelly battered population, attacked by those of his own race and culture.

Put Muir into the context of his time. Muir first came to the Sierra in 1868. At that point, there were places in California with a bounty on the native people: in some places, $5 a head, 50 cents a scalp; other places, $25 for a male Indian, $5 for women and children. One Indian hunter is reported to have said that while gunning down the family of the last Yahi Indians (Ishi was the last of those people), he "had to change his long rifle for a pistol because the long rifle blew the babies up so badly."[29] There was not enough left of the body to collect the bounty.

That was the California of Muir's time.

Muir respected the Tlingit people of Alaska and included African Americans as part of "the family of man."[30] Muir called Indians dirty even as he declared that "mankind is dirty." Muir associated with white supremacists who were on the Sierra Club's board but apparently did not support their views. Muir's racism seems to have grown out of the fact that he was a man of his time living within an elite, privileged white world. We are inculcated by our culture in ways we may not realize. That is a reason, not an excuse; his words denigrating Indigenous people are absolutely unacceptable and hold a racist tone, yet they don't hold the violent hate that stood behind the guns that blew up babies. But if he could have opened his eyes and seen the nonwhite people for who they were, if he could have celebrated their existence as much as he celebrated the natural world, Muir might have made a difference, for his words were widely read. But his Romantic ideals blinded and bent him.

The Romantic philosophy, the view of sublime, the idea of a divine wilderness pure and unsullied by humans, was constructed out of a privileged white European class. It came in response to Enlightenment thinking that degraded nature, reducing it to a machine. Muir followed in the Romantic tradition during a time when Euro-Americans destroyed swaths of the natural world of the American West in their greedy harvest, the idea of infinite resources sweeping across the land with a wake of loss behind it. In 1864, four years before Muir first set foot in Yosemite, George Perkins Marsh declared, "Man is everywhere a disturbing agent. Wherever he plants his foot, the harmonies of nature are turned to discords."[31] Marsh's work was widely known and likely influenced Muir's thoughts, either directly or through his teachers.[32]

Muir wanted to preserve the harmony of nature in his beloved Yosemite. People were a disturbing agent. But the Miwoks deserved greater respect and understanding from a man who had the sensitivity to relate to the natural world of their homeland.

With flake in hand, I remembered the complexity of these issues, the sadness, the tragic history—that the surrounding mountains were once home to the Miwok. I thought again how I am white and privileged and can afford to take my pack and wander in the wilderness of Yosemite for days on end, that I too harshly judged people I perceived as "dirty" and moved away from them to camp in peace. But there was no violence or hatred in any of our actions, me or the other campers; we are people of a different time. And sadly, as part of that time, as far as I know, none of those I saw or met during my Yosemite travels were of Miwok descent.

I pressed the inky black obsidian into a niche in the rocks, next to a mint plant whose pungent scent filled the air. Rolling a mint leaf between my fingers, I savored the plant's aromatic essence before placing the leaf on the flake. After a deep bow of respect, palms pressed, I walked on, another mint leaf in my pocket—which later I couldn't find, but digging for it, my hand came out smelling of mint.

~~~

Somewhere during those days, I slipped out of Yosemite and into the Mountain.

Pussy paws, blue dragonflies, the droop of the hemlock, the way the rocks lie in shelves holding gardens, the meadows and springs, pikas with their own language, black-headed juncos that sound like towhees, the hummingbird who paused and perched beside me one bright morning, enormous junipers with sweet-scented berries, the particular sound of the nearby stream that gifted me water to drink and cooled my face and body in the afternoon heat, squawking jays and calling chickadees, brilliant pink penstemon thriving in rocky crannies, striations stitched across ice-scoured granite, the heights and the cliffs, Temple Mountain rising in the distance, lakes shimmering with rejuvenating icy clear water, osprey, Mama Duck, Mama Deer. All came together. Perspective shifted.

Romantics—including Muir—embraced the new perspectives provided by mountains, knowing that views evolve in such high places, the world around taking on new form and depth. This I experienced. After careful awareness in such lively terrain, I found a sort of parallax of existence, a transition in perception from an unknown location called Yosemite, to the landscape of Yosemite, to a place of its own that has little to do with modern human society—except that that place is protected, thanks in part to Muir. Protected, it functions in a somewhat natural way, and the elements carry on while the nonhuman residents go about their lives in this mountain island, all in beautiful motion.

It is known as Yosemite. I came to know it a bit more, to find a place beyond nomenclature, labels no longer needed in a world that stretched from rock to stream, ant to mountain, trickling spring to infinite sky, majestic to frail, and all in between. The vastness of the
~~~

place comes not from the sublimely spacious views but from what the mountains hold, from the smallest molecule of water clinging in iridescence to the needle of a pine in morning light to the rising peaks that formed during great collisions of continents. The elemental forces flow through those mountains alongside golden-hued ducklings peeping behind their mama, all threaded together.

As a Romantic naturalist, Muir felt this, understanding Yosemite's sublimity at a level far different from the Romantic tourist who came to gaze upon Half Dome. His was a perception grown out of study, a knowing that begins with a name, builds on facts, then takes on greater meaning through experiential learning, when knowing blossoms into a leap of intuitive understanding of the interconnections of life, elementals, cycles, and flow, infinite and beyond. Through study, contemplation, and deep experience, it seems the Romantic naturalist arrives at a feeling of awe that is not so much about the sublime as a sense of the whole, a sense of belonging in which the natural world is integral to being. And so must be protected.

Muir, the Romantic naturalist, wrote of the natural world, completing volumes of work that brought the wonder of that world to the greater public. He was a reticent writer, but he believed his words could make a difference in preserving the earth he so loved. He met those who might help in the work, sharing his Yosemite with them, including Emerson and President Roosevelt.

In 1913, Congress passed the bill that would dam Yosemite's Hetch Hetchy, flooding the resplendent valley beloved by Muir. The following year, Muir died of pneumonia, a seemingly unlikely death for a man of the mountains yet perhaps not surprising, given the timing.

In that short Yosemite sojourn, immersed in his writings and his beloved mountains, I came to appreciate John Muir, though he remained an enigma. A complexity of concepts and characters resided within the man: just a bit of research will show different perspectives on his ideology as well as controversy over his actions, for his life is marked by questionable acts aside moments of sheer glory. As I read of him and about him, delved into his thoughts while looking at the very mountains that inspired them, I found a man who saw those mountains simultaneously through multiple lenses: sacred, scientific, Romantic. I found a man who—while most often traveling solo—set the physical world within the context of something greater.[33]

~~~

Regretfully, I packed and headed out, giving a last bow of gratitude to the place where the mountains had held me in benign peace, the elemental forces withholding any storm or extreme ferocity. I decided to camp on the high, broad sweep of Ten Lakes Pass on my way to the trailhead, though I had to haul water quite a distance to my site. Perhaps that is why I was the only person there that night, my tent set in a place where Temple Mountain soared on the far horizon. That evening, the full moon rose glowing, gleaming, setting all things to light yet not light. I stood on the high plateau listening, hearing sounds of the night. But never, not once, was there a moment without airplane noise. I would wait as one plane passed, but another would approach before it was gone, and the roar came and came, a sound I didn't remember from the camp on the ledge. As if I'd been elsewhere.

The next morning, knowing I was most likely leaving the place forever, I lingered, sitting with coffee and quiet sunrise, watching a ground squirrel harvesting various plants. The squirrel knew I was watching and so was equally watchful. A deer appeared, walking across the broad pass, golden bronze in the morning sun. She stopped at the edge of the slope and stood unmoving, her ears pointed forward. She stayed there for a long time, as if in contemplation of the rugged mountains that spread before her.
~~~

5
THE SOLO MOUNTAIN

Cairngorms, Scotland

Mountain I

Late in the 1920s, Nan Shepherd, already in her thirties, began an exploration of the mountains near her home. At first her treks were for "sensuous gratification,"[1] physical endeavors of elevation and ecstasy. Often, she walked solo. Nan watched and saw things: how mist amplifies the peregrine in flight, the way roe deer melt into the heather to become part of the slope. She heard the mountain's silence and the peak's crashing gales, drank of the purity of the high springs, inhaled the earth's peaty aromas. The excursions on the mountains took new paths, until eventually Nan moved into the mountains rather than simply walking on them. She was embraced.

Nan's mountains, the Cairngorms, lie in the Scottish Highlands, a vast massif of rolling ridges and sweeping plateaus punctuated by some of the highest peaks in the UK. There is a mood to the Cairngorms, a different sense than the jagged peaks of the Rocky Mountains. Perhaps it is their origins. The Cairngorm range is composed of mountains created by erosion, its core a granitic pluton, not unlike the granite mass underlying Yosemite. Yet its heights were revealed not by uplift but by the grinding away of softer matter around the resistant rock in an exhumation that happened only a short time ago in geological terms; erosion exposed the granite around 380 million years before the present, creating a lofty incised plateau rather than an uplifted mountain range. "One does not look upward to spectacular peaks but downward from the peaks to spectacular chasms," Nan observed.[2]

Does the manner of creation affect how one senses a landform? For there is an ancient pensive feel to the Cairngorms, mountains borne in the belly of the earth rather than raised up to the expanse of the sky. That outer landscape soaks inward, especially for contemplatives who wander solo within it.

It is the way of some people, seeking, finding hints and essences in the natural world, a wandering of sorts that seems to require an element of solitaire. The solo experience is cross-cultural; most peoples have lore of the lone person in the wilds, the monk who retreats into solitude on the mountain, the mountain wise man, the hermit on the crag, the eremite of the mount. Some of these solo journeyers follow the lead of their culture, walking into a long-honored vision quest. Others simply follow their spirit.

Such was the way of Nan. She was drawn early into the wonder of nature, mentored by her father, who took her on long walks, teaching of plants and animals and the way of things not human. Youthful Nan immersed in her own wanderings in a forest near her home, the Quarry Woods,[3] with no other people to keep her tangled in the human web.

This was not a woman who slipped easily into the mold society expected of her, though one might not have known that looking at her life from the outside. Most of her life, Nan lived in the Aberdeen suburb of Cults, eventually working as a lecturer of English at the Aberdeen College of Education, a professional middle-class teacher who wore her skirts and dresses. She declared her task as a lecturer was "to prevent a few of the students who pass through our institution from conforming altogether to the approved patterns."[4] In the mountains, she had her "secret life,"[5] beyond conformity, walking within another realm.

In the way of such people, Nan held a desire to know the facts alongside her yearning to delve into the mystery. She learned from friends and from the people living on the Cairngorm's fringe, gaining knowledge of plants, geology, and the mountain's physical systems. She read of more mystical ways of relating to nature, exploring ancient Eastern traditions, Buddhism and Zen. She was herself, at ease alone within the Cairngorm expanse; there, with only the company of the mountain, she leapt beyond self, losing herself to encounter her Self.

Nan journeyed into the Cairngorms, "walking out of the body and into the mountain,"[6] moving into a pure state of "being." One summer day, I walked into the Cairngorms following Nan's path, carrying her book *The Living Mountain*. I walked solo but not alone. I had Nan and the mountains as companions.

Water

There is a close kinship between water and mountain. Water appears out of air in the coolness of the heights, moisture condensing into mist, droplets, and rain that tumbles down to nurture the lowlands. The force of water carves as it falls, shaping slopes and removing rock. The mountain livens the water, gravity adding energy, turning transparent flow into frothing white. Water can also rest in the mountain's palm, in pools and lakes amid the currents. Throughout the Cairngorms, water resides in all its forms, for in these mountains, water seems ever present and holds attributes that caught Nan's attention. "The whiteness of the waters is simple," she wrote. "They are elemental transparency. Like roundness or silence, their quality is natural, but is found so seldom in its absolute state that when we do so find it, we are astonished."[7] On the high plateau of the Cairngorms, water flows from the Wells of Dee, feeding the River Dee from an altitude seemingly closer to sky than ocean. I imagine the Wells as a burst of crystalline liquid emerging from the earth, springing forth to stream across the alpine meadow, as if faeries had gifted the earth with a clear intoxicant from the underworld. For how else could so much water emerge in such a place? There will be geological explanations, perhaps bedrock layers that meet the surface at that point, sending the plentiful groundwater out from below to break forth with gusto just there. Yet the Wells of Dee hold a mystical quality—at least in my thoughts. They are a source. And here in the Cairngorms, I am not far from those Wells.

This morning, before walking into the Cairngorms, thinking of the Wells of Dee, I took out *The Living Mountain* and contemplated Nan's words: "One cannot know the rivers till one has seen them at their sources; but this journey to the sources is not to be undertaken lightly. One walks among elementals, and elementals are not governable.

They are awakened also in oneself by the contact elementals that are as unpredictable as wind or snow."[8] In the comfort of my hostel room, I mused that perhaps by "contact elementals," she means those that are tangible—water, air, earth, fire. Yet there is more to the elementals, including the elemental forces that enfold time, energy, spirituality, and beyond.

Now my tent stands below the rounded summit of Braeriach, the mountain where the Wells of Dee reside. The evening is chill, though the light will last long in this northern country, and so I set off, walking to generate warmth.

Moving upward along a ridge above camp, I see a route toward the summit and the Wells of Dee, where, as Nan knows, "water, that strong white stuff, one of the four elemental mysteries, can here be seen at its origins."[9] The elemental in pure form, newly emerged into this world. I decide to go there tomorrow, up this ridge, a symbolic start, walking with the elementals.

Two ptarmigan flutter up, spreading their white wings to glide in grouse fashion off and away. My blood runs strong now, bringing warmth to toes and fingers, and I stand for a moment on this rocky rise, alone and slight amid the mountain, watching the birds fade into the misty distance before descending to my tent on the edge of a cirque on the edge of this great range.

I am nothing so much as ptarmigan flight.

~~~

The fog rolled down off the plateau in the night, a wave of moisture glowing pearl in the dimness of the non-night of the north, slipping over the headwall of the cirque. Crawling from the tent, I watched the cloud bank arrive from the summit plateau of Braeriach, mist ushering in rain. Drops pattered on the tent for the rest of the night, and morning seemed no brighter than night.

The tent sits in Coire Ruadh, a cirque carved out of Braeriach by a long-melted glacier. Steep rocky slopes almost encircle the corrie's[10] grassy floor, a near-level green swath punctuated by numerous granite
~~~

boulders. Not quite a complete bowl, the cirque's far end drops off abruptly in a steep slope from whence I came. Thick fog has filled the bowl, and rain has seeped into the tent. All is sodden.

Here on the trek's first morning is a near-fatal flaw in my equipment, for there will be more rain, more damp, more penetrating moisture over the next ten days of my journey. To be wet is to be chilled, which is not prudent in the mountains, where the peaks create and hold the clouds, folding fog into their recesses and mist into their cracks. There seems naught for it but to go down, descend to lower climes, perhaps below the density of wet that surrounds me; there is little point in staying. I cannot walk anywhere but down without the risk of getting lost—it would be foolhardy to climb up Braeriach—and I cannot simply lie here in a puddle. I will pack up and move on.

Emerging from the tent, I move into a close, gray world, the corrie's grassy green floor a brilliant contrast to the leaden air that sinks into every exposed pore. It feels almost otherworldly, this fog, with a strange sense of being removed into a haven of sorts. I hesitate to pack, for to drop down out of this cirque is to move away from the heights, to turn from the path leading up to the Wells of Dee. To stay is to remain in the watery embrace of the mist, with no dry shelter. I cannot see across the cirque, cannot see the ridge above me, cannot see the corrie's edge, but I know which way it is, and the mountain's slope will lead me back the way I came, back toward the human domain. I am here with non-human entities, forces, feelings. Both reduced and extended, I want to remain here, alone in this wildness.

For a time I wander, following the clear stream where I fetched water last night, following its curves and meanderings. Yet the elementals have chosen this day's path, without force, without rage, a gentleness in the way of the blanketing mist that belies the strength of the vapor's effect on the smallness of humans. I pack up and make my way to the edge and descend. Only a short distance below, the fog dissipates, and I walk in clear air as I move down and down, headed for the Làirig Ghru, the long, deep valley that cuts through the Cairngorms, the valley that will take me deeper into the mountains.

Looking back, Coire Ruadh remains in its own space, hidden by cloud and wet, a world away from the brightness of the slopes below. Above it, flowing within the mist, are the Wells of Dee, a source. I turn away from that view and continue my descent.

~~~

Water cascades over the cliff, a churning whiteness that sends a current of sound into the upper reaches of Garbh Choire, the "rough corrie." The rush of the stream slows as it reaches the corrie floor, and the water fills dark pools, seeming completely still, an appearance belied by the burbling outflow that carries on downward. It is the stream that flows past my tent at my second camp to continue on into the Làirig Ghru, feeding the River Dee. These are the Falls of Dee; this is the water flowing from the Wells of Dee, the water I'd hoped to see springing from the source. This is the water that has traveled across the high Cairngorm plateau to spout from a notch in the cliff's crest, spreading in a sheet across the granite face as it crashes down, narrowing again in an incised channel cut into the lower talus slope. The heights are the birthplace of this pure liquid that tumbles in a raucous cascade.

Nan stood where I am now. She declared this side valley of the Làirig Ghru, with its cirques within cirques, "one of the most secret of the range." In places like this, Nan felt you could hear the "sound from the energies that have been at work for aeons in the universe."[11]

Having walked up from my second camp near the mouth of Garbh Choire, I have settled onto rocks beside the pools. The water's surface takes on motion, ripplings of raindrops circling outward, accumulating. I pull my raincoat tighter and eat lunch, stubbornly wanting to stay with the place. In a downpour, I sit with the headwaters of the Dee, rivulets running off my hood to soak the nuts even as I eat them. Between sips of hot ginger tea, I drink icy cascade water collected in my bottle. Musing on the plenitude of moisture that drops from sky and cliff, runs in riffles between pools, I say to it, "You will become plant, animal, or rise to the sky to fall again... or perhaps you will take the longest journey and reach the ocean." The waters around gently carry
~~~

on with their elemental essence of being, flowing from, through, and within these mountains.

Though I am weary, I do not feel alone within this wetness: there is the companionship of this place and its life, camaraderie found in stream-song meshed with rock, wind-whisper woven into peat, frogs that leap from the mossy ground, ptarmigan that wheel away, black grouse that cackle in the night.

Before filling the water bottle at the cascade, I cupped my hands beneath the tumbling froth of the falls and drank from the water in my palms. I am not sure what to make of this draught from the source. It feels as if the place has become part of me. Or me a part of it.

~~~

Nan reminds us that water "does nothing, absolutely nothing, but be itself."[12]

My third camp, far from Garbh Choire, lies beyond a rush of water. What had been a cheerful stream when I set off in the morning has turned to spate after a day of constant rain, and that churning flood runs between me and my tent. I spent the afternoon tucked in a bothy[13] near Loch Etchachan, first hoping for a break in the rain to visit that high mountain lake, then waiting for a break in the rain to have a relatively dry walk back to camp. When white ribbons of water appeared on every slope, I knew I'd waited too long.

There is just one stream crossing without a bridge between me and camp. Just the one. I stand on the stream's edge, watching the flow and then pick my path, finding a place to cross where a slip or stumble would put me into a relatively flat current rather than tumbling me into powerful rapids swirling around boulders. Each foot is carefully planted on slick stones beneath the flow, both walking poles planted with each step: plant foot, plant poles, move a foot to the next rock, repeat. I do not let myself feel trepidation.

Nan knew of such crossings: "In fording a swollen stream, one's strongest sensation is of the pouring strength of the water against one's
~~~

limbs; the effort to poise the body against it gives significance to this simple act of walking through running water."[14]

The water only reaches my knees as I manage to stay on rocks that normally would have provided a dry-footed crossing of the stream. And so I cross. When both feet land on the soggy far bank, I pause, inhale deeply—it seems I have not drawn a breath as I waded through.

The strength of water is pure in its form, for it is a force that holds no aggression yet can raise worry, even fear, perhaps more so because, though its violence is without malice, water holds no regard for the human in its grip. Alone in the midst of a torrent, there is no compassion at hand.

Later, tucked warm and dry in the tent, I turn to *The Living Mountain* to find the words I have been thinking of: "For the most appalling quality of water is its strength. I love its flash and gleam, its music, its pliancy and grace, its slap against my body; but I fear its strength. I fear it as my ancestors must have feared the natural forces that they worshipped. All the mysteries are in its movement."[15]

In the night in the tent, the sound of water reaches into my sleep from the stream below my camp. I am awakened by voices echoing within the flow of sound and lie listening to the earth sharing its thoughts.

Air

The sweep of the Cairngorm plateau stretches out under blue sky, the sun ablaze for the first time during this trek. I walk within the lightness of dry air, the colors, the scents and sights, the life, all awakening the senses. Moss campion (*Silene*) crouches in humps of pink, a familiar alpine cushion plant that's like a friend, one I've seen decorating mountains in Norway, Greenland, and my Montana homeland. A mountain hare bounces away over the rising slope, another stands watching on the horizon. Crossing the rock-strewn slopes, I encounter a small spring where clear water seeps from the peat, providing habitat for multicolored sphagnum moss, a spreading mat of colors—lime green, rust, and a dark purple that looks like liver, as if this is an organ of the earth. The moss holds the water, creating miniature pools of pure liquid. Grasses and sedges cling to the mountain and find shelter in the lee of lichened rock, all short in stature as dictated by the height's extreme climate.

A white ptarmigan feather lies hooked into the low plants, and as has become my habit, I pick it up, then release it into the growing wind with a wish and a word of gratitude. It floats, caught by the sky, a bit of bird once again in flight. For a moment I am spellbound by the dancing feather that flits high, dips, drops, and nestles back into the earth's embrace, as if stitching together mountain and sky.

I stand with the floating feather and remember Nan's words, wrought from her own journeys across the plateau, the sky with her as she walked, reaching down to entwine with the rocky earth beneath her feet: "The air is part of the mountain which does not come to an end with its rock and its soil. It has its own air; and it is to the quality of its air that is due the endless diversity of its colourings."[16] Her words ground me on this plateau, where the mountain holds my feet and the sky embraces my mind, my body stretched between the elements.

Watching the surrounds, moving upward through a new world, I reach a cliff edge of the plateau at a high point named Sgor a Lochain Uaine, the "peak of the green lochan." It seems all the Cairngorms lie before me, and there, just across the way, over the depths of the deep valley, are the Falls of Dee, a white streak tumbling off the plateau into Garbh Choire Dhaidh. I am still camped at my second camp in Garbh Choire, and it was only yesterday that I drank from that cascade and so consumed a bit of the mountain's lifeblood. Perhaps some of that water is now absorbed into my cells and some released into the mountain air with my exhaling breath or evaporating sweat.

There is another white feather tucked among the alpine vegetation, brilliantly bright, curved, and stiff. I raise the feather, its downy base fluttering... but don't let it go like the one before. It speaks to me. I have seen no birds. No ptarmigan, no snow buntings, no swifts or plovers or dotterel or any avian creature, for that matter. The feather is saying something, provides hope that birds are here despite their absence this day. Even as I pick it up, the ptarmigan feather becomes precious, a symbol of that which is felt in the beauty of bird flight, a strand of a wing that holds air in its coverts, heaven in its lightness, holds that which keeps us truly alive. I tuck it safely into my pack. It stays with me as a hope.

The feather will travel with me; once at camp, I will carefully stow the feathery gift in the side pocket of the tent. If I am to lose this feather that I have taken from the heights, it would feel a sacrilege.

~~~

On the plateau, I look for eagles.

Nan writes that the eagle "binds the strength of the wind to its own purpose, so that the more powerful the wind the more powerful is the flight of the bird, then one sees how intimately the eagle, like the moss campion, is integral to the mountain."[17]

This mountain beats with life, the unity of rock, plant, bird, air, the connections witnessed with something beyond senses. I watch this land for time, up here on high ground, sitting in the blustery lee of the mountainside, mesmerized by a bee traveling from one campion blossom to another. The bee leaves its perch, lifts into the air, flying off till it is but a speck, till it is nothing but sky.

I do not see an eagle. I did see the bee, integral to the mountain.

~~~

The mountains reach into the sky, and the air dances with them in breezes and zephyrs, gusts and gales. The air is never truly still in the mountains, though the wind is always changing the tempo of its waltz.

At my second camp at the head of Garbh Choire below the plateau, the wind strengthens. The wind, the wind, the wind! It beats on all things, bashes against my head as if harassing my thoughts. But it's just air moving across the land, not aimed at me—as much as it feels that way. I'm simply here in this place where the wind is up, and my camp happens to lie in its path. It is blowing a hoolie, as they say in Scotland, and even the rocks seem to have difficulty holding on as the gale rises. The tent flattens, then rights itself, in an odd tango. Extra guy lines and bracing hiking poles fail to make a difference. I'm having trouble finding a place where I can write, let alone cook dinner. With a sputter, the flame goes out on the little cookstove. I am tired. No. I am weary.

The wind is eating at me, this elemental force that is persistent and unforgiving. My campsite is chosen poorly and provides no shelter. I move with my stove to sit behind the biggest boulder I can find, with a view looking out over the glacial valley that is Làirig Ghru. The wind whips around the edges of the rock, finding me as if in pursuit, seeking. An image comes to mind from my year of research in the Great Rift Valley of Kenya decades ago, a memory of a young local woman who worked with us, running away from a twisting whirlwind, screaming in her native language. When the whipping gusts had fled the plain, she returned, explaining that such winds steal your soul if they blow over you.

The cookstove holds its flame now, set up against the tall rock in the most sheltered point possible. The quinoa-lentil mixture bubbles. A sip of brandy. A pause in the dizzying wind. Okay. My senses return.

~~~

The tent has collapsed. Gusty blasts flattened it time and time again, and I tried to hold it upright, using a walking stick pressed against the poles over my head. The wind was stronger than my arm, and nothing seemed to matter. I gave up, rolled over, tried to sleep. The wind flattened the shelter once again. It didn't pop back up.

"Shit..." said softly, in resignation. The wind makes it hard to inspect the damage: one snapped pole has slashed the fly with a long gash. I grab the intact part of the fly through the inner tent material and pull it over my head, protection from the rain that still falls and falls and falls.

Think solutions. Think... There's a pole splint somewhere, duct tape. Maybe this flimsy thing can be repaired, get me through six more nights. Because I'm not leaving. I am here for ten nights, eleven days. I cannot leave, for I came here to figure something out, to find something. I came to be alone and walk my way into something. To leave would feel
~~~

like defeat, like the world is against me, like anger and hostility have won. Over everything.

I am here during a hard time of life.

The wind is not hostile, but it *has* broken my tent.

I need to retreat. Retreat in many ways. To continue the dance. To fix this damn tent.

In the wreckage of the tent, I search for my journal, to make sure its dry bag has protected it from the wet seeping in. Then I find the map and make a plan. Drop down, down again, even lower, down to the Scots pine forests at the foot of the mountain, to shelter in the trees where the wind can't be as strong, where boughs will provide the shelter that this tent fails to do.

The wind carries on its raucous play. Huddled in the flattened heap of a tent, unable to sleep, waiting for dawn, I think of Nan, take the journal out of its bag, and scrawl without my glasses in the dim light of 11 p.m.:

A thought just came.
Nan didn't study philosophy.
Nan didn't study ecology.
Nan was an English teacher and a poet.
Her ideas—all is one—didn't come from Humboldt.
Her ideas on Self didn't come from philosophy.
Her knowledge and (belonging) didn't come from science—
They came from the land itself. From living with it with awareness.

The thoughts aren't strictly true; later I realize that Nan did study in many ways. But what I am remembering is the mentoring of the earth. What I'm remembering is something like the importance of Place.

Dim dawn light comes. Packing my crushed heap of tent, I lose the ptarmigan feather that was found up in the heights near the sky where it once flew.

Earth

Walking the earth, we walk where others have gone before. Most strongly, most poignantly, I have felt the presence of past walkers along pilgrimage routes, the passing of those seeking something, a quest to reach a sacred site. Etched into the land, these ancient paths hold a history of souls walking toward a tangible place for an intangible spiritual essence.

Medieval pilgrims moved toward the Holy Land, the original saunterers, according to Thoreau.[18] Thoreau's own walking was a movement of meaning; he called it a saunter. He thought that word was derived from pilgrims "going à la Sainte Terre"—to the Holy Land—making "sauntering" a holy walk, a movement of aware intention. He also considered that "saunter" might have come from those who walk *sans terre*, without earth, without land, without home, the peregrini, the wanderers, the wonderers.[19]

Thoreau sauntered. The "art of Walking,"[20] he believed, is an art of living with the earth, developed through the foot journey. When Thoreau spoke "a word for Nature, for absolute Freedom and Wildness," a word "to regard man as an inhabitant, or a part and parcel of Nature," he wrote of the art of walking as a way to *feel* as part of Nature. To move on foot through a place, to move slowly in a saunter so that one can be with the surrounding place, provides a route back into connection, a way for the human species to rediscover something slipping from modern life. Such a saunter or pilgrimage is often achieved while walking alone.

I walk through these mountains, a lone pilgrim, feeling truly *sans terre*, without land, without home. That is why this is a hard time of my life; my faraway Montana home is now homeland, a deep hurtful loss of Home caused by the anger and hostility of others, by the tragic side of human behavior. I am tired. Pilgrimage implies movement. Can there be rest? Stillness. Just for a moment. Last night's windstorm was like a Sufi whirling dervish, all motion on the outside, stillness on the inside, as I wrote in the journal in the broken tent.

Retreat to solitary wildness is an ancient practice, a removal from the "surface ways" of humanity—movement into stillness. In this modern age, to retreat alone into wild lands and listen, truly listen, might also be an act of defiance against the power-driven, angry egos that corrupt and destroy. To take time to hear the nonhuman voices is to step beyond the hostility, hubris, and greed that drive the crises of the planet. Retreat solo to a natural setting where you are only one small speck within abounding life on a vast earth, and a beautiful stretching occurs, a bond with that very life, an identification with the other beings. We are all in this together. It is a sense of the sacred that brings great peace, equanimity, and compassion. Come out of retreat carrying that and change may happen, not just for the peregrini.

Motion and stillness. Yang and Yin. It is all one thing.

I carry on, dropping down lower on the mountain, holding a vision of a forest in my mind—quiet, protected.

~~~

Look from above, from as high as spacecrafts can go, from where they send back pictures of our small blue planet; the mountains are reduced, not so easily distinguished from the lowlands. The planet is of one continuous earth, without such boundaries as humans might create. The forest is part of the mountain.

Dropping from the heights, I've fixed and set up the tent in the sheltering forest at the foot of the bare mountains. I have moved deeper into the earth. It feels like I've moved into an older time when forests and bears were common in this land. Here, the stony skeleton of the earth is ancient, older than the granite of the high plateau. That granite punched up through the psammite bedrock below me that is formed from metamorphized sediments laid down by shallow seas a thousand million years ago. The bedrock is invisible to the eye here in the woods, only seen where the water's force has scrubbed the land. Still, it is present, supporting all around. I stand on it when I bathe my feet in the creek nearby.

For days I've had only sky above, where clouds play, birds travel, and stars reside. Now thick tree branches reach overhead, and life surrounds in all dimensions. The pines are widely spaced, with an open feel that has a pastoral peace, green beneath, boughs above, the sturdy
~~~

trunks straight as pillars, creating a sheltering canopy where their limbs entwine. Farther out, lone trees take on an umbrella shape, with more room to spread. I have joined a forest culture that feels comforting for this lone human.

What it feels like is nesting. Just yesterday, wet and wind and elemental wildness pervaded; now it is the earth element, in a gentler mood. My tent—tacked together with splints and duct tape—presses against the base of a large tree, heather around it like a bordering garden. Another tree provides a place to cook, with a bit of built-up duff where I can sit and lean against the trunk and stay dry, even as the rain falls. The tree has a thick, intricate skin, patterned like puzzle pieces, the outer layer made of flaky bits, lichen lining deeper cracks of the pattern. The older exterior is gray and wizened with time; where pieces of the outer bark have flaked off, there is a deeper tone where fresh, younger brown bark is exposed. This too will weather and wizen.

On the ground next to my cooking spot, in poetic display, a few cones have settled into a bit of reindeer lichen, looking as if they dropped from a lodgepole pine, so closely do they resemble the cones of that Montana conifer; the two pines are apparently closely related, though the Scots pine is more robust and stately. There is something reassuring in the familiarity of these small cones, nestled into the forest beside me.

~~~

All my senses are cued to this woodland community, uninterrupted by human foibles or machine sounds. There is a vole living near my tent who rips my small washcloth into shreds, making me smile to think the material will be a vole nest. There are birds above and around, singing, calling, talking. There is a small wren. She has captured my heart.

Sitting at my cooking spot at the base of the tree in the morning's awakenings, I watch the busy wren as she flits around the heather, foraging, then flying to an ancient stump. Disappeared for a bit, she emerges from that moss-laden mound of wood to carry on with her busyness. The stump appears as a phantasmic creature of another world, with craggy face and peering eye, fur of heather and moss, muscled limbs of woody
~~~

tone. Wren repeatedly flits in and out of this creature's chest. She must have a nest in the depths of the stump's heart, a home of wooden warmth.

Once, only once, during my stay will I move close to the stump to see if I can find the nest entrance. There amid curling wood, lichen lines, and pits of decayed bark, I can make out holes and crannies, but the opening to Wren's home is well hidden, invisible in the heathery, mossy, guarded cloak of the stump creature. It feels an intrusion, and I move away. Simply to know she is here, that her home is there, that is enough.

~~~

The journal is set aside. There is soft evening sunlight and time to just sit with this place. A bit more brandy in the cup, which I might regret if I run out later, but I want this evening to stretch: sun, pines, peace, the sound of the stream, the clarity of the blue sky, the cliffs and green slopes highlighted by sun's rays, and all the life. Nobody knows where I am: only me, the birds, the heather, the trees.

Only the mountain knows.

~~~

On my last morning in the forest, I watch Wren forage and flit, back and forth from the troll stump who has stared at me with the wooden knot of his eye for the last few days. I watch as I eat and finish breakfast. Finish coffee. There's nothing for it. I pack and prepare to leave.

Wren carries on. Just now, just here, it seems Wren and her nest are all that matters, Wren and life and cycles, a purity that continues forward, that thrives in this nook away from all things, in the quiet, the stillness of my solo space. Tears rise as I shoulder the pack.

Goodbye… Go well, little one.

I step out of the forest, headed for Strath Nethy, where I will spend the last two nights left of ten.

~~~
~~~

Strath Nethy is a big open moor encircled by mountains, wide and open with little protection. No trees, though the refuge of the forest remains within, carried with me. Earth scent pervades the strath—thickly organic, peaty, boggy. For a time, I feel alone, with my small tent in this broad valley, for the tent is a shelter that has proven none too good of a shelter at all. For hours I looked for a good tent spot, testing the ground, sitting for a time on potential sites to determine exposure to wind, carrying the pack from here to there and back to find my final camp and settle in. The aromatic earth reaches up and around. The sweep of slope holds me but provides little for shielding against the elements.

The ground is so soft, I build a small stick platform like a raft to support the stove, fearing my dinner will tip. I am hungry. Splashing calories on the ground would be hard just now. I sift through the food bag, rationing things into remaining meals so I will walk out without an ounce of food in my pack. I need to consume what I have while I am here. I have been walking from lowland forest to mountain heights daily and have grown thin, like the wind has blown through me, like the water has rinsed my bones.

Looking back toward the route from the forest, over a high pass down a narrow valley, I find myself wishing I could have spent more time in the highest country. Yet the moors are part of this place too, and so be it. But this expanse… I feel small and exposed. I feel I've moved into something other. Walking today, I thought of sacred lands and felt sorrow at what we have come to in the larger world. Then walked out of that into this.

The cookstove lights up, a flame burns.

I eat quickly, escape into the tent as the rain patters down again.

When the rain stops, I think, *I should go back outside*. Instead, I curl into the warmth of the sleeping bag and fall asleep, smelling earth.

Fire

It was before Strath Nethy moor, before I said goodbye to Wren. It was the day when I set out from the forest camp to reach the heights that Nan wrote of. It was the day of The Spate, the day in the bothy, the day of rain, the day of the difficult stream crossing. It was on that day when I sheltered in that mountain hut up near Loch Etchachan that I remembered the poems.

The bothy was spare though welcoming in the way of such places, its walls bare pine, wooden planks for the floor, benches lining each side. There were three simple, unpadded chairs, a woodstove with a new-looking stovepipe, and the detritus of many visitors—bits of dried food, candles, midge repellant, salt, a whistle, a decrepit frying pan, an insulated travel coffee mug, a battered teapot. I settled into a chair, pulled out the well-worn journal, and wrote until I could write no more.

Still the rain fell. So I flipped through the pages where I'd recorded this Cairngorm journey, finding Nan's poems on the inside covers. It seemed so long ago that I'd written them there to carry with me as I walked; they'd not crossed my mind for days, my thoughts elsewhere as I retreated from water and wind and went into conversation with the forest. I'd forgotten the poems, to remember them with a start and a pause.

"Fires." The poem engrained itself into my memory on first reading. How could I have let it slip from this journey? In "Fires," Nan writes of moving from the mountains into a bothy, from the infinite to the immediate:

> In from the cold blown dark: from flame to flame—
> From the hidden flame of cosmic motion
> That roars through all the worlds and will not tame,
> Driving the stars on the crest of its own commotion,
> To the little leaping flame that our own hands kindled:

Later in the poem, she speaks to the fire within:

> The fire that smouldering deep in the heart of man
> Lies unfelt and forgotten under
> Our surface ways, till a swift wind rise and fan
> The covered heat to a blaze that snaps asunder

The strange restraints of life for a soaring moment
And we lift unquiet eyes and stare in wonder
At the infinite reaches…[21]

I read this over and again as I sat in the still bothy, listening to rain, knowing the air was in motion just beyond the walls. The mountains had sent a swift wind my way, kindling the flames, opening unquiet eyes to "stare in wonder."

Wonder, the catalyst, the kindling for inner fires, the spark that flames curiosity, the ember heating the desire to understand and exist within the intricate interplay of beings and earth and energy. Wonder is humble, bowing in honor before beauty and the unknown, unveiling joy as it nurtures modesty. Wonder presses palms together in the presence of mystery. Wonder wove me into the wilds of Montana, fueling my own curiosity, a longing to comprehend the vibrant surrounds with its diverse community. Just so here, in the Cairngorms, despite the short time of my stay. Watching ptarmigan in flight, sitting in forests of earthy scents infused with birdsong, listening to roe deer call and grouse chuckle in the night, swimming in the clarity of Loch Etchachan—such sights, smells, sounds hold a lyrical, inescapable call: *Come! Join the dance!*

The fire flickered, took hold. The solo journey toward nothing and everything continued.

~~~

The faint light meant it was probably around 2 a.m. The organic earthy scent of this final camp here in Strath Nethy permeated my head, made my eyes puffy. My joints ached; I was restless—I needed to stretch, I needed to pee, I needed to *get out* of the tent. Crawling from the shelter, I arched my back, stretching upward, and felt a presence. No motion, no sound, but a feeling of flow, like the current of a candle flame in a still room, a flow of energy streaming upward but not away, as if solid on the candle wick. Nothing tangible was out there, yet there was the feeling of great benign beasts moving about in the sloping moors.
~~~

This morning, I write,

I stepped out of the tent and felt I stepped into a different world. An ancient world, where this land was inhabited by bears and wolves and humans who understood.

Then an even more ancient land... one before any human knowing. The wind song, the stream rush, faintly in the background. The expansive Strath Nethy glen spread out in the dim predawn light of a far-north morning. The feeling was eerie, expansive. I went back into the tent relaxed and fell into a deep sleep.

This I've never experienced, a dissolution of temporal boundaries. When it happened, an electric adrenaline flush rose, then subsided. I was left standing in the midst of the world's heartbeat, with an inner peace that wasn't about my own tranquility but something larger. Perhaps it was what Nan once felt: "But now and then comes an hour when the silence is all but absolute and listening to it one slips out of time."[22]

Later, I described this to a Native American man, someone who mentored me in ways of knowing that provide paths toward peace when the immediate reality is untenable.

"It was the dreamtime." He said it matter-of-factly, looking at me with the soft smile that would brush his face after I unknowingly said something that fits into a larger mystery.

Yes, that moment rests in memory like a dream; the ephemeral light that wasn't night but wasn't day, the sounds of the elementals, the way the slopes and ridges rose and fell with living motion, the scent of dark earth musty and strong. All time. Unbounded time. Not modern human time. Dreamtime? A concept that bangs against our rational, objective thinking.

"If I had other senses, there are other things I should know," Nan believed.[23] Have we lost those other senses, or have they simply gone latent, shrunk inside of our diminished cerebral space? There are ancient ways of knowing, where time is not linear or absolute.

There in that moor in the motionless flowing current, I stood vulnerable and bare, minuscule within the "flame of cosmic motion." All boundaries dissolved.

~~~

Nan would lean over and look at the earth through her legs. Here in Strath Nethy, I follow Nan, standing astraddle, legs wide, leaning over, bending down down down till my hands press on the earth and I look out through my legs, viewing the world from bottom upward, from soil to sky, totally upside down. In some strange way, it changes the relief so up is down and down is up, ridges are valleys and valleys are ridges, like a reversed version of a stereoscopic photo. For a moment I am lost in this new world. The *things* of this world are seen anew. I am not where I am.

When Nan dropped her head down to peer between her legs, she discovered, "Nothing has reference to me, the looker. This is how the earth must see itself." Such a simple act that provides a different way of seeing, parallax creating a changed perspective, reducing the human and removing self-referentiality, ego swept away by viewing the earth from a standpoint unfamiliar to the human eye so that "each detail stands erect in its own validity."[24]

Seen anew, things once seeming static now flow with life, all in process, all in transformation, all things in relationship within an evolving universe. Change the perspective, wake from sleep, turn things upside down—literally or figuratively—and the world expands, no longer the universe that revolves around self, but a home where a greater Self may reside without boundaries or dichotomies, existing within an animate world that has the capacity to "see itself."

Standing up, the earth swims around me for a dizzy moment, then solidifies. Laughter bubbles up, a joy brought on by the playfulness of the motion, a beautiful joy with a wellspring born from last night's encounter with Mountain mystique. How ludicrous I must appear, upside down on the top of this ridge! I look around at this place, where the surrounds feel like an embrace, where all things continue in their eternal act of transformation. Water and stream, air and wind, earth and root, fire of
~~~

life: the elementals have done their work. Within this strath accessible to any hardy walker, a valley that might not stand out as remarkable in the larger picture of earth's topography, I rediscover the sense that goes beyond belonging and reaches into Being.

~~~

The footprint of humanity is easily overlooked in Strath Nethy, the valley conveying a wild, untamed essence sensed in the weight of my own insignificance. I sit comfortably within the immensity of this strath, feeling a sense of participation with things beyond comfortable… "unquiet eyes." Rising from my resting spot, I continue my walk upward along this ridge above my camp, the tent a flimsy orange speck in the distance. The slope seems to stretch upward for a long ways.

I move onto a main ridge, find an easily walked path, and tell myself, *Go! Go up, reach that ridgeline, and see this view, on this last Cairngorm day.* The growing elation—it's not about elevation, is it, Nan? The rising rush within is simply because I am here, in Nan's Cairngorms, after ten days of a walk that has been a walk beyond days. The world around expands with the ascent. A ptarmigan feather rests aside the path, picked up to be let loose with a wish. Then another. And I remember the lost feather from the day on the plateau, hoping it returned to its element.

I reach the summit, turn slowly, and feel as if the universe is there to behold in all the craggy mountains, deep valleys, rolling hills, buttresses, the creative workings of the earth unveiled, all in motion, the sky silver and light, playing with the planet, turning crags into molten mercury and meadows blazing green. Immersed solo in this place, I feel I've slipped into the cracks of its essence, feeling a part of it, it a part of me.

A long sweep of another ridge runs off from the top, green and rumpled by rivulets and hillocks. I traverse the stretch in my mind, following its curves and swales, back into the mountains, into the heart of that massif. The hour is too late to actually walk that ridge; it does not matter.

"Nan, you walked all these ridges, I suppose? I can see you out there, ridge walking…" And I watch her, me, walking our way through and into the mountains with an ease of motion, the swing of the stride
~~~

that moves with the earth. A smile spreads, and my arms fly up in overwhelming joy. Then I stand for a time, just watching.

The mountain here is essence of being—water, air, rock, and light imbued with a living sense, these inanimate elements seeming just as alive as the beings we think of as life: plant, animal, moss, insect. This is Nan's *Living Mountain*, and I have walked into it.

~~~

The feather rode with me, from windblown camp through forest and into moor. Packing on the last morning, surrounded by Strath Nethy, I find the ptarmigan feather from the high plateau in the tent pocket, right where I thought I put it, right where I thought I looked for it. It was there, as if only now was the time to find it. It was there, obviously in sight, the feather that was found and kept, that became precious and was lost, to be found again. Carefully, I take that found bit of bird wing that had skimmed through the sky and put it tightly into the journal, carried as a reminder of the high places where wind whips and life thrives in its own way.

Mountain II

When you are alone, solo, lean and spare and open like the alpine expanse, when you collide with the elementals and vision isn't about seeing—this is when the Mountain rises, a reminder of how little is understood and how much less is known. This is when I've felt the deepest truths, those that cannot be found through the telling.
~~~

6
THE PEOPLED MOUNTAIN

Assynt, Scotland

Rain continues, wind-driven drops drumming on the roof. I am in Inchnadamph, Scotland, the place I wanted to call home, looking out the window and watching the rain, thinking about how to write this chapter. I am holding the Montana family ranch, a mountain place, in my thoughts. I am thinking about how to write the chapter about "Mountain as Home" when I have decided to make my home in the desert.

It has been raining since yesterday, when I arrived from Ullapool on the little blue-and-white Rapson bus. So often in past years, I've watched those buses pass by while sitting on the Kirkton deck in Inchnadamph in this corner of the Scottish Highlands known as Assynt. Now no longer able to afford a rental car, I became a passenger on that bus. In my weariness, it felt a blessing to simply sit and watch the world pass by as the bus worked its way out of Ullapool, through Ledmore, out to the cluster of white houses, hotel, and lodge that is Inchnadamph. The mountains gained height along the way, a landscape of familiarity, though I could not see it all, for cloud covered the higher ridges and summits where I have walked and wandered over the years. Memories brought them to life, images in my mind.

The bus pulled over at the head of the Inchnadamph Lodge drive. I had dreaded the walk up that dirt road. Though it was only a quarter mile, it seemed insurmountable with the rain, my heavy backpack, a bag of groceries, and post-COVID fatigue. But there was Helen, her car parked at the end of the drive, waiting for me. Dear sweet Helen. Oh, Helen. My tears started, the hug was long.

"Come on then," in that cheerful way of hers, and all the luggage went into Helen's car, and we drove up to the little "Shepherd's Hut" at the lodge where I am staying for a few days, before moving my accommodation over to Jane's place at nearby Kirkton where I have stayed so often.

Getting to Assynt felt impossible while I was quarantined with COVID in Ireland only a few weeks ago, reaching this place of familiarity and friendship seeming only a wish and a hope. I felt stashed away like used goods in the hotel room, worrying I'd never return here, to where the people have welcomed me with kindness over the years and the Scottish mountains feel as if they have become part of me, settling into my soul alongside the Montana mountains. Yet I did arrive, and there was Helen, and here I am, warm and comfortable with the rumpling moors and rising mountains outside the window, with the lodge owners, Chris and his partner Jane—a different Jane than at Kirkton, as there are two Janes in this one small community—and the same good-hearted lodge employees, all still here. All looks the same, feels the same in so many ways, the people, the rain, the gales and green, the mountains a mosaic of rock, heather, and moss. But things have changed, and all is not the same. The world has changed. My world has changed.

Still, it feels like a homecoming.

Home. I would have made Assynt *home* in every sense of the word if I'd found a way to make it a permanent residence. For almost twenty years, I've been coming to Scotland, and in the last decade, I found something in Assynt different from my Montana homeland. Even as I came to know this Highland landscape, I came to understand the significance of community in our human lives. There in Assynt I found *both* community and a place where I could walk out the door and into the mountains, things that provide such depth and richness to my life. I sought employment in Scotland, looked for land, participated in the Assynt community in small ways, always holding on to the hope that I would eventually live here. Then the pandemic hit. COVID prevented travel. Scotland, once so close, became far distant. In those years away, I found a home in the American West, not in the mountains, not near the family ranch. I chose the desert. My world has changed. Within that is the knowing that true friendships and deep connections to a place endure, despite change.

The landscape surrounding this small community of Inchnadamph seems even more strikingly beautiful than I remember, though just now it's whipped by strong winds and pelted by rain. Curtains of wet sweep past, but I am warm and snug in the Shepherd's Hut. Four red deer stags browse out front, antlers waving as they tear at the rough fodder. Beyond, the hills lead into unseen mountains, shrouded with mist and cloud. I have just two weeks in this place where I would have lived for a lifetime if such a thing were possible.

How best to spend this short time? This weather and my lack of energy mean there won't be much hillwalking. There will be tea drinking and good conversation. Two weeks. Perhaps I can turn my thoughts to the idea of home, wrap my mind and spirit around that book chapter that is so challenging, for every topic flows with deep emotional currents. I've stopped thinking about it as "The Peopled Mountain," the working title now in my mind as "Mountain as Home." *Home* resonates, home is personal, it is individual, communal, even global when we wisely acknowledge Earth as home. *Peopled* is clinical, academic, a look from the outside, like seeing an inhabited mountainscape as scenery; even geographers note that much of what has been written about mountain people is "by flatlanders and mainstream institutions, whether government or private, business or academic, conservationist or political."[1]

Like all things precious, home is fragile. It can be taken away. Home can become homeland, with the bond remaining but different. Home is not a simple subject, academically or personally, especially since I write of "Mountain as Home" when I have chosen a home in the desert.

Yet I write not just from my personal perspective, so I will stick with "The Peopled Mountain" as the chapter's title, for it is the past peoples of this Highland place that first slipped something into my thoughts that was expanded by those now living here, something about human interactions with the land and its life, something about mountain as home. I cannot write of those historical peoples with intimacy, though standing by the broken remnants of their houses scattered amid these moors and mountains feels intimate.

I will also hold to "The Peopled Mountain" because mountain people across the globe play through this narrative of mountain communities.

To live within the mountains, populations need to adjust, and that happens in different ways—"mountain as home" is far from a uniform concept, just as people and peaks are each unique. And though I could write with more personal understanding of the people of this Assynt community, it does not feel my place to write of their lives beyond my own experience of shared warmth and kindness. And so "The Peopled Mountain" it remains, as I pull myself back a bit so as not to hijack the narrative into purely memoir. Yet even as I think this, I acknowledge that knowing the mountain as home is a more intimate connection than the other ways of knowing the mountain I've written about, though it might include sacred, scientific, and Romantic perspectives as well as solo ventures.

The rain has eased. I will walk. COVID robbed the stamina from not only my body but my mind as well. I cannot think anymore. I will walk. I don't know how far.

~~~

The dirt road beyond Inchnadamph Lodge wends its way up to Glenbain Cottage, where it becomes a track negotiable by the all-terrain vehicles frequently used here for stalking (hunting) by the land-owning estate. Farther on it becomes a trail that eventually forks, one path leading up toward Conival and Ben More Assynt, imposing mountains, though both are only slightly higher than 3,000′. The other path stays in the valley, deteriorating to trackless bog beyond the Traligill Caves. Keep going beyond the caves, squishing through soaked sphagnum, slipping down peat hags, marveling at the beauty of the bog even as you look for the firmer ground, and the way will take you to Breabag, a whale-backed mound of a mountain. Breabag is the only mountain I would like to visit on this stay, for it is one of my places within a Place.

After my morning musings, I walked up that dirt road, a gentle walk without destination. Stained by peaty tannins, a river runs chestnut brown under the road's ford, not as high as one might expect after all the rain. Above the ford, Glenbain still sits neat and white-tidy on the hillside, once leased from the local estate by a couple from Dorset,
~~~

now a weekly self-catering rental. That couple loved Assynt as a second home and came to this place for some fifty years; their lives too have changed. I gave Glenbain a nod, then made my way past the cottage to Traligill Caves, where the limestone rock has eroded to open up the hill, revealing a subterranean stream crashing below the earth's surface. Along the path are shieling ruins, roughly rectangular piles of rocks, the last remnants of herders' huts, the last whisperings of a lost way of mountain life.

I paused often, not because of COVID fatigue, but to take in a memory, reflect on a site where I have been before, consider the ruins, raise my eyes to where Breabag stood unseen, lost in cloud.

From my first visit onward, this landscape felt familiar, perhaps because of the geologic parallels between the mountains around Inchnadamph and the Montana mountains I know so well, something that creates a similar gestalt between the two places. The bedrock here also includes a large amount of limestone as well as dolostone[2] and quartzites, laid down around 600 million years ago when shallow seas covered this region. During the mountain-building Caledonian Orogeny, the land heaved upward, a continental crash driving up mountains over a period from about 500 to 390 million years ago as plates coalesced into the supercontinent Pangea. Breabag was part of that uplift, meaning Breabag, like Monument Mountain behind our ranch, was an ocean floor that lifted skyward; both are now high places holding fossilized ecosystems of marine remnants.

The forces of the Caledonian Orogeny created the vast Appalachian-Caledonian Mountains along the center line of Pangea, a massif that existed for only a fairly short geologic time. Just 155 million years after the uplift, Pangea began drifting apart as an upwelling of magma split the supercontinent, dividing that ancient mountain range even as it created the Atlantic Ocean. Today, the rupture continues along the vast Mid-Atlantic Ridge that runs along the ocean floor, the Atlantic Ocean continuing to expand as fast as your fingernails grow. Split apart, the Appalachian-Caledonian Mountains and their geological formations now exist as remnants running along either side of the sea. The east coast of North America, western Greenland, Svalbard, the United

Kingdom, Europe, and northern Africa are thus all connected by the same ancient geology and tectonic processes. Breabag is thus related to those Appalachian-Caledonian Mountains.

That ancient, divided mountain range became part of my life, for it is the foundation for an intercontinental, cross-cultural trail: the International Appalachian Trail (IAT), a global network of routes that runs through those countries connected by the Appalachian-Caledonian geology.[3] Years before COVID, I decided to walk a section of the IAT in all of its countries for my sixtieth year, a walk that was not meant to be about me, nor about covering miles. I wanted to physically experience how nature and culture are not divided by boundaries but rather bonded by our mutual existence on this Earth. The walk along the remains of the Appalachian-Caledonian Mountains was a hope to find and so show through my writing the unity within the diversity of our planet, both ecologically and culturally.

The pandemic changed all things, first making it impossible to plan for a cohesive, connected, yearlong walk across several countries. I carried on in bits and pieces, starting in my fifty-ninth year, the summer of 2021, at the IAT beginning in Maine, where the Appalachian trail ends and IAT takes off. From Maine I hopped over the Atlantic to Iceland, the country lying over the mid-Atlantic rift and so at the IAT's geological beginnings. This summer—the summer of my sixtieth year that finds me in rainy Inchnadamph—I set out on the west coast of Ireland, following the newly renovated Ulster-Ireland IAT, heading east with plans for months of walking and travel. Ten days in, shortly after crossing the Ireland-Northern Ireland border, COVID hit hard. Quarantined in the small town of Castlederg, I held hopes of continuing. I left the hotel, stayed for almost a week in a small cottage on Northern Ireland's north coast. Fatigue persisted. I had little stamina and had gone through most of my budget, so no energy, no money. I gave up the IAT dream, booked a flight back to Montana, leaving time to spend these two weeks in Inchnadamph to recover, visit friends, and be in the Place I would have made home.

Ironically, because Scotland's IAT section runs right through Inchnadamph along the long-distance Cape Wrath Trail, this place had been on the summer's itinerary already—but not as a COVID-recovery site. Meaning that in my short morning walk, out and back along the route past Glenbain and over the ford, I walked the IAT. Yet it was not what I had hoped for.

~~~

Like yesterday, the morning is wet, the air so saturated that standing on the small deck of the Shepherd's Hut, I'm accumulating a coating of droplets even though it's not raining at the moment. Constant moisture means the surroundings are green, though that single adjective fails to capture the terrain's quilting. Green of all hues covers the land, heightened by gray and black rock outcrops, a contrast not just of color but of dark stone set within vibrant life. There is bright green of moss and new leaves, deep green of rush and tree, forest green of heather, sweeping green, swelling green, early summer green of growth.

A song thrush sits on the fence post nearby. Each morning he sings, beginning in the first light of day—3 a.m. or so. These past mornings, I couldn't sleep, so lay listening to the notes, trying to predict which sequence would come next, turning my mind toward the quality of birdsong. Though still I was awake, I lay in peace. That is what this place inspires—Peace.

Now the thrush flies off. My eyes are drawn toward the sky, where two ravens fly. They are calling and sweep-soaring over the slope where I would see them in past years and lift my hand, calling back to them. Would they remember me after so much time? Would they call again? Will the ravens in Montana miss me? Will the ravens at my new home in the desert come to know me?

The morning asks for musings, and so I turn my mind to "The Peopled Mountain," the Home chapter, mulling over the idea of "Home" and "sense of place." *Home* seems a deeply felt connection to a place, though we toss the word around carelessly. I am lucky to have spent the majority of my life on or near the family ranch and to have been so close to parents and grandparents, meaning the ranch has felt like *Home* from earliest memory. There in Montana, it was land and family
~~~

together creating strong bonds to that piece of the earth as well as fostering my deep connection to mountains. So home includes human relationships, though any definition of home is essentially personal, built out of experience. Still, culture, community, and human bonds certainly weave into the idea of Mountain as Home.

Home, I believe, also requires a sense of place—that part of the bond growing out of the physical location—but sense of place is not dependent on home. "Sense of place" is another phrase used and overused to try to explain a connection to a particular landscape that reaches beyond physical. Still, it comes close to capturing what it is meant to define.

The ravens flying black against the gray sky take my thoughts to all the creatures who know me at the ranch, from raven to fox to jay and chickadee, and probably others, who are not so gregarious as to come sit with me on the back deck. These nonhuman residents have acknowledged and even accepted me as part of that Place, and so, because of my life experience, I've come to think of "sense of place" as more than feeling that a Place is part of you; it is when you are part of it.

The ravens wheel away. Watching the misty mountains, the green swath of the valley below the slopes invites me to wander up the road again, even as the clouds lower. I will venture out, taking notebook and pen, and go a bit farther, beyond Traligill Caves, to sit by the "beehive hut" and write of mountain as home, for that crumbling ruin of rock became part of my understanding of this place, simply because it's not a beehive hut, never has been. It is a shieling, a herder's hut long since decayed into history.

~~~

The "beehive hut" shieling was built with a large rock as part of one wall, a boulder embedded in the earth, waist high and just as far across, securing the building in a grassy glade. Hands skilled at constructing drystone structures built off that anchoring stone, creating a small shelter where young herders would live in summer. The walls have collapsed in, moss growing in thick cushions across the crumbled ruin. Nettles and rushes shelter there now, the shieling abandoned centuries ago,
~~~

that way of life that took herders and their animals to the mountain flanks for the warm months of the year long since beat out of this land.

As the shieling walls fell inward, the ruin took on a circular appearance. Years ago when Scotland was new to me, I stood by the structure for the first time, my curiosity piqued. I knew little of Highland history, had yet to learn of the Highland Clearances and transhumance. The land around felt wild and remote, a wilderness of sorts, though the small cluster of houses and the white lodge of Inchnadamph could be seen only a few miles away. What was this building, constructed of the earth's stone in a place where people would not live, on the edge of the mountain, tucked into its small meadow?

A beehive hut, I decided, the name for those structures that provided a place for monks to be away, a hermitage, a seclusion. The feel of wilderness led me to think of this place as devoid of people who might actually *live* here, calling it home. A monk's retreat: that fit with "wilderness." Such is the thinking of a young person from the mountains of Montana. Later I learned that no, it was not part of Celtic Christianity, nothing to do with wise men retreating to the mountains.

This valley, these mountains, were not empty of people a few hundred years ago when the structure was built. That shieling, along with the other shieling ruins not far away, was an integral part of traditional life in this mountain landscape prior to the early nineteenth century, before everything changed. Transhumance is the term used for this way of life, where a community in the lowlands uses high pastures for livestock in the summer months. It is a seasonal migration of animals and their herders and shepherds, cattle being the traditional livestock species here, not the sheep often associated with Scotland today.

One geographer described transhumance in the Alps this way: "Traditional mountain societies are commonly organized according to a mode of exploitation based on the complementarities of altitudinal biogeographic belts. These societies are mainly oriented towards the practice of animal breeding.... The presence of a series of dwellings spreading from the villages to the high pastures attests to a strategy of maximizing the use of vegetation belts and, more specifically, the fundamental resource of grass. Management is based on an annual cycle."[4]

That academic definition fits with "The Peopled Mountain."

On this morning's walk, I looked at the shieling ruins and thought of the herders, remembering stories I've read that were passed down through generations, how the young people thought of that high-elevation summer season as the best time of year. Theirs was not an easy life, but it most likely had its joys, and the mountain and its seasons were part of it, shaping the community and woven into people's lives. That is "Mountain as Home."

There are different forms of transhumance, even as there is diversity in mountain communities; people have developed many ways to inhabit the heights for at least part of the year.[5] Indigenous nomadic and more settled agropastoralist communities like those once here in Assynt have moved with the seasons for centuries; both are a form of transhumance. There are still some who maintain this lifestyle, but they are diminishing, increasingly transforming as traditional ways of life give way to new economies, particularly tourism.

There are also colonized regions—including the American West—where traditional ways of mountain living are simply gone. Tourism is often at the heart of such modern mountain communities, as in the Montana ski resort community I am familiar with, the sprawling Big Sky Ski and Summer resort. There, the mountain is a stage for recreation, providing sport and leisure within an economy populated by amenity migrants and serviced by a workforce. There, buildings, roads, and golf courses are planted on the earth, the natural world pushed aside, forests and habitat removed to create space for ski runs and hotels. It too holds a human community that functions seasonally but one that is so different from the Indigenous peoples of that region's past—those who left the occasional obsidian chip or tepee ring as a reminder of their existence—that to set them in comparison is to look at a blankness, a space, no answer. Yet within each population are people, emotions, hard lives, good lives, hierarchies, compassion, and conflict: within each population are people who know Mountain as Home.

Such thoughts held me standing by the beehive hut this morning. I did not write while I was there, as raindrops would have smeared the ink into illegibility. I did pause for a long time, considering "The Peopled

Mountain" chapter and how to approach the subject, how to speak to the complexity of home and the diversity of human adaptation to high places all within one chapter.

Then I simply stood with that round pile of rocks, holding memories, remembering the slow transition of my understanding of this land. In the ruins of shielings and townships scattered across Assynt is an archive of another time, the undeniable evidence that this wasn't and isn't a "pristine" wilderness in the sense of unmarked by human activity. As I learned of this history, what I saw in those ruins was a people who once lived *with* the mountains. In Montana, I lived *in* the mountains, knew them intimately, had my soul nurtured and my spirit lifted by that terrain—but my livelihood came from elsewhere, my food from the grocery store, my subsistence separate from the earth in a way that left a yearning for something different.

I did not stay long by the small ruin and returned to the Shepherd's Hut to write. The walk to the beehive hut made me tired. Such a short walk compared to my usual hill ramblings. I worry I am developing long COVID. Now I sit in this comfortable dwelling, warmed by a sense of place, for I can think of no better term for what I am feeling just now.

~~~

After a few days at Inchnadamph Lodge, I have moved from the Shepherd's Hut to Kirkton, just a hundred yards away or so, still in Inchnadamph. In her cluster of buildings named Kirkton, Jane lets out a house, loft studio bedroom, and a converted shed with an outdoor kitchen that provides "glamping" for long-distance walkers passing through. I am in the shed—now called the Kozy Kabin—as the loft studio is fully booked. In past years, I spent weeks, even months at a time in that loft, sat on its balcony watching the morning come and the Rapson buses go by. Recently retired from teaching, Jane's various short-term rental units are now her business income, listed online and often occupied. Things have changed over the decades. I find the Kabin comfortable and accommodating, even with the continued wet weather. It, too, like
~~~

most places around, has a history, as the small structure was originally the first telephone exchange in Inchnadamph.[6]

A mist crept down in the night, covering the mountains, tucking them away and out of sight. Describing that in my journal, a memory rises from my early years here, a recollection of climbing Assynt's iconic mountain Suilven in the fog.

Suilven is an erosion remnant, having once had a resistant cap of quartzite that preserved the underlying Torridonian sandstone from the glaciers that ground away the surrounding land, leaving the hulking dinosaur of a mountain standing remarkably singular within Assynt. Although encircled by other peaks like Stac Polly and Canisp that jut just as surprisingly from moor to sky, it is Suilven that seems omnipresent, seen from so many vantage points. I can't quite see Suilven from Kirkton, as the mountain lies closer to the sea, but hike up a bit, and there Suilven stands, just there, as if watching over the land.

Suilven's distinctive shape and dramatic rise from surrounding moors have inspired poets and writers through time, drawing one hiker after another up the exposed trail to the rounded crest—including me; I climbed Suilven on my first visit to Assynt. After a few miles of valley walking, the true ascent began with a hike up the mountain's steep side to a low spot on the ridge of the undulating backbone of the beast. The summit was lost to view, enshrouded in cloud. Still, I continued, to encounter the rock wall that stretches across Suilven's spine, a gap in the wall allowing trekkers to easily pass and journey upward.

I was stunned and puzzled. Here on this mountain was a drystone wall draped across this ridge in the "wilderness" of the Scottish Highlands. The barrier curls down Suilven's rocky slope, disappearing into the cliffs, leaving a question as to its practicality—or was it simply a human gesture of territory and ownership?

Beyond the wall, the trail to Suilven's summit is well used, easy to follow, yet the exposure can intimidate, especially walking alone as I did that day, no other hikers around. I made slow progress, up the rocks, along a ledge, moving from below the fog into the fog. The view of the heights slipped away, yet the sense of exposure seemed only to increase as I worked my way along a strand of trail suspended in gray with no view of earth below. At one point I crawled, before eventually reaching the rounded top.

A head-high cairn marked Suilven's summit, appearing in the fog like a ghostly vision. Standing next to it, the solid rock anchored my senses, and I started the normal summit procedure of stripping off wet, sweaty clothes, putting on dry layers. Comfortable, I stood and looked into the gray; the cairn and I were the only stillness within the mist that visibly moved and swirled in the breath of the mountain. Soft sounds sifted out of the fog. Most likely it was zephyrs and wafting winds, but there seemed words, flute notes even, out there in the unseen expanse of Suilven's summit.

The mystical moment hung thick in the air... and then it was time to retreat, chill setting in. Before reaching the saddle between Suilven's two humps, I'd dropped below the cloud, the world returning to material matter, so that I could see without any illusion the drystone wall slung across the mountain's back. The feel of the faerie still clung like the mist, yet the rock wall was a concrete thread, uniting history and human into that mountain.

Faeries dance on Suilven when the fog settles in. Sprites and spirits waltz unseen when mist covers the peak, free to frolic hidden from human eyes. That was the tale that spun itself in my head later that evening when I looked up to Suilven from below, the mountain's cap still lost to view. That is what I felt, standing on that mist-cloaked high dome overlooking nothing at all, in a land replete with myths of faeries, selkies, kelpies, and mystical happenings. That tale lingered in my mind and in my many trips back to Assynt, a myth I created out of a longing, a feeling; we seem to have chased the spirit of the land into the mist, where it dances only when we are not watching or cannot see, human eyes looking through a fog, only with luck hearing the breath of the dance as it swirls around. I created a tale, believing the stories and folklore of the land handed down through the generations are more than words; they are a bond, a weaving of human creativity and culture into the earth, often a part of Home.

It was Suilven that caused my heart to leap on my return to Assynt just a year after that first climb, the great stony pachyderm sparking the same emotion penned by poets through time. Oddly, I found the surge constricting my chest felt like the emotion of a homecoming, like returning to a place of connection. Which seemed soundly absurd, since all my deep connections to Place revolved around a region of Montana, where I spent so many days walking, wandering, and watching peregrines in the sky. Peregrini... the wanderers.

~~~

That hike up Suilven was almost twenty years ago, but the connection was made. Sitting in this little Kabin on this gray morning, it seems a long time ago. Today, I know it was the beginning of a journey into people and Place. It is curious though, what brought me back to Assynt, for it seemed almost as if I kept returning to find out why I kept returning. It started with the land, with the stories it told, for in those first years, the friendships and appreciation of the communities had yet to grow.

All landscapes carry stories, whispered tales of past events woven into the earth, reminders of the intricate connections between all things. This vast archive speaks of both the nonhuman world and the human populations, the earth recording our past as we reside on it, living here alongside the nonhuman. In the Scottish Highlands, that history is writ large, for stone was often more readily available for building than wood, and stone construction stands in testament to past lives. In Scotland, I walked within visible ruins from Paleolithic onward, each successive age marked by its structures. I saw the standing stones in enigmatic array, dipped my finger in ancient rock-lined holy wells to touch the moisture to my forehead, stood by ruins of castles and homes, and heard the stories that are part of the land.

Such stories and oral histories weave us into a place. All lands have their narratives, myths, and folklore that shape and are shaped by culture, told to make sense of what we have no power to control, to convey moral teachings, sometimes sculpting our concept of history. The
~~~

colonizing culture of the American West developed its stories based on only a few centuries of occupation, legends of cowboys and Indians, settlers and mountain men that evolved out of a history of dispossession and occupation. Across the West, the reality was more of everyday people simply trying to carve out a new life, following the siren call of a story that had no depth in the past, a Manifest Destiny that washed over the Indigenous cultures in a tidal wave that nearly erased those populations whose roots wend deep into the earth.

I wove my own thoughts of myth and mystery into this place in Scotland, where rock walls run over mountain backs and whisperings emerge from the mist. Out of it rose a desire for a deeper cultural connection, to somehow be part of that Highland landscape. There are deep roots in Assynt. In Montana, I am nothing but a transplant.

As I began to better know the region and my awareness of the ruins and their history increased, it became apparent the work of humans has touched Assynt's entire landscape, despite my perception of its wildness and the feel of the faerie. Within the open moors lie the ruins of past constructions, while much (though certainly not all) of Assynt's modern population now lives near the coast, in the village of Lochinver and in smaller coastal crofting communities such as Drumbeg, Stoer, and Clachtoll.

History constructed these patterns across the land. A critical point in that timeline is the Jacobite Rebellions, the uprisings of those who wanted James Stuart VIII and his heirs returned to the throne: many of the Jacobites were Highlanders. The Jacobites were defeated, and their Highland culture subsequently crushed. As part of this, the Scottish Highlands were carved into large estates of private property, the estate lairds coming from the winning side; the people who lived on the land became tenants, paying rent.

Yet sheep were more profitable than tenants, and so the Highland Clearances, a time when the lairds cleared the tenants to create pastures, pushing out the people who'd known the place as home for generations, forcing them overseas or to coastal communities. For some of those who stayed, small holdings called crofts were created—often near the coast—out of chunks of land too small for subsistence, forcing the crofters to work for the laird in order to get by. Sutherland, where Assynt lies, is notorious for the brutal removal of the tenants from their land, for the burnings of homes so the families could not return, for the utter misery and even deaths that resulted. The traditional transhumant way of life, the agropastoral existence that took herders to summer pastures in the mountains, crumbled into memory. The ruins within the moors stand as solid stone reminders that this empty land is not empty, that these broad sweeping moors and high romantic peaks are alive with ghosts and memories.

Wild places and lands known as wilderness are part of who I am. That great feeling of homecoming swept over me when I first returned to Assynt partly because of its wild feel, the open space, the rising peaks. It is all that I want to embrace. Yet the empty wildness is also that very element that makes me stand in stunned silence by the ruins of a shattered township or a crumbled foundation. It is the same penetrating stillness that envelops me on finding an obsidian spearhead in the Montana mountains, stumbling across an ancient tepee ring, or visiting the Sheep Eater Indian wickiup remains near our family ranch. Here in Assynt and in Montana, the mountains where I wander were the ancestral home to a people who walked before me, people who had a deeper kinship with the earth than modern society. In Montana, it was my culture who took it from them. By all rights, it is not my home but theirs.

Sometimes I question myself, wondering how to think about, how to *feel* about, those past peoples' relationship with the land, both in Assynt and in Montana—what is idealized, what is real. Then I wrap my thoughts around how I feel as a European descendant about calling Montana my homeland. Now, here in Assynt, I have found community and mountains, a place I would have settled into, but I am from America and have no Scottish ancestry. Do I fit into this historic trajectory, coming from the American West? The wanderer who wanted to come home to Assynt, wanting to have deep roots here, knowing that was impossible but still wanting to settle in this place—yet simply could not make that work.

On this misty morning in Inchnadamph, I sit with journal in hand, remembering Suilven but writing nothing, making no progress on figuring this Home chapter out, overwhelmed by the complexity of home and homeland, of sense of place, of the mountain landscapes that have for so long been under my feet—knowing I have chosen the desert.

I need to go walk. I will stand by the shieling and township ruins and think about home and loss, those who lived in these mountains, and those who were lost to these mountains. And I will try to make peace with Mountain as Home, for these shieling and township ruins of Assynt now hold a greater poignancy after what happened on our family ranch in the last few years, events that shifted my deep sense of place for the ranch and its surrounds from Home to homeland. Now in this gray time here in Inchnadamph, when weariness allows melancholy to bleed through my veins, I stand by the ruins and think of this challenging chapter I must write and wonder if I need to speak of those Montana ranch events? Or hold them distant.

Perhaps best to hold them distant yet note that time for the intensity of the situation. Suffice it to say there were major issues on the ranch, conflict and controversy beyond what I ever could have imagined might occur in a place that had always been peaceful, a complex situation involving both employees and relatives, the details of which are not necessary for this narrative. As the only family member residing on the ranch at the time, I was central to the maelstrom that felt so dark, a blackness in a place that was once of light. My mental and physical health deteriorated, and living on the ranch became untenable. I sought peace and kindness in other places—in Scotland, in the desert. Things had forever changed on the ranch that was Home, that was my foundation, that is the place where the Mountain still cups me in the palms of its hands.

After spending a vast majority of my life living on or near the family ranch, I came to know how deep connections to both family and place create Home, so that now, standing in front of the ruins, I grieve for those who lost their home, reflecting on the cruelty of dispossession. Across the planet, history holds the stories of entire cultures forcefully removed from their lands, violent brutality, attempted genocide; it is beyond what I might imagine, though now I can better sense it after those painful years at the place I knew as Home.

In the Scottish Highlands and in the American West, where the emptied mountain landscapes ring with sorrow, those who are long since gone left their print on the earth. Yet in the mountains of Montana, that print is so light, it is easy to overlook, for the people were nomadic and used wood for their structures. From the beginning, the ruins I came across in the Assynt moorlands spoke to me, stories of stone for a woman of wood. And I stand by them thinking of the laughter and the tears and the footsteps of those who walked out of the broken doorways for the last time, never to return home.

Today, I will stand by them again and remember. The gray of the rock will blend with the color of the sky.

~~~

A few days onward from that gray day, and morning has arrived clear and bright. Breabag arches across the horizon, inviting me to its heights, and I feel I must try, though clouds and rain are predicted again for the late afternoon and that fatigue haunts me, a tiredness unlike any I've known. In my head, I hear the warnings of those who had or who've known people who had COVID: *Don't push it. You will get long COVID.*

Still, I will go. Walking the path toward Breabag will also take me along part of the IAT, for what that's worth—perhaps a continuation of something I started that now feels impossible. And I will think about "The Peopled Mountain." Perhaps these few weeks in Inchnadamph could be the chapter's framework so there is a time frame, a specific journey, a journey within the larger journey. If I don't get to Breabag, then that could be a metaphor. For what? Letting go of hopes that didn't and won't come to pass? Like the IAT? Like this Scottish mountain region as home?

As my bond with this Highland place grew, I started to think of Breabag as my Scottish version of Monument Mountain, that mountain behind the ranch, a place oft visited, holding many markers of memory and familiarity. Breabag too has such markers, though not so many and not so deeply felt. There is that small lochan on the way up, beneath the last rise of cliffs, where I once plunged into the cold waters to wash
~~~

away weeks of working on a tourist boat. There is the spring on the far side that bubbles with clear cold water that holds no trace of peaty tannins, my place to sit for lunch by moss-lined pools, where I once saw a fox—"And don't tell the gamekeeper," a local told me, because foxes are hunted, and I learned more about this place and its ways. There is the high ledge that takes me to a flat quartzite terrace, that I first walked in wonder with the discovery that such geology exists. And there is the drystone wall so carefully constructed right on top, a wall I can see so clearly in my mind, remembering when I first found it and the impact of that wall's presence—the same as finding the wall on Suilven. So today I will try to reach Breabag, for to see that wall and write beside it would fit well in "The Peopled Mountain" chapter. Though honestly, to visit the wall seems of no significance compared to the joy of being on Breabag again, after years of pandemic-forced absence.

Breabag's summit wall holds significance. I've been told it was probably part of the creation of sheep farms, when the dispossessed estate tenants were put to work building walls that created pastures and boundaries. I've thought of that wall as a fragment of a sentence, a few words of a thick book, an entire story growing out of its stones. I've thought of the hands that built the wall, thought of those who lived here before the estates, the people who did not have such walls, when much of the land was communal.

Thinking of that crumbled curve of stone wall on Breabag, thinking of Mountain as Home, makes me consider: there are no dwellings in the heights, the highest places are not for the human in the depths of winter, when the wind rakes the land with sharp crystals of snow and temperatures freeze tears in eyes and mucus in nose, when snow hides earth that provides pasture in warmer times. In Assynt, the shielings are on the mountain flanks, only the stone walls running higher; the town and house ruins sit below. In the Cairngorm mountains not too far away, archaeologists find remnants of Mesolithic hunting camps in the high regions but not homes, those past people temporarily immersed in the highest mountains as part of subsistence, not for constant inhabitation. Even Assynt's Neolithic ruins are near the valley floor. Likewise, in Montana, I've seen arrowheads at 10,000′ above sea level, but even in summer, those hunter-gatherer nomadic people stayed down around the elevation of the ranch, about 7,000′, venturing higher to hunt but not to stay. The high elevations of the mountains I know have not been permanent living spaces; rather, they were places traveled into and through for hunting, pasture, or migration.

Looking for more information on high-elevation communities, wondering if any existed within the highest of peaks, I came across articles on the Dokpa nomadic yak herders, a people who have turned the usual transhumant journey around, moving *up* into the alpine Tibetan Plateau in winter when wind scours the land free of snow, providing forage for their livestock. The Dokpa stay in stone huts or temporary tents along their migratory route. Also on the Tibetan Plateau is the highest traditional mountain village, Tuiwa Village. But this is an alpine plateau, at an elevation below where vegetation gives way to rock and snow and grassless mountain peaks. Those high, rocky points are not even included in the term *mountain* or *alp* by traditional societies in the Valaisan Alps, as they are of no use for summer pastures and so are left out of any designation. These people of the Alps didn't even consider themselves "mountain people" until politics and tourism made that desirable; they reserved the term for the herders who seasonally journeyed to the higher parts of the mountains.[7]

All this provides support for Thoreau's belief that the high peaks are unsuitable for human existence and are "among the unfinished parts of the globe, whither it is a slight insult to the gods to climb and pry into their secrets, and try their effect on our humanity. Only daring and insolent men, perchance, go there."[8] Thus, people simply should not be in those high places.[9]

It complicates my thought of Mountain as Home. For the high mountains are, with a few exceptions, not a place of human abode; that is where the ptarmigan and mountain hare live, where the eagle hunts and the plover cries in summertime, where the rock is bared, and the feel of the faerie lingers in the mountain mystique, the Mountain holding and sometimes revealing its deeper secrets.

"It's a place where you put your foot down and wonder if anyone else has ever stepped there," Jane said.

"That's how the Montana mountains often feel," I replied.

Then you find the obsidian chip or run across a stone wall and remember: this was an inhabited land, The Peopled Mountain.

~~~

Skylarks sing above, notes sprinkling down from the sky. These birds are the moor to me, with a song that plants me in place and remains in my mind after the bird has long gone. There are meadow pipits here as well, flying up to parachute down in courtship display, their thin tweeting calling me to watch as they descend. A snipe is winnowing. I can see the bird, fluttering, swooping, its tail feathers stroking the air to create that magical fluting sound of the winnow. The mountains surround me, rumpled and rocky yet green, rolled over and smoothed by ice, their curves and ridges, summits and valleys familiar by sight if not by foot, for I have not walked all of these mountains. Breabag arches to the east, clouds above it, lowering as I watch.

The heights of Breabag will have to wait for another time. Clouds moved in, but more it was the dragging COVID fatigue, the difficulty of getting a good lungful of air, that turned me back. I did not even make it to the lochan below the cliff.

Now I sit sipping ginger tea on a dolostone outcrop between Traligill Caves and Breabag's first steep rise, examining the pattern and rainbow colors of sphagnum moss, the way the moss clumps on the rock, the elegance of its "fronds."

The sphagnum moss brought me home, in its simplicity and its kinship with these moors, this ancient species sparking a subtle inner joy grown out of that moss, the birds, the notes filling the sky, the thrumming of the snipe resonating into the bone. Sitting here on this soft rock, a sense of belonging warms me, a homecoming of sorts, home in the greater sense of the word, for it is not the home of dwelling within a human community but rather a comfortable sense of settling into belonging.

There is time to sit, time to reflect, my thoughts turning to the Home chapter. It will be an emotional challenge to write, given the
~~~

complexity of my wandering desire to find home, the lows and highs along that path, the deep pain and sense of loss suffused into Montana memories juxtaposed against the joyful connections to this place in Assynt that grew out of that oddly striking similarity in emotion evoked by the Montana wildlands and the Scottish Highlands.

Sitting on a mossy rock in the midst of familiar mountains, I consider again how I kept coming back to Scotland to find out why I kept coming back. It seems obvious now. I'd found something here I'd not experienced at the ranch, something that feels integral to home. Community.

The historical communities first caught my attention as I read the history of shieling and township ruins. No longer monks' abodes and faerie haunts, I came to know that the land holds people's lives in its stone—laughter and tears and a knowing of place. And I thought that to live in the mountain's shadow, to know its pastures and springs, the comings and goings of plant and bird as seasons shift, where and when the grass grows, and what lives and blooms, to hold a knowledge of ecology and geology built through time and experience—that is a belonging marked here in crumbled walls and vacant doorframes, a relationship to the land that set me to yearning for a different way of living.

It seems that such a connection to the earth must be especially tight for mountain communities that lie within an ecology that can be unforgiving, thus requiring adaptation. In fact, it is not just my romantic dreaming to consider mountain communities as connected to the land, functioning in a sustainable way. A study of two transhumant communities in the Indian Himalayan region—including the Dokpa yak herders who winter on the Tibetan Plateau—considered how their *modern* social system based on traditional ecological knowledge adapts to the harsh and changing conditions of the extreme mountain environment. The governing system of these communities focuses on natural resources, forming "an important link between social structures and natural systems," thus "providing social, economic, and ecological security to the community."[10] The communities' governing system only dates back to the early nineteenth century, but their way of life is older, just as the historic agropastoral transhumance of Assynt reached back generation after generation. In the past, both nomadic and agropastoral populations had to be sustainable, for to live otherwise was death. In the Himalayan populations, their ways have carried forward in the continued ability to adapt to changing conditions, fostered by a modern social structure connected to the land, something that could provide insights on how to mitigate the impacts of climate change. We need to remember how to live *with* the earth, not just on it—which was chiming in my thoughts on first seeing the ruins and learning of the traditional lifestyle in Assynt.

These ecological connections are also demonstrably tight in some communities where livestock have grazed for millennia in traditional ways, a coevolution occurring with the unfolding of time between people, place, and nonhuman life. Dispersed and moving, grazing animals created a patchy vegetation mosaic, seen in parts of Scotland and other regions (including the Tibetan Plateau), resulting in a heterogeneous habitat that promotes biodiversity, allowing a greater variety of species to survive. Butterflies and birds start to disappear when livestock are removed, sometimes done with the best of intentions when creating a nature reserve; when the land loses its grazing and browsing, it loses the heterogeneity associated with *dispersed* pastoral practices.[11] People and their animals were part of the land, a part of the ecosystem.

The traditional life in this Highland landscape was hard and not one most people would choose today—at any rate, there is no going back to it in its original form. I do not think of it in those terms. But the tangible presence of those past people in these moors and mountains set a thought in my mind that rippled across my way of knowing the earth, a hope that people are not always "Man the Disturber," as George Perkins Marsh wrote in *Man and Nature* in the mid-nineteenth century.[12] The more recent history of the Himalayan people supports that rippling thought: if we once could live in a more sustainable manner, maybe we could do so again.

Sitting on this dolostone rock in the midst of the moors, I note that "Man the Disturber" has made his mark in what I see around me. This land now suffers not from lack of grazing but from the impact of too much grazing and browsing, historically from sheep and now from red deer. It has been centuries since any large predator prowled this landscape, and the red deer numbers have exploded. Wild trees cling to protected sites, while trees planted to create new woodlands survive inside stout deer fences almost two meters high. I remind myself not to romanticize, for the wolves, bears, and lynx were slaughtered and are gone. Past populations were not in complete harmony with all that is wild.

This land's history, the transhumant people, the idea of lifestyles intimately connected to the mountain's ways and cycles—all that nurtured my yearning for a different way of life. Standing by township ruins, I could not help but think that those who were cleared off this land lived together in a community *within* the mountains. Yet history is just that, something of the past, and as the years passed, I found a living, vibrant community in the people who live here *now*. Experiencing the modern community solidified my bond to Assynt, the people and place of the present—not the ruins of the past—pulling me so strongly into the Scottish Highland landscape.

"The ranch is my wild community," I used to tell Jane. "Assynt is where I find a human community."

When a move is made, there are push and pull factors. My move away from the ranch was related to the push of painful events, yet a more subtle push had long been at work: that desire for community. The mountains draw people, and southern Montana has suffered a population explosion along with an uptick in the cost of living. Like so many other awe-inspiring locales, it isn't the same place I grew up with, and the towns and cities near the ranch are places where a connected sense of community eluded me.

The pandemic hit while I was here in Inchnadamph, staying at Jane's, and so I returned to Montana. Not able to get overseas, the next autumn, I rented a place in southern Utah, in a small community I'd come to know during the black years at the ranch when I fled from the situation. In the odd way that life takes us in unexpected directions, I found the human community I yearned for, one small and kind and accepting, in the midst of a high desert, adjacent to wildlands. I found what I'd discovered in Assynt, what I'd learned is so important to settling and finding Home: community. A place where I walked out the door into kindness *and* where I could walk out into the surrounding lands and wander all day. Life is once again suffused with joy.

For my entire life, I thought I'd end up in the mountains. I would have made Montana home. I would have made Assynt home. And I have chosen the desert. But the Desert is not so different from the Mountain as one might think.

Sitting with the moss, I've remembered the joy of what *is*, letting loose of what was and will not be. Still, it catches me up with poignancy that could hold me in utter stillness, and so I will walk down and later share the evening with those I've come to know here in Inchnadamph, the people who showed me the beauty of community that makes life whole, as much as the song of the skylark and the way the moss grows.

~~~

My last morning at Inchnadamph came. I sat with coffee, watching the mountains, thinking how much I loved that Place and its people in that way of love that rests solidly, warmly within you. Suddenly, as if a veil lifted, I saw the mountains for what they are, what seemed their essence, the mountains that have no name, the bedrock Mountain beyond humanity, where the people and culture are a thin veneer, an ephemeral blush over the land. Just as I came to think of Yosemite and so many other mountains, knowing them beyond the labels and meaning we give them, so these mountains became themselves. For so many years, I explored this place and there beneath it all was the Mountain.

And now I know that Breabag will never be my Monument, and Assynt cannot be homeland, but that does not negate what I feel for that place and its people.

My big backpack was overstuffed, all the IAT trekking gear smashed in with as much as I could carry of things I've stored at Jane's over the years. Packing the bag was hard, for the IAT was done, that journey about connections, a journey of hope planned over years—just done, so abruptly ended by COVID. Then to pack the mug, flute, slippers, and other cozy things that for so long stayed at Jane's place, to take
~~~

them back to the States seemed like the end of a chapter, and I wasn't ready to turn the page.

I plopped the heavy backpack on a bench out front and went to find Jane of Kirkton. While I was in back, the other Jane from the Lodge put some cards made from her paintings on top of my pack—she was running late and didn't have time to find me, thought I might be out walking. Those cards are precious; I will probably never mail them.

The cards were there when I came out front with Jane of Kirkton, who had shared her loft bedroom so generously with me over the years, who made it possible to stay in Assynt for week after week after week, who'd said to me when the pandemic hit, "Just stay here and wait it out. You can help me with the garden," even as I packed and left thinking of my parents. Years of separation followed. Jane provided a shelter and a haven for me. Now her loft room is a major part of her business and so income. I am moving to a desert. All things change.

We chatted while waiting for Helen to arrive. Dear Helen, who'd met me when I'd arrived only a few weeks ago and who would now take me away to Ullapool to catch the bus to Inverness.

"Remember I always said this was my human community?" I asked Jane.

"Yes."

"Now I found a human community in Bluff, where I can walk into wildlands."

Jane understands.

"You will come back," she said, and I think I scowled, for I wonder: nothing seems to happen as planned anymore.

"Of course you will." She stated it. And I smiled. I'd left a few things still stored there—of course I will.

Helen arrived. It was time to go. I hugged Jane tight, once, twice, and just before I got in Helen's car, we looked at each other and hugged again.

At the Ullapool Ferry Terminal, where the bus would arrive, I hugged Helen just as tightly, not knowing what to say, how to take my leave from the warmth of this friend who had so welcomed me to Assynt. "Haste ye back," she said, adding, "when the time is right." Then I watched Helen drive away, off to her appointment.

There were hours before the bus would come. With my big bag kindly stored by the harbor master, I set off for a walk up Ullapool Hill, for here on my last full day in the Highlands, the sun shone out of a clear blue sky.

Halfway up the hill, a bird shadow passed, a fleeting bit of flight marked across the earth, lifting my awareness upward. A sea eagle, broad and dark except for the brilliant white tail lit through by sunlight, soaring high enough that its great size was lost in the uncommonly blue depths of the sky. That sea eagle circled directly overhead, circling above one lone hiker on a ridge with a view toward the place I'd come to know. All the years in the Highlands and I've never seen a sea eagle soaring like that, softly soaring just above. It felt like the land's gift, an acknowledgment of my love for the Place, all the connections and threads, relationships and dreams forever embedded in that Place, wild, human, mountain, and moor, all embedded into who I am.

The eagle circled twice, three times, again, then floated north, disappearing into that cloudless sky just where the mountains near Inchnadamph rose in the distance, not so far in miles but now a long way away. For a time I watched the sky where the bird had been, thinking of Scottish poet Norman MacCaig, who had a "love affair" with Assynt,[13] thinking of MacCaig's poem "In Everything," which ends:

> And I don't remember
> The eagle going away. But I'll never forget
> The eagle-shaped space it left, stamped on the air.
> Absence or presence? . . . It seems I'm on a ledge of seapinks
> All the time, an observing, blank-puzzled cliff-hanger.[14]

Everything seemed changed in life. Absence or presence?

I walked down the hill to catch my bus and start the long journey back across the Atlantic.

Months later, I took out my journal of that time in Assynt and wrote the chapter you hold in your hands, "The Peopled Mountain." Mountain as Home.

7
THE WHOLE MOUNTAIN

Hallingskarvet, Norway

Philosophers

No other passenger left the warm train, with its comfortable seats and readily available food and drink. Not one other traveler stepped out onto the battered asphalt platform of Ustaoset with its windowless rusty-red station house that had only one door marked "WC." Only the conductor and I left the train, the conductor taking his usual stance to monitor people coming and going, making sure all was safe before the train doors closed—but no one else was coming or going. The Ustaoset train station was deserted except for me, the conductor, and the puddles rippling in the cold wind. The display in the train had told me the temperature was seven degrees Celsius. Translating that to forty-five degrees Fahrenheit, I inwardly shivered. It was midday in mid-July. When I set out, I would walk up in elevation to camp in colder climes.

The conductor watched with a sympathetic expression as I heaved my pack onto the only station bench, as if he felt the solitary isolation of the lone traveler on a windswept train platform, where the gusts whipped through everything, twisting around the concrete and buildings and bench and cutting deep into me.

"Cold here... but I think it's raining farther on," the conductor said in a kind voice.

"I hear there's sunshine in the forecast," I answered with a smile, sounding hopeful for my own sake, even as I dug out wool hat, mittens, neck gaiter from the top compartment of the pack, all easily accessible with expectations they would soon be needed—this was typical weather for this place at this time of year.

The conductor blew his whistle at the empty platform, wished me the best as he stepped back into the warmth of the railcar. The train moved off. Silence bore in. The world shrank down.

Me. A pack. A hut. A ridge.

A ridge that is a mountain that is Hallingskarvet.

The Hallingskarvet massif runs across south-central Norway, just north of Ustaoset. From below, it presents a formidable cliff front that stretches over the softer terrain below, its rock facade broken by dancing ribbons of water, its crest—when not lost in mist—rolling green above the dark crags. This is not the green of alpine meadow softness but the lighter green of lichen that coats the rocky land. Like the Scottish mountains where I've walked, Hallingskarvet rose up during the vigorous mountain-building time of the Caledonian Orogeny, some 400 million years ago. Ice and time subsequently worked on this land, carving Hallingskarvet into the creature it is today, a forty-kilometer stretch of rugged ridge seeming devoid of vegetation. *Skarve* means naked mountain in Norwegian, and *Hallingskarvet* refers to the naked mountain over Halling Valley.

Hallingskarvet is moody, and the first morning I met this mountain, it had a dark mood, a cloak of mist drawn over its crest, a somber-hued, snow-patched bench of earth running below the ominous cliffs that rose into unknown heights within deep-gray fog. Hallingskarvet might be a mountain, but in my mind, it will always be the long Ridge, an edge, a boundary to cross, standing out there solemn and still, cold and warm all at once, like a guardian watching over all.

On Hallingskarvet's flank, on the earth bench below the cliffs, is a small cottage named Tvergastein Hytte. Built, loved, and lived in by philosopher Arne Næss, this building allowed Næss to reside within the mountain's embrace in all seasons and immerse in that mountain landscape that shaped his life and so sparked the deep ecology movement. Tvergastein Hytte was my destination for the day, the mountain and its near surrounds to be my place for the next ten nights and days. Hallingskarvet was where I was going, solo, just me with my massive bag, following the lead of Arne Næss.

I hefted the pack onto my back and began the journey.

~~~

The sojourn at Hallingskarvet may best be described as living a question, an exploration of the significance of connecting to a Place. The quest evolved out of my own connection to the mountain landscape of my Montana homeland and the understanding of how deeply that Place had shaped my very being. This led to the realization that at the heart of many of the world's influential environmental thinkers is a particular Place, a physical, geographic muse that inspired ideas, emotions, thought, and wonder, such as John Muir's Yosemite or Rachel Carson's Maine coast. The Place these people knew was an integral factor in molding their worldview and fostering a life philosophy in which they felt connected to and part of the natural world and so were devoted to caring for the greater-than-human community and the earth as a whole; this was simply how these people lived, their actions born out of compassion and deep bonds rather than moral obligation or ethical duty. Intuitively, one can understand why this may be, yet I wanted to delve deeper, unravel the importance of Place through the eyes and lives of others. And so when I stepped onto the Ustaoset platform, I began the first of what I called my "shared path journeys," a project to revisit the inspirational Places of naturalists and nature writers, carrying their words and thoughts with me. These shared path journeys would eventually take me to diverse landscapes, including the Tetons with Olaus Murie, Yosemite with John Muir, and Scotland's Cairngorms with Nan Shepherd. Hallingskarvet, "home" to Arne Næss, was my first such journey.

Næss intrigued me, for he directly attributed his life philosophy (what he called an ecosophy) to Hallingskarvet's mountain landscape and so had written much about the significance of that Place to his life. Yet choosing to immerse in Næss's Place and his worldview turned out to be a complex undertaking, for there was nothing simple about the man. His life spanned almost a century, from 1912 to 2009, two weeks shy of ninety-seven years of living. He was an accomplished academic, already a philosophy professor at the University of Oslo in his twenties; he was a skilled mountaineer, known internationally for some of his first
~~~

ascents; he was a curmudgeon and cantankerous by some accounts, provoking some while enlightening others. Joyful is a word he used often and is a characteristic that others often apply to him. "Life is a process," Næss said. "Going strong is joyful all the way. You just do things until you have practically no power."[1]

It seems deep ecology is what Arne Næss is mostly known for, at least across the globe.[2] Although he established himself as an academic through his publications and explorations of the philosophy of science, semantics, and skepticism, it was deep ecology that made him one of the most influential philosophers of the twentieth century. Deep ecology is not a science; it is both a philosophy and a movement that enfolds ecological principles into a deep philosophical inquiry into our very existence on this earth. The deep ecology movement emphasized values and worldview as they shape our actions, its eight-point platform[3] meant as a guide to living that could shape cultural norms and foster actions to create a sustainable, just, and environmentally responsible world; the movement inspired and motivated people across the planet. Catalyzed by Næss, developed and promoted in association with other like-minded people, deep ecology might be said to be grounded in Tvergastein on Hallingskarvet. There, Næss did a great deal of his deep thinking, and there, his connection and compassion for that Place led him into a life of caring for the earth.

Because of this, I believed Næss and Hallingskarvet would provide insights into the larger significance of what might be called "sense of place"—exactly as to what and how was a bit unclear as I moved from comfortable train onto windy platform and upward, through Ustaoset and out toward the Mountain and Tvergastein Hytte.

Not a long distance to go, less than six miles. Once I left the small town, familiar flowers appeared, plants I knew from time spent in Scotland: butterwort, meadow buttercup, birch willow. A bluethroat landed nearby, a brown sparrowlike bird with a brilliant sapphire throat set alight by the sun's rays. As I climbed from Hallingskarvet's feet to its knees (Næss's terms, I seemed to remember), the plants shortened in stature so that I walked through a suite of alpine vegetation—dryas, moss campion, vaccinium—all hugging the ground.

The gentle incline of the plain broke at a steep rise, the beginning of the bench on which Tvergastein Hytte sits. The bench is a geologic feature, a shelf with an edge that drops steeply down to the south, that south-facing slope forming the north side of a broad valley. At the base of the bench, a tattered, ripped sign stood on a tilted post, marking the edge of Hallingskarvet National Park, the sign's stately royal dancing-lion emblem contrasting with the metal's worn appearance. Looking up I saw Tvergastein Hytte perched on the bench crest, silhouetted against the gray mist behind, looking black except for the silvery glint of the windows. This was no shack of a hut but a substantial building, large and long, the straight lines and rectangular shape distinctly set apart from the surrounds.

I lost the trail on the last pitch and made my own route upward, between a turbulent stream and a snowbank, pushing down my poles to take the weight of the pack off my back. Yellow violets blossomed, sheep appeared—sheep!? I hiked over the edge of the bench and reached Tvergastein Hytte.

Me. A pack. A hut. A ridge.

A hut. *The* hut. The Hytte. There. REAL.

Having looked for so long at internet pictures, the building had a sense of familiarity. Now it was a reality before me. Solid. Arne Næss's Tvergastein Hytte. Real.

The heavy pack fell onto Næss's doorstep, rolling awkwardly under its own weight. I pulled shirts out of the pack, removed sweaty layers, replaced them with dry warmth. The mist hung low, the top of Hallingskarvet still lost in cloud. Quiet. No one else was there.

Surrounding me was an alpine landscape of rock, mat vegetation, snowbanks, cliff, and cold streams. A waterfall plunged from the crags, feeding into a small lake to the west. Fog swirled in and out, dropping, rising. That environment would surround me for the next ten days—environment all too sanitized a word to describe the place, where the mineral scent of rock merged with the aroma of mist, where the sound of running water seemed a backdrop to a permeating quiet stillness.

I stood by the doorstep for a very long, still moment. I was there. I had made it to Tvergastein Hytte. And now?

~~~

In 1937, Næss, only in his twenties, built Tvergastein Hytte, situating the building below Hallingskarvet's cliffs, just on the bench edge where the slope drops steeply into the valley below, where you can see it from a far distance, if you know where to look. Tvergastein referred to the area extending out from the cottage to the immediate surrounds, or as Næss said, "to a greater gestalt" encompassing that part of the bench visible from Tvergastein Hytte, including the little lake Tvergasteinjernet that lies in a low spot below the building (*jernet* is Norwegian for lake). Constructing the hytte was no easy feat: sixty-two loads of building material, pulled in by horse on autumn snow. Today, the hytte is a well-maintained, dark-brown structure with several rooms, its windows bordered with red. Rocks of varied colors and striations, including a block of quartz, are built into a stoop in front of the door. Cables stretch over the roof to keep it from blowing off during gales (in older pictures, there are just rocks on the roof), while a massive stone wall curves around the western side to protect against the prevailing winds. Peering in the windows, I could see the comfortable homey rooms, with sitting chairs, woodstove, bookshelves, bed, cupboards. The walls and floor are light wood, the dining table and inside door painted light blue, a wooden chest on the side decorated with traditional Norwegian design, a comfortable-looking couch strewn with pillows, all giving a feeling of brightness and warmth—a home, not a shack, a cottage rather than what Americans might think of as a "hut." Today, the building is privately owned[4] and closed to the likes of me, no matter how much my softer side wanted to curl up on that couch in front of the wood stove.

A sign was posted in the hytte's window, put up on the inside so that numerous small insects and flies were trapped between the laminated paper and the window, obscuring some of the letters. The top of the 8½ × 11 sheet was in Norwegian, with a small picture of Næss in his later years. The bottom was in English:
~~~

DEAR HIKER!

You are now standing next to the philosopher and founder of deep ecology Arne Næss' cabin Tvergastein at 1505 m above sea level. The cabin was built by local carpenters in 1937. Arne Næss has spent all together 14 years of his life here, and wrote many of his books here. He said that it is difficult to think "small thoughts" in a place like this, and we hope the view can inspire us all to be as open for a life more in tune with nature. Arne Næss was especially fond of the vulnerable vegetation around the cabin, so we hope that you will admire and respect all life while you are here and tread lightly, mostly on stones. The cabin is managed by a private organization. It is not open to the public.

Stiftelsen Tvergastein Arne Næss' hytte

Fourteen years. Næss died at almost ninety-seven years of age, meaning around eighty-three years of his life took place elsewhere, but *this* Place inspired and changed him.[5] Fourteen years is long enough to learn the greater rhythms of the mountain, especially when you have the keen senses of a field naturalist and the mind of a philosopher, a mind that observes the "what" in minute detail and then asks the "why." Næss had a mind and heart that could put the "what" and "why" together and come up with wonder.

Næss's way of life and thinking evolved where that expansive view stretched around, where the mountain landscape tested him even as he embraced it; here, there could be no "small thoughts." Næss named his life philosophy after this Place: Ecosophy T, where *T* is usually interpreted as T is for Tvergastein. An ecosophy, as explained by fellow deep ecologist Alan Drengson, is a worldview that takes "careful account of ecological responsibilities... a word coined for ecological wisdom."[6] Such a life philosophy is inspired by the ecosphere, by the earth with its rock, water, soil, air, and creatures and all their intimate complex interactions. Næss emphasized that those who live by an ecosophy are *inclined* to care for the earth, *inclined* to live according to the deep ecology platform, and thus their actions are "beautiful actions," directed not by environmental ethics or moral duty—what one is supposed to do—but rather by a view of reality that puts humans as part of a "whole," along with all life.

The basic tenets that Næss lived by were established in that place where I stood, an alpine world, a bench below a cliff below a plateau of lichen-coated rock. Not an easy place. The reality of Tvergastein—with its inhabitants from lichen to lemming to reindeer, its rocks, water, and weather—became part of who Næss was. *T* is for Tvergastein. That did not happen with short visits or just looking at the view.

I pulled out my camera from its protected pouch buried under layers of clothes and photographed the hytte from all perspectives, returning to the sign in the window, capturing it in a photo as well.

A couple appeared, having walked up from below. They watched me looking at the sign. I smiled, nodded at them. They looked a bit older than me, gray-haired, wearing jeans, battered wool hats, and good raincoats, fitting in with the place. The man sat down, leaned against the hytte, and said something in Norwegian.

"I'm sorry, I only speak English..."

He peered at me through his glasses with a professorial look. "You know of Arne Næss?" he asked.

"Yes." I smiled. "He is why I am here."

"You have studied him then?" the man queried, curious.

"Yes..."

"You know his philosophy then?"

I knew enough to know that my knowledge of Næss's work was limited. "My studies are environmental history and environmental ethics. Mostly I know his work on deep ecology."

Even that knowledge was slim. At that point in time, what I really knew was what Næss wrote and thought about our relationship to landscapes, "place," and the earth, having focused my pretrip reading on Næss's ideas about Tvergastein and his own connection to Place. That seemed beyond explaining right then.

"Ah." The man looked at me, frowned. I couldn't tell what he was thinking. He didn't seem approving. Of me or of Næss? "So his later studies."

"Yes..."

The man changed the subject and stopped frowning, asking, "Do you know of his ideas on skepticism?"

I think he said skepticism... or was it positivism? Something familiar, from the limited philosophy I knew. Stoicism? I struggled to remember later, re-creating the conversation. At that moment, I just smiled again, feeling ignorant. "Not much..."

He talked about Næss's philosophies then, how he'd sent a paper to Næss, and how helpful the older, acclaimed philosopher had been, responding kindly and offering to help get the paper published. The man seemed to cherish the memories, enjoyed relating them to this rapt American woman.

"You've met him then?" To meet someone who had interacted with Næss, there by the hytte...

"Oh, yes. He was a professor at twenty-seven, you know."

"A brilliant man, yes."

Wanting to hear what this living philosopher thought of Næss's environmentalism, I asked, "I understand he read Rachel Carson and decided he wanted to do something about the environmental movement. That's why he left the university?"

This I knew. Joining the environmental movement was a new direction for Næss, who'd spent decades at the University of Oslo. In 1968, a student and friend from the United States told Næss about Rachel Carson. "Eureka! I have found it," Næss declared about Carson's *Silent Spring*, a chronicle of human devastation of the natural environment through the heavy use of pesticides. In Carson's tough words lay hope, for Næss believed, "At last there was a real possibility of fighting to save free nature and to save the planet."[7] In 1969, Næss retired early, devoting himself to deep ecology.

"Yes," the philosopher before me said, scowling. "His thoughts shifted." He did not seem all too pleased by the shift. So it was Næss that caused the disapproving frown? He added, as if to change the subject, "He was greatly interested in Spinoza, you know."

"Yes! I think I should read Spinoza to better understand."

"Spinoza was a pantheist," he said suddenly, as if it was an essential fact to know, explaining how this and Spinoza's ethics fit with Næss's thinking.

Of course. Pantheism. The belief that all the world, especially the natural world, is one and the same with a greater spirit, that all is both within and part of an immanent divine presence. Spinoza's ideas catalyzed Næss's own thoughts. Spinoza was a pantheist. And Næss? Certainly, he must have fallen within that framework, even if not claiming it, holding to a unity of all life, that all things are connected, "all things hang together,"[8] as he said. Yet in my readings from Næss, I rarely came across any reference to spirituality.

"Was Næss a pantheist?"

"Well..." The man did not give me a definite *yes*, rather, "He saw a connection in all things."

Again, a rapid subject change as the man looked up toward the cliffs, the rocky face enshrouded with clouds. "Næss wrote a book about Hallingskarvet—it's only in Norwegian.[9] He related the mountain to his mother."

This surprised me; I'd read how Næss referred to the ridge as his father figure; I'd heard Næss in an interview describing that at ten or eleven years old, he already "looked upon this mountain as a kind of benevolent, great father."[10]

"He had tension with his mother. They did not get along." The man knocked his fists together, "Like this," his knuckles meeting.

"So he had a tension with Hallingskarvet?"

"Oh yes." The living philosopher before me pointed up toward the hidden cliff face. "There's a tiny cabin up there. You can't see it right now, of course." The mist swirled, hiding Hallingskarvet's heights. "Næss was up there with a friend. His friend fell. He died on the rocks below."

Was he telling me that was why Næss felt a tension? Or maybe this was yet another subject change, that this pleasant, generous gentleman was trying to convey as much as he could in the limited time we had?

He looked at me, studying.

"Not many people who come here know of Arne Næss. It's a common destination—there's a shorter trail than the one you took, but you need a car to get to the starting point." He chuckled, adding, "You had to climb more.... Many people come, but most people don't know about Arne Næss."

"I think," I said, smiling broadly, "that I am very lucky to have come on this day, when you are here."

The man's wife came over from around the corner of the building, where she'd been looking out over the expansive view of the Hardangervidda plateau. She smiled at me, then spoke to her husband in Norwegian.

"Will you join us for something to eat?" he asked.

"Of course, yes. I was just going to have some food."

They loaned me a comfortable pad to sit on. They ate stacked open-faced sandwiches the way Norwegians do: a slice of bread with meat, cheese, tomato on top, a piece of wax paper, the next slice of bread with more toppings, another bit of wax paper, and so on. I slowly chewed my ration of nuts and raisins for that day. We chatted casually as we shared our mealtime, discussing more mundane subjects. I learned they had a cottage just outside of Ustaoset, that they come up to Tvergastein at least a few times a year.

"Where will you stay?" the man asked.

"I have my tent," I told them. "My plan is to camp near Tvergastein for a while."

The man's wife ended our conversation. "The mist comes down," she said in halting English. "The weather is changing. We must go."

"I think I should camp lower," I mused aloud.

"Yes," the man said firmly, his wife nodding in agreement. "You will camp lower. The mist will come down, and the wind will come up... it will be very cold. Very cold. You *will* camp lower."

They left, walking down the trail, disappearing into the mist, returning to their cottage below, to warmer climes and a wood stove. I packed up and left as well. I'd hauled that heavy pack up to the hut, and now I hauled it down—just one step though, one step down from Hallingskarvet's shoulders to the base of the bench.

The chance encounter with the philosopher who'd known Næss was not taken lightly. Chatting there on the stone doorstep of Tvergastein, it felt like Næss himself was joining the journey. I played the conversation through my head, again and again, so I could write of it later.

Remember, I thought. *Especially remember pantheism and that tension.*

Næss felt tension with Hallingskarvet: this intrigued me, in an unsettling way.

Then another thought. *Remember Joy!* Despite the weight of the pack, the chill in the damp air, the prospect of setting up camp in the inclement weather, that brought a smile, thinking of Næss's words: "Going strong is joyful all the way."[11]

Camp One

Wheatears sat on rock tops all around me, calling, *Chik! Chik! Chik!* Identifying them was easy, as they flashed white rumps when in flight, a saucy-looking hind end that gave the bird its original name of white-ass; the Victorians rejected that for a primmer label. Lovely wheat-hued streaks run from the bird's bill, curving over the eye like eyeglass arms reaching behind the ears, so "wheatear" seems fitting. The wheatears cocked their heads, eyeing me, *chik, chikking*. They fluttered off, returned, fluttered off. Were they calling a warning, alarmed by this odd creature who'd come into their territory, to sit on one of their rocks where no one may have sat before? I wanted to think they were addressing me, telling me something about their home, but I think they were simply curious. *A human? Here? Check her out! Chik! Chik!* Behaving like the chickadees at home, who *chickadee-dee-dee* in the trees where I walk, flitting in close, talking among themselves, checking me out. *She okay? Maybe*... If only their language was something I could better understand.

Wheatears are hardy little birds, living up in northern climes from Europe to North America in the summer, surviving in arctic-alpine conditions, and doing this quite well, it seems, as many of these birds came and went around my camp. No matter where they spend summer though, most if not all wheatears go to sub-Saharan Africa in the winter, some traveling from Alaska across Russia and then Europe to arrive in the winter warmth of Africa. The birds that surrounded me on the slope in July would be many thousands of miles away only a few months later. Like many humans, they do not find the high mountain a good place to reside in winter.

On this, my first morning at Hallingskarvet, I too sat perched on a stone, journal at hand, surrounded by enormity. Heeding the philosopher's advice of the day before, I'd dropped down to set up my tent in a small meadow sheltered from the wind, with a spring, small lake for bathing, and unexpectedly, many signs of domestic sheep. My tent was not far below the Tvergastein bench but was in a much more comfortable clime; last evening, I'd watched the cold mist bear down and swallow Tvergastein Hytte. It never reached my camp.

This morning, I sat with my leather-bound journal in hand, a black notebook holding Næss's thoughts on my lap. Over the preceding months, I'd filled that notebook with transcribed readings from Næss, along with my comments on his work and the upcoming trip.

I stared out from the journal, watched the birds, watched the sky. Then wrote down the thought that had been a troubling undercurrent through the morning. It had been my question as I filled the black notebook in the comfort of home in Montana, and still it dogged me.

What am I doing in this place?

Arne Næss's Place, not mine. Where it was cold, wet, with wheatears and sheep for company. Across the valley, the endless Hardangervidda plateau spread southward out and out with almost as much snow as earth visible, a land of white ice, black cliffs, gray talus, and a cracked mass of a glacial cap. Behind me, that looming mass of a mountain, Hallingskarvet.

Wheatear chipped. I chuckled and flipped through the black book, to remember what I wrote back in Montana, my homeland, my Place, and found what I sought:

Why are YOU HERE?? ~~ "here" because hopefully I will read this at Tvergastein. What's the point of Being in the Place? In Arne Næss's Place?

I set the journal down and thought, *Why are **YOU** here?? Why are you **HERE**??*

Perhaps because so much is written, said, discussed, deliberated about the *people* who made a difference—Næss, Carson, Thoreau, Leopold, Muir, and so on—without much reflection on or intimate understanding of the *Place* that inspired them. That Place is a character too, an influence, a factor in those people's lives. Many have noted that Tvergastein is the place that inspired Næss. People have interviewed Næss about Tvergastein, visited with him at Tvergastein. I wanted to immerse in Tvergastein and its inhabitants one-on-one, to know this landscape well enough—in conjunction with Næss's own thoughts and ideas—to begin to understand what "Place" means, why the mountain Place of Tvergastein mattered to Næss in particular. Why "sense of place" matters at all. Why it creates an ecosophy and nurtures beautiful action.

And if I sat there all day, I'd never know the Place. I set off and up, to meet the Hallingskarvet community.

On my route upward, a plover appeared at a break in the slope, then another, fairly large, almost crow size, and elegant. Golden plovers' backs are a complexity of feathers creating an intricate mix of butter, mocha, and cream spots. A porcelain *S*-shaped band separates the pointillistic upper from an almost black breast, neck, and face, the band sweeping from below the mottled wings, up along the neck curve, ending in an arc over the eye. The birds are common residents in Hallingskarvet, common in that they are fairly abundant but not common in the sense of dull, not with that striking plumage and penetrating, melancholy call. With those intricate, lovely hues, the bird can blend in with the arctic-alpine land, camouflaged. The plovers appeared, all pointillism and porcelain, doing anything but blending in, as they strutted and called as I passed by, their voices echoing long after I was out of sight.

Moving up from what I came to know as "The Place of the Plover" to reach the slope's crest, Hallingskarvet reached up in front of me, overwhelming at first, the dark cliff abruptly rising from the gray-green-brown bench, the world opening up in all other directions. To the southwest, the view spread endlessly outward over Hardangervidda's rugged snow-flecked terrain. Dryer, lower mountains rose in the southeast.

In the east-west directions, the bench stretched both ways along the base of Hallingskarvet's cliff. Tvergastein Hytte stood anchored on that bench, not far from lake Tvergasteinjernet, which shimmered silver under gray skies.

The wild-feeling land seemed barren and bleak until I started meandering. The ground cover where I came over the crest and onto the ledge was a brown, gray, and cream mosaic of low-growing highland rush, rock, and lichen, a contrast to the green meadow surrounding my camp below. I headed west along the bench, away from Tvergastein Hytte, the bench easy walking, the flora and terrain always changing. There were more areas of rush, rock, and lichen and also bare rock fields. Most eye-catching were the brilliant green patches in those places where grass stretched over moist earth, moss ran along small streams, and feathery ferns sprouted from stone joints.

This was far from a "naked" mountain; it was a place where every niche available for a plant held growth, where birds, lemmings, reindeer, foxes, and insects found home. Rock dominated, yet the stone entwined with plant and animal in a way that it seemed part of the life, for such a place turns the elementals alive, their forces and energy flowing as strongly as the blood through the plover's veins. Boulder, cliff, stream, cloud—the surroundings felt a wholly living landscape, a complex web of being.

Næss made it a conscious project to explore every strand of Hallingskarvet's web, an undertaking based on his attachment to his Place. He set out to learn the factual information of the landscape in order to love everything about it, studying Tvergastein in the manner of what he called "the great naturalist tradition,"[12] motivated as much by feelings as by any abstract scientific knowledge. His amateur research spanned the disciplines, from geology and botany to glaciology studies based on the ice that formed on the walls inside his cottage. In his studies, Næss felt an animacy in all things, his compassion and care including mountain, stream, and boulder along with the breathing, blood-circulating, photosynthesizing life. Science, Næss felt, did not deny such compassion, did not negate emotional, sensuous feelings for the natural world, but only added to it as a way to know a place, to understand and identify with it. Næss said of his studies, "Hundreds of questions were formed, few were answered. This intensified wonder."[13]

But it was more than wonder that came out of scientific inquiry. Næss knew that unraveling the complexities of the natural world through science can spark a *felt* way of interacting with the land, believing a field researcher develops a "respect, even veneration" for all life. It is an understanding that develops through intimate association with the entire ecosystem, creating a connection that reaches beyond humans and a limited array of species.[14]

Næss had fourteen years of exploration. I had ten days, and every step, every breath was taken with a curiosity fed by that idea of learning about the place so as to love it.

~~~

Evening. The sun had warmed the land, still high in the sky at 7 p.m., allowing for a sponge bath in the shallow lake nearby. Washed, warm, with a small ration of brandy in my cup, I filled pages in the leather journal. The sheep were on the move, making their way down the little valley, filling the air with bell tunes as they passed close to camp. They stared at me, an oddity in what is perhaps their daily routine. The woolly beasts reminded me—as did the presence of Ustaoset far below—that this is an inhabited land. Down lower, the human stamp is large, yet up at the higher elevation of Tvergastein Hytte, where the dark cliffs loom, humans do not dominate. Still the sheep were there.

In the soft evening light, a white bird lifted from the cliffs, a flashing brightness against the gray stone and heather. The long straight tail, the curve of the wing, the flight pattern suggested a falcon. The very tips of the wings were black, as if the bird had dipped those end feathers into paint. The bird soared, tilted, hunting, hovering, a swift turn and gone. A gyrfalcon, lit by the sun, luminescent in the evening radiance, seeking its prey.

As the sun lowered, I walked around camp to better know the surroundings. A ptarmigan and her chick flushed from willows by the stream. She clucked and fussed, putting her white wing out in a display,
~~~

a contrast to her brown body, scuttling off in one direction, luring me away from the tiny fluff ball of a chick who tottered off into the bushes. I backed off hurriedly, noting the spot. *I'll avoid her place now.*

All was still, but not without sound, the song of life rising from water, gnat, and bird, emanating from stone and the blossoming of campion. Warmed by brandy, food, and the last rays of the setting sun, diminutive me sat in the expansive neighborhood of gyrfalcon, ptarmigan, plover, wheatear, mountain, and sky, grateful for all the quirks of life that brought me to that one place at that one moment in time.

~~~

Rain, mist, and a deep chill descended on my third day in Hallingskarvet. I battened down camp and hiked up to Tvergastein Hytte to find shelter on the stoop. The previous day I'd wandered within a gentle moment of the alpine environment. Today was not so kind.

Settled on the stoop, I wondered what Næss would have thought about this person, this unknown American, sitting on his doorstep, pushed up against the wall to keep her journal pages dry, writing about him and this place—*his* Place. Me, a strange identity, not even an acquaintance or academic colleague, let alone friend. Me on the outside looking in, peering through the cloudy windows to see the material life, where his thoughts brewed and flowed from mind to page, peering into this man's life to better understand some vaguely defined idea about Place.

The rain spat down, my journal writing happening in bursts during the moments when the wind came firmly out of the west and the building successfully worked as a shield. When it was too wet to write, I tucked the journal under my raincoat for protection and watched the surrounds.

Flowers bloomed in abundance around the hytte, all pressed low to the ground. There were dryas spreading their petals in rays of white, buttercups sparking the ground with yellow, pink campion gathered against stones in tiny rock gardens, the rusty tinge of rushes, leaves and grass adding green amid the gray and marble white of stone. A comforting cheerfulness exuded from the colors in contrast to the gray of
~~~

the sky and the dark cliffs rising overhead, where foggy tendrils wisped down into crevices and crags, the rock heavy and solemn.

Of this alpine world Næss wrote, "There are worlds of minerals, rocks, rivers, and tiny rivulets, plants, hardly visible animals or big ones, plant and animal societies, tiny and great ecosystems.... Within a few yards from the gnarled wooden walls of the Tvergastein cottage, there are rich and diverse changing worlds big enough to be entirely unsurveyable."[15]

Droplets spotted the journal page. I gave up writing to simply sit with Tvergastein and the alpine. I considered Næss's statement that "all things hang together" and started consciously weaving together the crags and flowers, mist and stone, place and self. There is no separating anything into isolation; all is unified, connected by processes, flows, and time. Rock swirls with the earth's energy, heat and movement and eons of forces clearly written in the sweep of minerals in metamorphic stone. The stature of the cliffs, the stretch of the land, the sound of water falling from the heights as it carves into stone: all stand witness to those great processes shaping these surrounds. The resulting terrain provides the nooks and crannies where life takes hold, the plants and animals morphing, shaping, intertwining in an intricate dance with the earth and one another, so that all the niches are filled as minerals flow into plant, sun into leaf, and the delicate flowers bloom and lichens spread across stone. The shape of the plants, their brightness and beauty are attuned to the alpine setting, where limited soil and severe climate shortens stature even as the brief growing season boosts color and scent to quickly lure in pollinators. The vegetation transforms the sun and soil into sustenance, feeding the plovers who call in their meadow, the chipping wheatears, the hare that moves through boulder crevices, who then feed the fox who left her scat near my tent.

At first there seems a contrast of time and space in these ecosystem elements: eon-aged stone sits beneath ephemeral alpine blossoms, looming cliffs rise over blades of grass wafting in the breeze. The sound of water and wind is as old as the planet, while my breath taken in the mist of the immediate present feels so small in this place. Yet all is of one flow of time, coevolved, dependent, interdependent, one unity in a great community that has come together to this point, the here and now I felt watching the gyrfalcon. The heritage of the pink campion clump is as ancient as the rock beneath my feet; the yellow spark of a buttercup is not so different from the black crag as it may seem.

This was Næss's world surrounding me on his stoop, the Place he explored through science, so that he knew the bacteria, the protozoa, the littlest things are essential for the larger things, that the base of the food web is critical for the existence of the upper levels. But Næss was a philosopher, not an ecologist, and he *felt* the world in ways beyond the material connections. He extended his knowledge of connections beyond physical, ecological associations, taking it into emotional, sensory relationships to the land, considering even our human way of being as part of the natural environment.[16] Given the smallest things connected upward, nothing, not even the intangibles like ideas and spirit, could exist without the minuscule. Næss's view has a feel of Alexander von Humboldt's "order and adornment," the material and the intangible meshing together to compose the cosmos: there can be a material universe without art, creativity, intuition, spirit, emotion, but there cannot be the cosmos, "one great whole... animated by the breath of life."[17]

Næss's way of thinking also echoes the Romantic philosophy of the unity of nature. Like Næss, the Romantics did not reject all science and embraced studies akin to organic ecology that provided better understanding of nature's intricate connections. And they, long before Næss was born, felt a sensory appreciation of the natural world knit together with a factual inquiry, the two nurturing each other. Thus, deep ecology holds elements of the century's old Romantic tradition.

This place and Næss's thoughts challenged me. Enough thinking. The cold of the rocks beneath and the air around crept into me, and I walked for the remainder of the day.

~~~

Ptarmigan, gyrfalcon, and warmth were absent from camp that evening. Dinner was a quick affair. I washed dishes in heated water, letting my hands linger in the pot, even as the cold of the evening bored into my core. I shivered and shook, filled my water bottle with hot
~~~

water and stuck it into the bottom of my sleeping bag. But I knew I would never feel warmth that night unless the stagnated blood in my veins started to flow. Curling into the sleeping bag would be like wrapping an ice cube in insulation; I would only stay cold. I set off as fast as possible in my balloon of layers and heavy leather boots, out from camp, away from the cliffs, up the hills and ridges to the south, moving, moving, my eyes by necessity on the earth below to navigate quickly over the rough terrain.

The colors underfoot shifted and shimmered, caught my attention, took on a voice, all the rich hues burgeoning into a mosaic: green of moss, gray of rock, creamy-beige-green of reindeer lichen, pink of flower, rust of rush head, red of seed pod, black of crustose lichen, yellow of petal, brown of dead willow leaf. The colors passed below, each a word of life, speaking of species, cycles, and rhythms, telling the story of a plant, the narrative of rock, what stage of living, what step toward dying, what nourishment fed the plant from below, what process shaped mineral grains in their journey toward stone.

I thought about how color is the rich vocabulary of the land, turning my mind to quotes printed black on white in my notebook, Næss's idea of a "dialogue with nature," how "the 'things' express, talk, proclaim—without words."[18] Now the words slipped from idea to reality, the surrounds vivid and conversant, my thoughts moving even as I walked. Dialogue is communication. Communication is a web weaving a community together. *Communis* means "shared by all," common root of both communication and community. The thought passed through my mind even as I kept moving: *If we cannot sit in conversation with Nature, cannot communicate, we have removed ourselves from the greater community.*

The intricate world flickered under my feet in a beauty beyond aesthetic, a beauty that spoke of a realm beyond comprehension. *Beauty in a sacred sense.* The Irish poet-philosopher John O'Donohue had described beauty that way.

Then a question came.

What does this all have to do with the sacred?

In my readings, it seemed Næss avoided any talk of his own spirituality, yet there was a comment he made in the interview for the documentary film *The Call of the Mountain*, saying he had, in "a broad sense, a religious attitude towards that mountain"[19] and would later comment that, "It's holy, you see... the mountain is holy."[20] These feelings rose in reference to Hallingskarvet itself. The philosopher I met on that first day wouldn't say that Næss was a pantheist, not somebody who held to a belief that all things are part of a divine whole. Yet I sensed Næss had an intuition of *something*. The vastness, the infinite. The sacred? *And how does that fit, juxtaposed against the science? They merge, don't they? Maybe?*

I watched my feet, watched the churning thoughts, felt that I moved through a medium alive with energy that engulfed me in something just beyond my grasp. Up I moved, over the crest of a hill, pausing only long enough to look at the expanse around, then dropping down, up an adjacent slope, down, until the blood pumped into the very tips of my toes.

And then back to the tent, quickly into the sleeping bag, carrying with me the warmth generated by the walkabout, joining the warmth of the hot water bottle in the bag. Wrapped in lofty fibers, I lay back, not quite ready for sleep, mind still moving though body had come to rest. I took out the leather journal, scrawling a quick note:

I had not brought the sacred into this journey until this evening. Now it is with me. A sense of the sacred. It's too hard to write in the tent—to sleep now.

The natural world tells its stories of the eternal flow of time and the infinite stretch of space, seen in the shape of a stone and the twinkle of a star. The earth holds processes and material formations that preceded humans by eons, stretching back long before any species stood up on its two legs and walked as *Homo* on the earth. To immerse in a wild place of far-reaching horizons and challenging extremes is to hold a conversation with that place, perhaps even participate in it. It is a waltz with the eternal and infinite, a dance with a spirit that lies beyond touching but so close, so close—it is something one might find also in a flower or grain of sand. And so the sacred questions cannot be avoided.

It made me wonder then, it makes me wonder now: Is the reason spirituality has been marginalized in the culture I live in, that a "sense of the sacred" is hard to carry in everyday life and often even hard to discuss—is this related to today's increasing disconnect from Nature? Does this distance from natural environments—not just the extreme but simply those places not dominated by human doings—put blinders on us, framing our world around individual human selves, bound up in a world of human constructions, ideological and physical, veiling the expansive reality beyond the human, making the Nature/Culture dichotomy real, negating the spiritual questioning that I could not avoid, solo in the shadow of Hallingskarvet?

The Mountain is Holy, Næss said. It is a whole that should not be broken.

~~~

Four days into my venture, I tried to reach Hallingskarvet's summit, using the topo maps to sleuth out a likely route that might take me to a high lake nestled on the crest. Ascending the slope, I followed a ribbon of muddy sediments along a small stream picked out on the map, the wet earth allowing good footing, the grade steep but navigable, the trickle of water keeping me company with its song. Reindeer tracks paralleled mine, heading downhill, giving me hope that the route would indeed let me reach the lake above—maybe the reindeer had been there? Visions rose of a cleansing afternoon dip—possible on such a sunny day—and a picnic next to sparkling blue water. Upward! Purple saxifrage, the same as what grows in the alpine meadows of home, decorated the stream's rocky edges, brilliant green moss tucked in between the stones. The slope steepened as I clambered upward. I started using my hands to help with the climb, the little stream bubbling and vigorous now. At the stream's origin, where water flowed out from the earth, the slope turned into a steeply angled field of rock, each stone looking like it was ready to roll, most rocks of a size too
~~~

big to simply walk across, too small to walk between—unstable, precariously balanced rock as far as I could see. A broken ankle waiting to happen. And me alone.

I don't need to do this. With one hand in thumbs-down position in front of my camera, I took a picture to record the moment I turned back, chuckling to myself, thinking of what Næss had written about his mountain-climbing adventures, a paragraph copied into my black notebook:

> When I started climbing, I felt that the walls and ridges *invited* me cordially, saying "Come on, little speck of dust, come and partake in the greatness of both of us together. I have cracks and many more holds than you can see from where you stand. Trust me! I shall warn you when storms are near. I shall warn you when my snow or ice is ready to move down. I shall warn you of any so-called danger! But focus on me, not on achievement!" When bad things happened, it was by ignoring warnings, by not lovingly having the mountain itself in focus, but some silly question relating to our own success.[21]

Næss did not climb to conquer. My studies made this clear, and the evidence lay in his work with Sherpas in the Himalayas, who he helped in their efforts to protect Gauri Shankar, a peak held sacred by the people of Tibet and Nepal. The local communities wanted to make the mountain off-limits to conquest rather than reap the rewards and cash flow of the mountain-climbing industry, voting to save "their Mother of the Good Long Life from being degraded."[22] The efforts failed. But it says something about Næss's character and his attitude toward mountains that he worked hard to protect the sacredness of a mountain, says something about his belief that there should be "modesty in human relationships with mountains and with mountain people."[23]

Humbled by the Mountain, thinking of Næss's words, I dropped down. The day was young, and I had time to swing east and visit Tvergastein Hytte before returning to camp. Walking along the bench, Lake Tvergasteinjernet came into view, sparkling cheerfully in the sun, then Tvergastein Hytte itself. Just past the small lake, a large flat rock beckoned, calling for a sit-down in the lush, marshy green meadow. Earlier I'd seen a frog near that rock. A frog. A brown-green, umber-flecked frog, on the flats below Tvergastein Hytte. A frog sitting looking happy as can be in a watery nook between the rocks, his long fingers stretched across the moss, his bulging yellow-black eyes fixed on me. A thin-skinned, cold-blooded amphibian who looked like the frogs we caught in the pond as kids, lounging in his niche here in the arctic-alpine. It felt like discovering a frog on the top of an alpine meadow at home—which has never happened, at least not for me.

"Hello, frog." He just stared at me, blinked.

If the frog was around that day of my aborted climb, he was hidden, but wheatear, sheep, water, sky, and cliff provided company. Tvergastein Hytte stood prominently on the skyline against a blue sky, soft summer clouds floating past. In the clarity of the bright day, the tiny cabin Næss had built high up on the cliff face was also clearly visible. I considered the building, its location, what it took to construct it, what it would take to get there. I wondered, *Why?*

Given Næss's words about modesty and the mountain, a question nagged me. Why build Tvergastein Hytte at such a conspicuous location, set on a little knoll on the edge of the bench, visible for miles around? And more so, why build that small cabin perched high on the cliff face, as if flaunting the Mountain—*See this? I can build this and dwell on you, I can. No cliff will stop me.* And his friend died falling from that place. Modesty? Humbleness? There it stood, that small cabin tacked to the cliff face in an action that seemed more about hubris than humility. And Næss's friend made a fatal misstep, tumbling from the perched hut, crashing down the cliff face to land in a mass devoid of the spirit of life. What warnings did Næss ignore? Or his friend? What part of the conversation did they fail to hear? The cabin stood there, like a morality tale constructed of wood and stone.

Peace held sway in the meadow, seeming a great distance from mountain conquests and fatal falls. The silhouettes of a few people moved around Tvergastein Hytte. I wanted to go to the cottage, as I planned to move camp the next day. A solo moment at the Place that brought me here seemed appropriate for my last visit to the hytte, so I waited, hoping the hikers would move off. Then I realized, *Næss would correct me there. The Place is not Tvergastein Hytte. I'm sitting in the Place.*

And in that thought, I possibly found an answer. Did the fact that Næss planted the hytte on a conspicuous site and the cabin high in the crags have less to do with an arrogant ego-self than with planting himself in the heart of Hallingskarvet? Those buildings situated so that Tvergastein Hytte held a view across the expanse of wild country that includes both Hallingskarvet and the Hardangervidda plateau, the smaller lofty cabin perched like a peregrine nest viewing all, both in a position that put Næss, like the tiny figures in the Romantic paintings standing before the immensity of the mountains, squarely in the human's place in the universe: small.

Meaning that in Tvergastein Hytte and in the cliff cabin, Næss could dwell within his belief that "the smaller we come to feel ourselves compared with the mountain, the nearer we come to participating in its greatness."[24]

~~~

My last night at Camp One provided a soft close to the day, the calm air holding the sounds of evening—the tonking of sheep bells in the distance, the trickle of the stream, wheatears chipping. Bathed in the nearby pool, muscles relaxed after a bit of stretching, I sipped my brandy ration, tried to pull a few midges out of the amber liquid before they drowned—too late, but maybe they died happy. The sun slipped out from where it had been lost for a time behind the puffy clouds that filled most of the sky, the rays adding their warmth to what the brandy provided. The small stream by camp caught the sun's light in a glittering dance.

Surrounded by the peace of this small corner of the world, removed from the rush and clatter and violence of our times, I considered that idea: "The smaller we come to feel ourselves compared with the mountain, the nearer we come to participating in its greatness."

Intuitively I knew what Næss stated is true, but what exactly is it to "participate in its greatness"? How, as humans existing in a modern, Western civilization, can we truly, deeply "participate" with the natural
~~~

world: participate in a way that connects us with the mystery that is the mountain's "greatness"? We are no longer hunter-gatherers or subsistence farmers living off the land. Many people in modern societies can only briefly visit wild landscapes, and it seems that in such a short time, there is limited opportunity to develop a deep relationship with the natural environment.

To be a participant is to be more than a spectator or bystander, is to feel a *part* of the natural world, even a part of something greater. And that is enhanced by feeling small in the face of the mountain. I know that. But why?

I wanted to ask him, to talk with Arne Næss. Something was shifting, my way of seeing this Place, my way of seeing the world. I wanted to talk with him. *Hey, Arne, what do you think about this?* And so I wrote a letter.

July 20, A "Letter" to You, Arne Næss[25]

I wrote the date, the salutation . . . and then there was a moment when I felt a peculiar energy, as if something was there with me. I paused, listening. Perhaps it was simply a sound that had caught my awareness. After a long pause, I put pen back to paper.

Why this Place, Mr. Næss?

Did you feel the presence that just now I felt, before the word "Why"—subtly but there, the intangible made tangible for a moment, weaving all things into one. Life consists of "knots," you said, Mr. Næss. I have felt that life is where spirit knits itself into something visible, material, a hummingbird the nexus of invisible spirit bound into a beauty of a bird, a thought inspired by Teilhard de Chardin's "Matter is spirit moving slowly enough to be seen." Is that how you think of knots of life?

Why this Place? Arne . . . maybe I can call you that, having walked here and thought of you . . . I can guess but will never really know.

Perhaps it is rooted in that childhood call,[26] *the mountain the symbol of good and wholeness when your childhood was not so good. This I can relate to, for the place I know in Montana became the same for me [though my childhood was wonderful]. But was there something more calling? You wrote/spoke of Hallingskarvet as a Godlike being, and who could resist that call? Godlike—and perhaps fearsome.*

I sense it is the contrasts and immensity of this Place that provide a kind of enlightenment. The high, massive cliffs looming darkly overhead, so often catching the ghosts of wisps in its crags. And there on your doorstep, the delicate blossoms of campion, dryas, buttercup, seeming so fragile yet surviving there in that harsh environment where you, a mere human, must construct a cottage to survive in the face of what Hallingskarvet can throw at you.

That contrast speaks to the way of Nature—a nature you say we should be "in dialogue" with. The immensity, the fragility, sparks an awareness of something greater. There in those cliffs, capped in lichen-coated rock, where rock falls and the layers are stacked: the cap, the vertical black, the horizontal (is that the shiny schist?), the talus, boulder slope, the bench of gneiss (??). Those layers stand witness to the immensity of time, of earth's formation and transformation, even as the tiny blossoms speak to the miracle—yes, miracle; is that the right word, Arne?—of evolution, so that in a sense, those flowers are as ancient as the cliffs.

And they are all woven together. Was there an "aha" moment when you knew that? Or was it something Felt from the beginning? And once known, it—this knowing of interconnectedness—carries out to other places. So that I, from Montana, from a Place that has shown me the interconnectedness, can find that here in so few days.

*There is something more here. All things are connected... and we are part of it. Is it about **Belonging**? This is what I feel. Is that what you meant by saying, "The smaller we are, the more we participate." [Barry] Lopez called our disconnect the source of "existential loneliness."[27] By connection, we become part of a greater community. Part of something greater... and so we belong.*

Is that why that crazy tiny hut perched so high on the cliff? So that you could feel even smaller? But the bounds were overstepped, it seems. Did you return to that hut after your friend died?

Arne Næss. I will never know you, nor you me. But I have come to know your Place just a small bit. I think in many ways, we experienced things in the same way. In many ways, we held different views.

I wish now I could talk with you, walk along that high bench that is Tvergastein and hear your words.

Maybe in the sound of the water, the voice of the rock, the whisper of the plants that I shared time with today, I did hear your voice too.

Would that you would know that, Mr. Arne Næss.

~~~xxxxxxxxxxxxxxxxxx~~~

Camp Two

A cloudy but dry morning. Good conditions for packing up camp, a process of compressing the sleeping bag into a small ball to be jammed into the backpack's bottom compartment, rolling up the sleeping pad into a little cylinder that fit horizontally over the sleeping bag, pushing clothes into stuff sacks, pushing stuff sacks into pack, stowing pot and stove in the large outside compartment, tearing down the emptied tent and arranging that within the pack before organizing the food sack and tying that across the pack's top, then finally stashing rain gear within easy access—all without rush, only a small sorrow that this was the last morning to share with the trickling stream and the green meadow in the small vale that provided a channel for the sheep's daily movements. Would there be as many wheatears westward along Hallingskarvet?

A bird chipped. "Wheatear!" I called in a sort of farewell, hand raised toward the bird perched on a nearby rock.

The wind had shifted directions, coming out of the east now and feeling colder, foretelling I knew not what, but at least it would be at my back as I walked west along Hallingskarvet's long stretch of cliffs. My hope was to reach a cluster of small lakes that, after studying the map, seemed like a good campsite. The lakes were on the same bench at the same level as Tvergastein Hytte. It seemed right to spend time at that level, and I suspected the lakes would be surrounded by the same rock-flecked alpine heath of lichen, heather, sedge, rush, grass, and blossom as grew around Tvergasteinjernet lake. Plus, the lakes appeared
~~~

somewhat sheltered, tucked in below the cliffs at the opposite end of the shelf, maybe twelve kilometers away.

I debated the route I would take in my move: walk the bench below the cliffs or follow the valley floor? Examining the topo map, the bench seemed to hold potential barriers of cliff or torrent; the valley appeared marshy, rocky, rugged when viewed from the slopes above my camp—but negotiable. I took the low route along the valley.

The wind picked up, chill and biting but refreshing for a trek through the rough land with a full pack. The clouds thickened, the shade of gray deepening. I walked with a light step, despite the terrain and the pack's weight, buoyed by the feeling of exploration, the exhilaration of setting off into the unknown. Such a small expedition really, yet holding so much for one solo person in such a landscape. A small flock of sheep came running out, probably looking for the food and salt their shepherds brought them, but in my mind, they were a farewell entourage. "Goodbye, sheep! Hope you have a good life." A raven flew over, calling, a black arc dropping avian words from the sky, the message drifting in the wind as it descended.

This was not terrain for quick passage: bog, stone, stream, marsh, grass, boulder field, mixed in an intricate mosaic, painted with the now familiar hues of reindeer lichen, heather, flower, rush. Walking was a matter of reading the colors ahead to determine where the solid ground was, making for a weaving, erratic path, with a few sloshy moments, many leaps and bounds, a bit of rock hopping. A reindeer antler provided a reason to stop, drop my pack for a time, and pause to appreciate the beauty in the pearly arc decomposing into the earth, lady's mantle and buttercups entwined in its tines, budding life wound around decaying bone.

Eventually I reached a fast-flowing creek tumbling down from the bench above, according to the map an indicator that it was time to move upward toward the little lakes. Physically, this was not a far distance; ecologically, it unfolded into a wholly different world from the valley I'd just traversed. Colors diminished as stone dominated, snow patches increasing in size and frequency, until it became a realm of gray spotted with white. And there sat the little lakes, mercury-sleek under darkening skies, surrounded by rock and more water, ice, snow, wet moss, and clumps of sedge, cold and bleak without any possibility of pitching a tent anywhere near that spot that had looked so inviting on the map.

The clouds were dense now and ever darker, bleeding strands of moisture from their bellies, gathering gloom into their folds even as they lowered, sinking earthward. I needed to find a site for Camp Two before the weather went wild and wet. I took off the pack to lighten my step, leaving it on a conspicuous boulder, face down with rain cover on, a turtle abandoning her shell, then set off in search of a camp that could be a home for several days.

The land was hummocky, shaped by frost heave and gravity, piled rock here, sunken basin there, soil accumulating in places, allowing for small patches of sedge and lichen, occasionally a bit of green. The gray sky continued to sink, hunkering down over the land. A second look told me that anything near the little lakes was truly impossible, with only rock and snow, water sometimes heard bubbling below the rock. A look back eastward along the shelf and close to the cliffs showed tantalizingly green grassy swales that offered softness but no protection from the wind currents that careened up and down the bench.

On that midafternoon in July, the chill air bit deep, the scent of rock and snow spoke of winter rather than summer. It felt decidedly "Arctic," the word Næss used for the climate of this place; not for the last time I wondered why he would choose such a world for his home. Næss though might have reminded me that he didn't come for the climate but for the Place: "But it is Hallingskarvet that I'm for. It is not the Arctic climate, it is Hallingskarvet. I'm obeying, obeying the urge of Hallingskarvet to come!"[28]

There were times during those Hallingskarvet days when my mind and thoughts moved into a sheltered space, when the situation turned uncomfortably bleak, gray, chill, when dwelling on the uncomfortable could turn to lonely desolation. Then by letting my senses take it in, simply opening awareness to the scents, sounds, sights, feelings, the moment turned into a wild poem and allayed any fears, tears, or cringing despair.

This was such a time, and something welled up, and I embraced the surrounds, embraced the sheer magnitude of the whole wild extreme.

Pausing in my fast-moving survey of the surrounds, I looked back to where the pack lay inert on the boulder, a green spot on a rock, a tiny speck in that world. That pack was all I had, and it was nothing, surrounded by the elemental arctic-alpine.

For an hour and a half, I searched that land, carefully keeping oriented so as not to lose that pack of food, clothes, warmth, imported comforts. One spot, *one* spot only, offered a place to pitch my tent: a tiny lake—even smaller than those I'd picked out on the map—with a small grassy depression next to it, just big enough for a one-person shelter, the hollow providing a wind break, the little lake creating a water source. The site was just at the edge of the bench, where the slope slipped down into the valley below and the view reached across the Hardangervidda plateau. Hopefully, it was far enough from the Hallingskarvet's cliffs to escape the worst of the freezing mist that collected on the summit and rolled over and down the face, spilling across the shelf in a flood of chill vapor.

The clouds turned from steely gray to indigo gloom. In the distance, sweeping curtains of rain descended from the dark heavens, approaching quickly. *This will have to do.* I scurried over the hummocky ground back to my pack, strapped it on, stumbling in haste back to the chosen campsite, a turtle reunited with shell-home, moving at turtle pace in the face of the storm.

Calculating, guessing how long until the storm set in, it seemed I could get the tent up rather than just hunkering down until the rain passed—if it did in fact pass. Efficiency. Dig into the pack, remove tent, cover pack tightly to keep its contents dry, inner screen of tent out, staked, poles up, inner portion up and secured, waterproof fly unrolled—and wind hit, cold and sharp, picking up into blasting gusts, playing with the fly as if to torment the human struggling with the whipping material. The fly went over the inner tent as rain hit, marble-size pellets of thrown water, splashing against all things. The wind had twisted the fly, which was now upside down, the waterproof coating underneath, and so off it came as the deluge beat onto and into the tent's inner screen, and the wind again took the fly and tried to wrestle it from my hands... and my mind left that sheltered space, and I yelled at the sky, "**Shit! Stop it!** Will you just **STOP!!**" The wind increased, the sky throwing buckets of water at me. I screamed again, "**Stop it!** Just give me a minute!! ONE Minute!... **please!**"

Perhaps we don't want to admit that we have no control. Perhaps somewhere inside most of us is a little hidden idea that we can dominate, that whatever is going on here, somehow it's about us—about humans—and we have a say in things. That idea, admitted or not, allows us to behave as we do. And apparently it lurks in me, for it seemed to be what exploded out of me, a lone frustrated human yelling at the gods.

Knowing it made absolutely no difference.

This was Thoreau standing in the face of Ktaadn, the high mountain in Maine that shattered his comfortable transcendental idealism, that belief that nature is somehow about us.[29] This was Thoreau facing a Nature that didn't center on any human being, leaving him in "the presence of a force not bound to be kind to man... to be inhabited by men nearer of kin to the rocks and to wild animals than we."[30] This was the Thoreau who came to the conclusion that high peaks are "among the unfinished parts of the globe," not suitable for human existence or "place making" or perhaps even the mere presence of humans.[31] And Arne Næss built his hytte there.

This is not about humans. Definitely not about me. The wind was not tormenting me, nor was the sky throwing water at me. There was no "me" for the wind or rain. This person who is me stood in a wild place, touched by humans, but mostly functioning outside of human thoughts and activities: the sky releasing its tumultuous weather, the rocks tumbling, the alpine flowers blooming, the water gathering in its pools and nurturing the frogs—the way of things prior to human presence. And I stood alone and wind-whipped, pounded by the place, pushed one step closer to understanding my kinship with rocks and wild animals, with those beings who reside in that alpine extreme, who would never raise their faces to the heaving sky and demand that it just **Stop It!!**

I knew my cries didn't matter (didn't I?), so perhaps it was only a release of frustrated fear that set me to yelling at the gods, for it certainly felt good and provided the *umph* to get that tent up, creating a bit of shelter, where I could huddle in the vestibule until the worst of the storm passed, not wanting to take my mud-smeared self into the soaked inside. Returning to a quieter frame of mind, I smiled at my outburst, wondering that I would react in such a way. Rain pounded, drummed, thumped against the tent, its rhythm slowing, becoming more of a pulse, coming and going until it reduced down to a soft, gentle drizzle. I clambered out into a world of mist and moisture, dug out my tiny towel and dried the inside of the tent, dragged the pack into the vestibule, stripped my wet stuff off and pulled out my comforts, crawling into the sleeping bag for warmth, lying back in rain-soaked exhaustion.

Hours later, the light increased. Lifting the flap of the vestibule door, I could see the small lake glittering under brightened skies while sun flecks and misty streamers danced across the land. I crawled out of my warm cocoon, coated myself in Gore-Tex, and ventured out. The nearby cliffs of Hallingskarvet, just north of camp, reached upward into the fog as if they continued forever into the heavens, while far to the west, mist poured over the ridge crest like a waterfall of foam. To the east, sun played across the dark cliff above Tvergastein Hytte, close to where I'd been just that morning.

With obvious signs of sheep still around, the lake's water was left for cooking only; I set off to find drinking water and explore my new surroundings. This higher clime was far more arctic than Camp One, a wide expanse of rocky alpine tundra. I crossed the rough, stony terrain, nearing the cliffs, where a rushing stream poured off the foot slope, filled my bottles from that clear torrent and drank deeply, wondering at the alpine water that tastes like nothing at all yet holds a flavor of purity, almost mineral, more like air. In other places, the water tasted of snowmelt, a unique flavor all its own—but not there, where it must have come directly from springs and seemed simply to taste of mountain sky.

With water bags and bottles full, I returned to camp, nodding in pleasure at the site that had appeared during that harried rush of the afternoon. Time to settle. A kitchen evolved on two large flat rocks next to the lake, where I could sit on one stone with my feet in the crack between the two, place the stove before me on the other stone, and spread my sacks of food around me. From there, the views east and west ran along the Hallingskarvet ridge and out south across the Hardangervidda plateau as far as the eye could see. The lake reflected the sky, expanding the sense of spaciousness so that I could look up into the towering clouds that still sauntered around the heavens and then look *down* into the sky, seeing the same undersides of the clouds, billowing mounds of moisture plummeting into the lake's undersurface.

This was home for the next five nights.

~~~

Morning arrived gray but dry, clouds hanging low yet holding their moisture. Crawling out of the tent into the day, the campsite felt welcoming, the miniature basin protected, my tent tucked into its niche on the north side of the little lake that always held the color from above. I washed cold water over my face, sending ripples across the reflected sky with my cupped palms. Stove set on the kitchen rocks, water collected in the pot, the day started to unfold as the water boiled. Muesli, protein powder, coffee, that same meal somehow gaining flavor over the days.

Breakfast done, I took thermos and journal to the south edge of the lake, found a small, flat rock, carried it over against an outcrop to create a seat, and settled myself looking south across the Hardangervidda plateau. Wool hat, gloves, puffy jacket, rain pants, the layers warm enough to allow for sitting and writing. The tea trickled in lively tones falling from thermos to cup. I savored the rich Lapsang Souchong and its warmth.

Comfortably ensconced on the rock seat that would become my writing spot, with only the distant *baa-baaing* of sheep to remind me of the busy rush and chaos of humanity out beyond, I comfortably contemplated the past Hallingskarvet days, where I lived without distraction, solo and quiet, filling days and journal pages with thoughts. What to make of this…
~~~

This is why the monks removed themselves to isolated places. This is what solo on the Mountain means.

A few years later, I would read in Nan Shepherd's *Living Mountain*, "I believe that I now understand in some small measure why the Buddhist goes on pilgrimage to a mountain. The journey is itself part of the technique by which the god is sought."[32]

My mood was not for writing. I examined the earth around me.

Reindeer lichen covered most of the ground between the rocks, but also bits of alpine heather, crowberry, vaccinium, and a scattering of other lichens and plants. The reindeer lichen's creamy beige-green hue added lightness to the land. This lichen stands over an inch tall, leafy and intricate in its growth, some of its "leaves" as narrow as a thread, others broader—a few millimeters across—looking almost like something that would grow under the sea. Reindeer depend on this lichen. I had seen reindeer tracks and found large antlers but no fresh sign or actual sightings. I doubt the sheep have any interest in the reindeer lichen but wonder how their presence affects these last herds of Norway's wild reindeer.

Where there was no soil and only rock, lichen still dominated, crustose in form, closely coating every rock surface like scabs on the stone. Green crustose lichen that Arne Næss identified as *Geographicus* is so abundant that it gives the rock fields a green hue, like that of the lichen-coated crest of Hallingskarvet. I peered at the lichen on a nearby rock, thinking it looked like modern art, a study in light and dark, with black encircling the green in many places, a sort of pointillist painting without any subject. Other lichen species—both crustose and leafy foliose—grew in shades of gray and black, in nearly as great a quantity as the green, but without the striking color and so making it seem less abundant. Some of the lichens had put out fruiting bodies, cups perched on stalks half-inch high, clustered like a bouquet of blossoms yet far more ancient than the complex bloom of a flower.

I left my rock seat to lie flat on my stomach, in among the lichen, heather, vaccinium, looking through the miniature fruticose forest, smelling the organic pungency of ancient fruiting bodies, from lichen cups to a wee brown mushroom sprouting nearby. I buried my nose into a heath plant, breathing in a scent like alpine air on a dry day, shifting my position to take in the fragrance of a rock, a wafting of minerals and time. The air itself had the scent of old fog, a smell of mist mixed with organic fungus permeating the morning.

For a long while, my tired body relaxed into the world that usually lies below our feet—lichen, mushroom, leaf, rock, stone. Overhead, stretching across all things, the gray sky moved in gentle swirling billows. I stood, raising my arms up toward that cloud ceiling, twisting my torso to loosen muscles, changing the viewshed from east to south to west, toward Tvergastein, across Hardangervidda, along the far cliffs. Where a moment before I lay with an intimate encounter with minuscule life, now I stood with the immensity.

During my time at the second camp, I would return to that writing spot, again and again, always to look down at the one little brown mushroom in its bed of lichen, then up across Hardangervidda, to feel the stretching of mind, emotion, and self. The black notebook stayed packed away. Næss had been my guide into Hallingskarvet, opening thought and awareness. Now the Mountain took the lead. Tvergastein seemed far away.

~~~

The water of Hallingskarvet holds its own life, its personality varying with how it bubbles or falls, rests or ripples. Along the bench, small streams rise from the cliff base, flowing quietly and crystal clear over stone and bedrock, their banks alight with lime-green moss. The falls are the opposite, crashing down in a tumultuous plunge from the unseen void of Hallingskarvet's summit, frothy white ribbons against dark stone. These cascades send their voices into the world, the ancient voice of running water.

Water sometimes runs beneath the rocks, glimpsed when hopping from boulder to boulder, occasionally heard as an echoing trickle beneath my feet. This water is hidden, secretive, hinting that another world exists below the veneer of stone, a flowing universe all its own.
~~~

Solid water is present, resting in the snowbanks that highlight the landscape, curving in miniature glaciers over the rock along Hallingskarvet's cliffs, glistening in the great ice cap of the Hardangervidda plateau. An abundance of water overfills the land, pooling and creating innumerable lakes that glitter in sunlight, sit dark when clouds cover the sky, and dance when the wind picks up. The little lake I camped by showed me myriad ways that surface water can frolic with the wind and sky, flickering, rippling, silent, smooth, letting sun rays filter in and through. Like the sky it mirrors, it was never the same, always changing.

My second night at the camp, I sat looking over that little lake, writing of water while the lake kept me company as it played with the wind, creating tiny waves, a shooting wake, before settling into a calm stillness.

Then voices. Voices floating down from Hallingskarvet Mountain, distant and faint. The wind amid the crags? The water singing? It did not sound like the cascades. A bit eerie, unsettling. Frozen by the faint words that were not human, I listened, wondering. Sentences, fragments of thought, but not from a person, not from any species. The elements speaking? Sharing thoughts that carried across the land in an ancient language, drifting, fading. Gone.

It was like standing on the border of something, knowing that a step in a certain direction would lead on, over into another... another what? And I leaned toward that edge, and... the wind picked up again, the lake rippled, the sun slipped behind a growing billow of cloud. I rose from my lakeside seat to prepare dinner. No time to waste: the clouds were accumulating.

The evening meal was routine now: get the water heating, measure in the lentils, measure in the quinoa, crumble in the bouillon cube, throw in the nuts—specific amounts measured out before my departure for exactly ten nights of hot meals. I stirred the evening's quota and took a first bite, reminding myself not to wolf it, to carefully chew so that I could digest more of the food but also so that mealtime could be a relaxing, contemplative moment, watching the world around me. The little lake continued its antics while the sky moved in its own cloud dance. I took another bite and noticed a bit of vapor, a dark slip of moisture in direct line of sight between camp and the Hardangervidda plateau.

First it was only a dark wisp, just a bit of cloud—but such a deep-gray bit, floating there at eye level. The wisp took on some weight to become more of a strand, ever darkening. The strand writhed and grew, there in front of me, shaping itself into a black mass, not a storm rolling in, but a great beast building, stretching down and up and toward me. From the bottom of the mass, a new wisp appeared that became its own strand, twisting so that it seemed it would snake itself into a tornado. This behemoth advanced, approaching not by moving but by growing in size, bigger, darker. Behind me, mist was taking on its own shape, a different creature than the cloud but still thick, dark, growing, forming right there in the midst of Hallingskarvet's cliffs. The entire sky was now a heavy mass of cloud and dark.

I wolfed the food, then gave up eating as the sky closed in. My heart pounded, though I didn't think I was afraid, even as instinctual adrenaline accumulated, telling me otherwise. In a rush, I tucked things away and retreated, taking the remainder of my meal into the tent, shaken.

The storm passed without as much drama as it came, sending down just a scattering of heavy drops of rain. They reverberated against the tent, where I sat holding my pot of food, waiting for the maelstrom. Then a sudden quiet, the percussive beat of the drops hitting the fly gone, the storm done. Now my emotion was a bit of regret and near embarrassment that I had retreated so hastily.

Yet still the storm tossed the earth.

Emerging from the tent was to enter a world of turbulence and motion, storm clouds shuffling above, fog drifting, waterfall voices floating, a single dark bird sailing past, carried by the restless wind. I clambered up on a high rock and stood to witness the elements of air, water, earth, mixing in a mélange. I stood emptied of the everyday in a place far beyond me, cracked by the immensity of the surrounds. I was nothing, a fleck on the Mountain, where horizons stretch, where time runs in other dimensions, where space loses dimension.

This was the mountain distilled to ancient elementals, the stark contrast of ephemeral existence against the immensity of the surrounds so intense that everything crystallized, each flower, rock, the shape of the cloud, the movement of a bird, the way the water sounds travel through air, the feel of my foot on rock, clarity in this expanse that stretches from one little brown mushroom to a sky that reaches both upward to heaven and downward into lake depths.

All was fundamentals and foundations, not about any one being, one species, let alone any one person. It was in a strange way a homecoming, with a deep sense of belonging, standing there alone on a rock in the mist with the elements.

~~~

The next day, I dropped down off the bench to explore the valley below. This land was a vibrant medley of green and color, lush fields of alpine lady's mantle and purple geranium, flowers bunched amid low gray-green willow and grassy patches. I walked for a while, then lay on my stomach in the glory of the foliage that grew to stupendous heights—sometimes over a foot tall! Wheatears chipped, *Chik! Chik!* A golden plover called from the crest of a nearby hummock. A falcon-like bird flew over, so delicate and small, sparrow hawk size, wings curved in a narrow arc, long straight tail. The sun broke through the clouds.

I wandered along a lake's edge, stopping often to marvel at a blossom or take in the waters' play, the grasses' dance, the rocks' way of sculpting the land into a milieu of diversity. Clambering up to the top of a small hill, I sat amid yellow blossoms of wild dandelion under a blue sky that stretched out to the south and over the ridge where I could see a big sapphire lake with green shores far below. But to the east, dark clouds and gray mist hung over Hallingskarvet, over Tvergastein, over my campsite, perhaps even a drizzle descending on my tent.

A great weary sigh bubbled up, and I let myself admit that I wished Næss had built his hytte in the valley below the bench, situating the focal point of his Place lower, where the green, the flowers, the birds
~~~

abound. Where the sun brought warmth and I did not always feel so small and vulnerable.

"Arne," I cried aloud, there in the sun, watching the mist clinging to Hallingskarvet's crest. "What? Why the *high* alpine? Why?"

Stoic silence.

But that's just it, isn't it?

The line of thought continued. *The lower climes are comfortable. They don't stretch you.*

Did you even think about it, Arne? Why the alpine? Probably not. It seems the extreme places draw the extreme people. That's just it, isn't it? It's the extreme, the Mountain, it's "the smaller you are" . . . and the Mountain makes you small . . .

Time to move. Walking toward the bench where my tent sat perched somewhere along the edge, I took pictures of the green, clicking images of the meadows, wanting to remember the lushness, bring it with me. Then up the last slope, the vegetation diminishing, rock increasing. The mist and cloud had dissipated, the sky now a mix of blue and gray, holding a brightness, even a few rays of gold.

Just over the crest of the bench, where the slope leveled out, a plover fluttered up in a rush of feathers, crying *Twooee! Twooee!* and scuttled off, running across the rough ground with wing dragging, the broken-wing-wounded-bird act meant to decoy me from her young. I turned to avoid her, trying to remove myself as quickly as possible, only to have my foot come down so close to a tiny chick scrambling across the moss and lichen, all fluff and speckle. I turned off in the opposite direction, hoping mama and child would quickly reunite. A short distance away, a cracked eggshell lay huddled amid the stones, a rich creamy shell dotted with brown, the chick it had sheltered now running after its mother, there on the shoulders of Hallingskarvet.

The golden plover's nest is just a scrape in the ground, shallow, lined with plant, moss, a tad of reindeer lichen. The plover breeds in the arctic-alpine, successfully hatching its eggs and rearing its young in that scratched-out bit of a nest. A chick smaller than my hand, there in the alpine, surviving in the land I'd just thought of as extreme. I wanted to carry that eggshell with me as a totem, a reminder. But I did not touch it, left it where it lay, and moved on.

There was the little lake, its water glistening in the sun, my tent secure in its niche by the shore. I looked down toward the lower elevations of the day's wanderings, appreciating the relative lushness, thankful for the glorious time in the green. But there, with Hallingskarvet hovering overhead, the lake shining in its bowl, the plover nearby caring for her chick, the lichen to soften the land, and wheatear for company—in that alpine setting, *there* was the place that I was weaving myself into. *There* was the place woven into me.

Næss hauled me along on an immense journey during those few days in the shadow of Hallingskarvet, his ideas toted along in the black book. Arriving in Hallingskarvet, I'd delved into many different ways of knowing the Mountain, of thinking about place, consciously considering Hallingskarvet's ecology, experiencing the land's Romantic sublime vastness, feeling the sense of the sacred. Scientific, Romantic, Sacred: I have felt the tension between these perspectives. It is that unease—especially as perceived by the public—that is the main reason I left academia.

At Camp Two, I stopped analyzing Hallingskarvet. I walked with the curve of the land, walked with the feel of the ever-changing earth beneath my feet, walked with the sound of the wind harmonizing with the tumbling water, walked with the glacier buttercup for company, walked with a growing sense of what could be called participation. There was no longer any separating the Mountain into facets or dimensions: all the ways of knowing became a single way of knowing, the boundaries dissolved, the tension I felt *trying* to mesh them gone.

What I wrote in my letter to Næss sitting in Camp One seems true. It is about belonging, the kind of joyful belonging I felt that day as the lake appeared, the rock, the water dancing, the sound of bird call, the lichen smell, and my own domestic items for cooking, sleeping, writing there on the shore. And it is about the wild belonging of the evening before when I stood on that rock in a wind-washed world. Yet this was not a sense of belonging to Hallingskarvet; my time there was all too short for that. It was a larger sense, perhaps what Thoreau meant in his outcry on meeting the elements at Ktaadn, after venting about a "force not bound to be kind to man," when he declared, "Rocks, trees, wind on our cheeks! The solid earth! the actual world! the common sense! Contact! Contact! Who are we? where are we?"[33] Immersed in the Mountain, situating oneself in the cosmos, it is clear the human is nearly nothing yet is there, *part* of it. Contact.

We are here, in this singular moment at this particular place, so incredibly small. As Næss said, "Reality has nothing in particular to do with humans."[34] Nothing much at all. Reality sings songs of distant universes, dances with the infinite, allows the fragile frog to flourish where man must build a cottage to survive for any length of time. Reality tells tales of times outside of human knowing and weaves sea floors into rock that are sewn into mountains. Reality has nothing much to do with you, or me, or anyone else—or any species at all. Reality is about all species, all time, all space.

Yet humans, all of us, are part of it. We are part of that reality. We belong within it and can participate with that Whole. This is Næss's Whole, what I believe he meant by his Ontology of Wholeness, a way of being and perceiving reality that weaves each person into that Whole. To feel that is a homecoming.

That deep sense of belonging is why "sense of place" matters. The simple answer to the quest that brought me here. To reach that point of belonging is to feel a part of the greater community of life. And then the only way to live is to care for it. To act beautifully.

Næss attempted to put that in words; I have attempted to share it. There on Hallingskarvet, I simply lived it—the sweet sense of participating in something "greater" where there are no boundaries or dualisms, a point that can be reached along many paths, from science to spirituality. Later, I tried to explain by saying, "Now when I look up on a clear, moonless night into a universe with its countless stars, a universe that is expanding into what we do not know, that was created within that unknown, I do not feel overwhelmed. It is a feeling that I belong within that. And it is beautiful." A belonging brought about by the Mountain.

~~~

My topo map showed a trail that went up and over a pass on Hallingskarvet. On the pass is a mountain hut, Lordehytta, the "Lord's Hytte." I decided to explore, thinking that by reaching the pass, I could see Hallingskarvet's far side.

The well-worn trail felt odd underfoot, without the constant need for careful boot placement to balance on a rock, avoid a bog, or sidestep a blossoming bit of beauty, but it made for good walking. Soon the pass came into sight, a relatively flat area of rock, snow, water, tumbling streams, and a large lake lined with ice and snow that reached into the water, creating aquamarine colors vivid bright against the indigo depths. Cliffs rose in both directions, high and dark. Black rock, white snow, aqua ice, indigo water, blue sky, silver glints off the lake itself: stark hues separating the elements, defining the world by color, with no movement except on the lake surface where zephyrs brushed ripples.

The surrounds brought me to a slow halt. I was aware of a feeling, almost a fear, not of the Place but of the experience, as if I had finally grasped what others have tried to describe: Næss, Thoreau, Humboldt, Muir, the monk in his beehive hut off the coast of Scotland. This was a knowing that I stood within something I could not articulate but could now "hold in my hand, unwrap my fingers and find it in my palm, not an unknown but a *known* unknown"—what I had yearned for years before on the day of my cut hand, standing by the alpine lake. I felt an unease standing within that moment in a material world understood through ecology, experienced as sublime, intrinsically sacred.

I stood alone, a ways off the trail. I'd seen other hikers on the way. Early in the day, a group passed me, so intense and fast moving I thought they were part of a mountain race, then realized they were just "hiking." Later, hikers of another type appeared, joyful-looking people, some probably headed over the pass, others out for a shorter day, likely just to Lordehytta, then turning around, the size of their packs indicating the difference. There were couples and families, quite a few young kids, all cheery. Their pace was not hurried, parents explaining something to their child, children bouncing across snow fields, stopping now and
~~~

again to take in the surrounds. Good people, I thought, and good to see the youth.

Good people—who seemed like they had appeared from another world. People had not crossed my path since Tvergastein. I'd been living in a different space. Communication felt awkward, so I skirted the people, leaving the trail to meander off and let the other parties pass. Maintaining space. They might ask in congenial conversation what I was doing, where I was going...and I would say...?

I skirted the lake of aqua and indigo heading toward Lordehytta, a hytte that at first looks more like a pile of stones capped with wood than a shelter, hunkered into the mountain as if rock had tumbled down from surrounding cliffs to land just there and somebody threw a plank cover over it. On approach, the building took shape, resolving itself into walls and roof, doors on the narrow ends of the rectangle, windows looking toward the north. The Lord's Hytte is named for the second Lord Garvagh. The first Lord Garvagh built hyttes around the area in the mid-nineteenth century, and his son followed suit. The Lords Garvagh were part of the English tradition, gentlemen coming to the wild Romantic Norwegian mountains to hunt and fish and pit themselves against the peaks.

I arrived at one of the building's narrow ends, a windowless wall of stone built with boulders half the height of the door, a weathered wooden sign pounded into the roof's peak: *Lordehytta anno 1880, 1622 moh* (Lordehytta built 1880, 1,622 meters above sea level). A modern black box stands by the door where people could sign in. I didn't open the box, considered opening the door, until voices floated out, sending me around the hut, quickly past the windows where figures moved behind the translucent glass, and up the slope beyond, to a vantage point protected from the wind, views south and north to the far side of Hallingskarvet, cliffs all around, towering mountain pressing in, tiny Lordehytta below looking so insignificant, like another fallen boulder.

Settling in for food and hot tea, I sought the internal calm of the past days. Yet the unease continued, as if I should be part of the humanness found there, enjoying talk with the hikers. Or that the humanness shouldn't be part of this place. Or that I was part of the nonhumanness. Or all of that, all of that.

I ate while identifying the surrounding flowers, keeping an eye on the hytte below. Eventually, the people inside left. I went down to see what those stone walls contained. Approaching the other end of the building, Lordehytta seemed to be tilted, squashed to one side as if the mountain's gravity was bringing it down. Swinging the hefty door open, daylight revealed a dank, dark room, nothing more than a shed, lined with bare bunks and filled with wood shavings piled up from some animal gnawing at the timber, a critter who also left plenty of scat.

A newer door at the room's far end swung open to present a different scene: a clean, bright room with stone walls on two sides and light pine paneling elsewhere, light pine chairs, light pine table, and light pine cupboard. Light. Comfortable. Kettle sitting on the wood stove, with wood for burning stocked neatly in the corner. On a windy cold evening, the hytte would be warm, welcoming, wrapping itself around a weary walker. On that day of sunshine, despite its well-maintained pine interior with rays scattering through the window, splashing across the table into the corners, the room seemed dark and less comforting than the world outside.

Out then, out. I left the human domain of Lordehytta and went to the lakeshore.

I could not shake that unsettled feeling—*I've done something wrong; something is just not right.* Throughout the morning, my life questions, frustrations, disillusionments, self-deprecating thoughts flitted in my mind. Not the emotions of connections, belonging, joy so recently experienced. It was that feeling that I don't fit in, that so many don't understand my life lived outside of the mainstream, outside of what many might call "normality." Perhaps the feeling plagued me because in a few days, I was out, away from the Mountain.

When philosopher and author David Rothenberg interviewed Arne Næss at his hytte, Næss told him that he didn't particularly like to be alone at Tvergastein: "If I'm alone, my imagination takes over, and I leave the surface of the earth, in the sense that I forget time. I lose myself too much. I must be drawn back into normality and duration."

When asked if he had any unsolved problems, Næss responded, "I have trouble fitting in." Næss drew a sketch, a line with vertical lines crossing it to mark off the boundaries between the range of the norm on the left and the enigmatic area beyond the norm on the right. Using an arrow to demonstrate, Næss explained that he moves to the left just into the norm to reach a point of compromise that allows him to live compatibly with his wife—into the realm of normality.

"Why," Rothenberg queried, "don't you go further to the left, back toward normality?"

Næss answered simply, "Well, that would be the death of me. Even to get a tiny bit closer."[35]

And therein lies tension: the solo person in the mountains, caught up in something that cannot be articulated, even as they hold onto the love and warmth of community and "home."

Maybe this was the tension that kind man spoke of, that very first day at Tvergastein Hytte, when he said that "Næss had a tension with the mountain," knocking his fists together. Something Næss felt from youth? Around ten years old, Næss first climbed up to face the rising cliffs of Hallingskarvet, feeling even then that the "only dignified way of life would be to remain on the mountain, not to descend."[36] Up there, he stood with a vast view and a broader perspective on human existence.

Was this the tension I was feeling? The tension of immersing in life high on the Mountain, participating in the Mountain's ways and its truths, then to drop down and return to the human world of media and shopping and cars and materialism. This is not just difficult; it is painful.

For to watch the miraculous lichen flourishing even as the sky fills with clouds that billow toward heights that lead ever outward, to see the fragile chick fluttering after its mother as the faint roar of the distant cascades echoes off the ancient cliffs, to sit with sunlight dancing with water, to hear the sound of the elements singing off the crags, to be immersed in that world of wonder and return to a modern world where wonder is too often lost, where Beauty in the sacred sense of Beauty is crushed and destroyed as we pump our oil out of the earth even as we pump our pollution into the air, as we poison our land with herbicide and pesticide and tear down the forests and build up the concrete sprawl that steals habitat from the innocent, as bullets rip the life from creatures so that someone can hang the animals' heads on a wall... and I cannot—*cannot*—find the meeting point of the deep Mountain experience with the horror of what is happening here on earth. It seems to negate the very idea of anything like Næss's idea of a Whole. Of what I'd experienced.

I did not want to leave, did not want to lose what I'd found on the Mountain. But I cannot turn away from the earth as it is, and I cannot turn my back on the *Now* of my own existence, of those I love. I have come to know that Home is about community, people, loved ones, and so for me and seemingly for Næss, compromises are made. I moved to the desert for community. Næss would return to Oslo and his life within the city. The mountains are still there for us to Be within.

Standing by the lake, I watched birds walking along the ice on the water's edge, white birds that looked like they should be strutting by the sea. I took a photo at high zoom, then expanded the image on my camera. Yes! Seagulls! Mountain gulls? There on Hallingskarvet's pass, gulls crying with their melancholy, memory-inducing, emotion-invoking call. Gulls strutting along an alpine bank, acting just like seagulls, like they belong there, like they are in charge.

At my feet alpine buttercups blossomed white with a sunshine center. Along the shore, deep-pink flowers of the same species mixed in with the white, the color changed after pollination to better collect solar heat and so keep the developing seeds warm in their ovary. Such amazing evolution, such a beauty of color resulting, painted in amid the rock. Gulls and pink buttercups. I hunkered down to examine the flowers, watched the gulls waddle across the ice, their blue-gray wings melding into the lake beyond, white heads mirroring ice hues, swinging black tails and beige feet markers of movement, strut strut strutting. A smile smoothed away my scowl.

I left the lake to climb higher, to a point where I could see Hallingskarvet's lichen-green crest, reaching the highest point of my journey. The ridge stretched out in both directions, all of Hardangervidda spread to the south, and just visible down below was the tiny pool of water next to my tent. I crawled onto a boulder and stood, perched on the rock like a roosting raptor on the hunt, still and silent at that high point where the Mountain spun all around. Tension left.

"I get it, Arne," I whispered.

It? Really, honestly, I didn't know, still am not sure, if "I get it." But what I felt on that rock was an acceptance of the difficulty of living in the world of our everyday lives, with all their loves and sorrows, beauty and horrors, while always and *consciously* holding that deep sense of belonging within something so much larger than we can know. Yet it is possible to always carry that within, maintaining all that goes with such a sense of belonging; for myself, that includes a deep sense of the sacred. To hold that sense makes the day-to-day relationships of the here and now even more important, for the relationships we have in this immediate reality of *now* carry out, build up, micro to macro, starting at the smallest of things and reaching out to all things.

And though that sense of belonging and of the sacred are intensified by extreme conditions and thus often felt in places like the arctic-alpine, they are available to all of us. Frequent moments with what Næss called "free nature" show us the workings of larger things. Pausing during a walk, showing children the small beauty around, be it in the mountains or in a park—oh, the joy of those kids near Lordehytta!—simply finding a sit spot to consistently visit situated anywhere the sky reaches overhead: the pause, the reflection, can set one free of the chains of ego. Thus, the natural world shows us not just what is *beyond* human but what *is* human and so develops compassion. This is why deep ecology, Næss's legacy, is about caring for all life, at all times, including our fellow human beings in the here and now. There isn't any conflict, just a balancing act. There are tensions but not contradictions. And there is joy.

As Næss explains, "Feeling extremely small in the dimensions of the cosmos, you yourself get somehow widened and deeper, and you accept with joy this thing that others might perceive as a duty: to take care of the planet. The care of the planet becomes something joyful and not something that is done merely to survive."[37]

Tears welled. For the first time in a very long time, I lifted my arms to the sky in a joyous celebration of belonging to the endless, infinite, eternal, wild "something" that we live within.

In the ensuing years, that tension rises within me, whether I admit it or not. And I cannot speak for Næss, but his tension with Hallingskarvet? I wonder if it was that the Mountain demanded of him to see the world in ways that stretched him, that pulled him away from the warmth of community. That set before him a cosmos that he could not articulate but could only experience, something that went beyond academia. Something that meant he would spend the rest of his life doing what he could to protect and nurture free nature.

And I too try to do what I can to help protect it. I am not an activist and do not like conflict or controversy. So I write. It is small, but it is something.

You are reading the words that I write.

~~~

Rain came as I walked back to camp from Lordehytta. I tucked into the tent as it pattered down until evening.

Then the clouds moved away, not gone but moving elsewhere, and I emerged from my hermit hut out into the world, to watch the sky and the drifting storm clouds in their towering majesty. One cloud approached, dark, growing, looming, stirring emotions that wouldn't have been raised except for the monster storm of a few nights before. I made a conscious effort to relax and leaned back to watch the storm come, journal at hand.

Translucent gray sheets appeared below the thundercloud, moisture traveling sky to ground. And still it came on. The sky moved with light, the play of cloud and sun, rain and rays, chill and warmth, invisible currents stirring grays, creams, a dash of indigo, pearl across the heaven's palette, a shaft of gold slipping down to splash across a far-off mountain slope, a silver glint growing across Hallingskarvet's western cliffs before the gray returned, cumulonimbus sculptures rising over all. I
~~~

caught myself taking note of me, seated in that Place with all that dancing around, me worrying about the coming of the rain. Consciously, I blew the worry away with an exhalation and wrote,

Thanks be to all circumstances, gods and goddesses, whoever, whatever I might thank, that I am here, experiencing this…

Not much more writing happened that evening, eyes to the sky rather than down on the page. Another thunderstorm grew, approached. And another. The towering clouds split ranks as they came my way, moving to the west or disappearing to the east to dump their load of rain over Tvergastein Hytte.

… as if I sit near some nexus, where things divide and come together.

The clouds came on, floating my way, building at eye level. I did not turn away.

~~~

Eventually the rain came. The clouds converged and merged on a nexus point overhead to drop their moisture through the night. Morning came, and still rain fell even as fog rolled in. There was a lull, long enough to get out and pee, make sure the world was there, that I was there in it. The world was simultaneously shrunk and enlarged by the fog, compressed to me, my tent, and the lake by walls of mist that closed in all around, expanded by the sense of what lay unseen beyond those gray curtains of wet.

I stayed in the tent until midday. I walked for a time, first in a brief pause in the storm, then in a density of fog. Late afternoon, I retreated into the tent. Occasionally, I looked out. Bird. Sheep. Lake. Stone. *Chik! Chik!* Chime, *baa*! Rippling sounds of water. Stone silence speaking as loudly as the rain on the tent. The community's presence reverberated.

I pulled out the journal, lay back, awkwardly writing with the pages held above me, hands still wrapped in fingerless glove-mittens, the upside-down pen cantankerous with gravity pulling at the ink.
~~~

Not exactly the ending I had hoped for . . . but I have made it. My last night.

The ink stopped running. I shook the pen, tried again, managed a few words before the ink stopped running again, ending my writing even as the fog rolled in again and the entire world of Hallingskarvet was reduced to shadowy shapes within murky gray.

~~~

The next day, I walked down off the mountain. A pair of plovers followed for a while, calling, calling, staying with me for a long distance. The plovers turned back, flying north toward the Ridge. A small bird flew out and fluttered over my head and hovered just there above me, silhouetted against the gray sky, floating. I lifted my hand to the bird. "Thank you, Wheatear."

My last camp was outside Haugastøl, the town where I would catch a train the next day. Far off I could see the point on the bench where Tvergastein Hytte sat perched, surrounded by the Place that is Tvergastein.

T is for Tvergastein. Ecosophy T: Næss's worldview, his life philosophy based on that Place. *T* is for Tvergastein. That is what all my reading and research showed. Except for one sentence, a thought from Arne Næss himself: "I call it Ecosophy T, and people think it's T is for Tvergastein. I don't think so."[38]

T is for just what then? Was it what the wild places allow, an unveiling of the layers of meaning and mystery that comes from immersing and belonging within the complex beauty of the natural world? Is *T* for that gestalt that wraps the material world into a greater sensed world, connects all things in a Whole, and *T* is where Næss found that, felt that? So that *T* is any Place that allows for that deep connection and so compassion: "If you hear a phrase like, 'All life is fundamentally one,' you should be open to tasting this, before asking immediately, 'What does this mean?' There is a kind of deep yes to nature that is central to my philosophy."[39]
~~~

Perhaps Næss meant that *T* is where a small person can feel that *Yes*, feel the deep belonging, not a Place at all, but an experience. Something like what I found while I walked, slept, ate, laughed, cried, and wrote, solo beneath the great cliffs of Hallingskarvet, in the shadow of the Mountain.

EPILOGUE

Near the crest of Red Mountain, I found a small, rounded volcanic rock, a composite of black crystals blown out of a nearby volcano millions of years ago to land there on the limestone bedrock, the same strata of ancient seabed that underlies Monument Mountain only a few miles to the north. Holding the rock, I considered the geology of the land around me, a story of time, uplift, and erosion.

Rock in hand, I heard the frantic call of a pipit just before the bird passed by, a falcon close behind in a twisting chase of fluttering wings. The two birds flew only a foot or two apart, a distance that closed, expanded, closed, expanded, till the pipit made a fatal twist as the peregrine made the killing turn and caught the bird, taking it to the ground to squeeze out its life. The silence of the hunt cloaked the mountain, the hush that descends when all life bows down, hiding from the predator. Within the stillness grew a rushing, like a hundred wings; a whirlwind approached, a small twisting of air, sounding like the beat of huge, stiff, feathers. The twist of wind passed by, and I remembered the words told to me in Kenya: whirlwinds are souls of the dead. *A soul has just died*, I thought. In the following quiet, I looked across the expanse. *How should I feel… ? I don't know what to feel.*

"Oh…" I remember saying it out loud, so confused was I by the beauty, the horror, the wonder of what had just happened. There had just been a hunt, a death, a falcon nourished, vibrant life killing with grace, vibrant life crushed out.

The falcon took flight, its prey clenched in sharp talons, leaving the mountain still and hushed even as it departed. As the bird disappeared, I scanned the horizon. Four mountain goats came into sight, walking across the high edge of the alpine meadow, white against the gray-blue sky that was laden with smoke from western wildfires, a leaden color that shouted *climate change*. The goats dropped into the mountain's cirque and were gone. Into the silence floated a bird call. Pipits in flight again. Birdsong again.

All ways of knowing the Mountain folded into that moment: sacred, ecological, sublime, philosophical, even home, for in such moments, I find my greatest sense of belonging, grown out of my wanderings in that homeland. The entire event took perhaps two minutes, probably less, but it was all time, stretching into all space. To stand within such a moment, and be with it, is to participate in that which is beyond us yet where we can belong. It is, very simply, to be.

ACKNOWLEDGMENTS

Given that *The Mountain* taps into a lifetime of experience, it is impossible to mention everyone who in some way participated in its evolution. My deepest gratitude goes to all those good people who reside in my past and present who in some way contributed to this book.

The Mountain very simply would not exist if it had not been for the mentoring and encouragement of nature writer Mark Cocker. Mark has supported my writing life in many ways over the years, and it was his guidance that shaped this book from the beginning.

Jedediah Rogers at the University of Utah Press shepherded *The Mountain* through the publication process while providing insightful commentary. Always patient and kind, Jed was a joy to work with, especially given this is my first book and I was fairly naive about the process. Thanks also to the University of Utah Press team for all they have done to make this book a reality. Scott Olson and Edwin Bernbaum provided valuable critique during the review process with the University of Utah Press.

Behind *every* chapter is the loving strength of my parents, their influence most clearly described in chapter 1, "Beginnings." That first chapter is also a tribute to my grandparents. It is truly beyond my ability to express the depth of gratitude I feel for both my parents and my grandparents, who allowed me to create the life I have lived and so spend time trekking into the mountains that are part of the journeys within this book.

Also within the first chapter, subtly folded into mention of my good years at the University of Montana, lies the mentoring of my UM master's degree committee, the people who ushered me into the writing world: Phil Condon, Dan Spencer, and Dan Flores. Sections of the first chapter are drawn from my master's thesis written during my time in the UM Environmental Studies Department.

Chapter 2, "The Sacred Mountain," greatly benefited from the comments and writings of Edwin Bernbaum. His knowledge of sacred mountains as well as Māori culture and history brought accuracy and depth to the New Zealand story.

My studies and early experience in the Grand Tetons, as related in chapter 3, "The Scientific Mountain," were founded on the support and guidance of my master's committee. I greatly appreciate their patience with a free-spirited thinker, with special thanks to Dennis Knight. Without Dennis, I might not have made it through that degree.

Kim Heacox provided valuable insight into John Muir for chapter 4, "The Romantic Mountain." His review of the final version of the chapter is much appreciated.

Chapter 5, "The Solo Mountain," is a condensed version of a longer manuscript that recounted my Nan Shepherd journey in more detail. Charlotte Peacock, Nan Shepherd's biographer, reviewed that manuscript. Her thoughts, both in our email communications and in her book *Into the Mountain*, gave me a better understanding of Nan Shepherd as a person. Bill Glassley was another who read and supported that original narrative. Bill was an excellent writer who became a good friend, supporting my writing efforts on the long road to publication. Sadly, Bill passed away a few years ago. I would have liked to thank him in person. Thanks go to the others who commented on my Nan Shepherd travels and supported my writing: Ron Davis, Sara Maitland, and Gary Ferguson.

For chapter 6, "The Peopled Mountain," I hold overwhelming gratitude for the good people of Assynt, Inchnadamph in particular. Assynt and those I came to know there literally changed my life, adding depth, richness, and warmth to my days even when I was not in Scotland. There are those I mention in the chapter that hold a special place in my life: Helen, Jane, Chris, and Jane. There are also others outside of Inchnadamph that I came to know over the years, including Andy, Roz, Mandy, and Bill; Mandy provided helpful critique on some early essays, parts of which made it into this chapter. And there is Claire, a dear friend. Claire died suddenly and unexpectedly just as I was finishing the first draft of chapter 6. She knew I could get this published and helped make it happen in her own ways. Perhaps she is looking down and knows the Assynt writings finally made it into a book. So too might Allan and Evie Hamilton be watching from those places we cannot know. Allan and Evie were good friends who lived in Argyll, the people who first welcomed me to Scotland and helped make it feel like a second home.

Alan Drengson, friend of Arne Næss and an integral part of deep ecology, was there behind chapter 7, "The Whole Mountain." More than anything, he provided moral support when I reached out to him after my Hallingskarvet journey, as I began to realize the complexity of Næss's philosophy and what I had walked into. Drengson's first response to my initial email was, "Your project is a great one. As Arne would say, 'Two Thumbs-up!'" That gave me the courage to carry on. Sadly, Alan Drengson passed away in 2022. I hold as precious my short time of communicating with him.

After moving to the desert (as described in chapter 6), I found myself in a wonderful community where people support one another. Thanks to Andy Gulliford for getting this book on the road to publication and neighbor Christine Schillig for providing editorial advice. There are many in Bluff who have supported my writing and many friends there who make life a joy. I won't list them all, but I must press my palms together and give special thanks to Stewart Aitchison and Ann Kramer. They contributed to my life and so to this book in many ways, far more than I can say.

Of course, there is my acknowledgment of and gratitude for the Mountain, who will always be there whether I am in the heights or not.

~~~

Grateful acknowledgment is made to the following for permission to reprint previously published material:

Excerpt from Norman MacCaig, "In Everything," in *The Poems of Norman MacCaig*, 3rd ed., ed. Ewan McCaig (Edinburgh: Birlinn,
~~~

2010). Copyright © the estate of Norman MacCaig. Reproduced with permission of Birlinn Limited through PLSclear.

Quotes from Edwin Bernbaum, *Sacred Mountains of the World*, 2nd ed. (Cambridge: Cambridge University Press, 2022). Copyright © 2022 by Cambridge University Press. Reproduced with permission of Cambridge University Press through PLSclear.

Excerpts from Nan Shepherd, "Fires," in *In the Cairngorms* (Cambridge: Galileo, 2014). Copyright © 2014 by the Estate of Nan Shepherd. Reproduced with permission of Galileo Publishing.

Quotes from Denis Cosgrove and Veronica Della Dora, ed., *High Places: Cultural Geographies of Mountains, Ice and Science* (New York: I. B. Tauris, 2008). © Denis Cosgrove and Veronica Della Dora, 2008, "Introduction: High Places"; © Bernard Debarbieux, 2008, "Mountains: Between Pure Reason and Embodied Experience"; and © Gilles Rudaz, 2008, "Stewards of the Mountains: The Poetics and Politics of Local Knowledge in the Valaisan Alps." Reproduced with permission of I. B. Tauris, an imprint of Bloomsbury Publishing Plc.

Excerpts from *The Living Mountain* by Nan Shepherd. Copyright © 2025 by Nan Shepherd. Reprinted with the permission of Scribner, an imprint of Simon & Schuster LLC. All rights reserved.

Quotes from Olaus Murie, *Journeys to the Far North* (Nashville: Alaska Northwest Books of Turner Publishing, 2015), 227. Copyright © 1973 by Olaus J. Murie. Reprinted with permission from Turner Publishing.

Excerpts from David Rothenberg and Arne Næss, *Is It Painful to Think? Conversations with Arne Næss* (Minneapolis: University of Minnesota Press, 1993). © Copyright 1993 by the Regents of the University of Minnesota. Reproduced with permission from the University of Minnesota Press.

Quotes from Margaret E. Murie and Olaus J. Murie, *Wapiti Wilderness* (Boulder: University Press of Colorado, 1987). Copyright © 1985 by Margaret E. Murie. Used with permission of the University Press of Colorado; permission conveyed through Copyright Clearance Center Inc.

NOTES

Introduction

1 Peter Matthiessen, *The Snow Leopard* (New York: Penguin Random House, 2008), 121.
2 W. H. Murray, *Mountaineering in Scotland and Undiscovered Scotland* (London: Diadem, 1979), 4.
3 Nan Shepherd, *The Living Mountain*, 2nd ed. (Edinburgh: Canongate, 2011), 108.
4 Shepherd, 8.
5 Denis Cosgrove and Veronica Della Dora, "Introduction: High Places," in *High Places: Cultural Geographies of Mountains, Ice and Science*, ed. Denis Cosgrove and Veronica Della Dora (New York: I. B. Tauris, 2008), 1.
6 Robert Macfarlane, *Mountains of the Mind: A History of a Fascination* (London: Granta, 2004), 156–57.
7 David Hinton, *Hunger Mountain: A Field Guide to Mind and Landscape* (Boston: Shambhala, 2012), 4.
8 Edwin Bernbaum, *Sacred Mountains of the World* (Cambridge: Cambridge University Press, 2022), 1.
9 David Rothenberg and Arne Næss, *Is It Painful to Think? Conversations with Arne Næss* (Minneapolis: University of Minnesota Press, 1993), 65–66.
10 Rothenberg and Næss, 65–66.
11 Matthiessen, *Snow Leopard*, 208.

Chapter 1

1 *Pedicularis cystopteridifolia* has the common name Fernleaf Lousewort, which happens to be a common name my parents and I used for a different lousewort.

2 Gary Snyder, *The Practice of the Wild* (Berkeley: Counterpoint, 2010), 101.

3 This was the phrase Nan Shepherd used in her poem "Fires," which became part of my Cairngorm experience, as told in chapter 5; see Nan Shepherd, "Fires," in *In the Cairngorms* (Cambridge: Galileo, 2014), 4–5.

4 Grandma's journals were handed to me with the words "keep these safe." They are something I treasure, holding many life lessons.

5 Robert Macfarlane notes, "So drastic was this [the Romantic] revolution that to contemplate it now is to be reminded of a truth about landscapes: that our responses to them are for the most part culturally devised. That is to say, when we look at a landscape, we do not see what is there, but largely what we think is there. We attribute qualities to a landscape which it does not intrinsically possess—savageness for example, or bleakness—and we value it accordingly. We read landscapes, in other words, we interpret their forms in the light of our own experience and memory and that or our shared cultural memory." Macfarlane, *Mountains of the Mind*, 18.

6 I use *Euro-American* in reference to people of European descent in North America. This is different from Western culture. *Western* and *Euro-American* are both vague terms, but Euro-American fits here.

7 William Cronon, "The Trouble with Wilderness: Or, Getting Back to the Wrong Nature," *Environmental History* 1, no. 1 (January 1996): 10. "Where were these sublime places? The eighteenth century catalog of their locations feels very familiar, for we still see and value landscapes as it *taught* us to do. God was on the mountaintop, in the chasm, in the waterfall, in the thundercloud, in the rainbow, in the sunset. One has only to think of the sites that Americans chose for their first national parks–Yellowstone, Yosemite, Grand Canyon, Rainier, Zion—to realize that virtually all of them fit one or more of these categories" (emphasis added).

8 Macfarlane notes, "Seven centuries before Romanticism revolutionized Western perceptions of mountains and wilderness, Chinese and Japanese artists were celebrating the spiritual qualities of wild landscape." Macfarlane, *Mountains of the Mind*, 56.

9 Ecophilosopher Arne Næss mused about how philosophers can negate the reality and essence of the natural world, in part turning to the idea that we are products of our own culture and perceptions. Næss disagreed with this line of thinking, "where you end up saying: 'Nature is without colours, even without shapes, and even without cause and effect. Because relations of cause and effect is something created by

humans. So there is nothing there. In short: there is nothing in nature in itself! You have no access to nature in itself.' You see, you end up in complete nonsense. That's what many people do who are in philosophy. Even in contemporary so-called 'postmodernism,' nature is something, only a limiting thing, which you never can really see or appreciate. You appreciate only your own ways of thinking and feeling and you are completely determined by your culture, and so on. So, this protection of nature is a sham in a sense. There is something there, but you don't have any access to it." Jan van Boeckel, dir., *The Call of the Mountain: Arne Næss and the Deep Ecology Movement* (ReRun Productions, 1997), https://www.deepecology.net/blog/2022/03/16/the-call-of-the-mountain-arne-Næss-and-the-deep-ecology-movement-full-version/.

10 Matthiessen, *Snow Leopard*, 121.

CHAPTER 2

1 I feel this description is far too brief and apologize for its superficiality and any inaccuracies of this and other discussions of Māori culture. All cultures' cosmology and spirituality are nuanced and deep, far beyond what fits in a few paragraphs as told by a visitor. I speak of this and other Māori cultural topics from what I have gleaned from my studies and visits to the Whakapapa Visitor Centre, the Auckland Museum, and the Museum of New Zealand in Wellington. The papers and books I learned from are included in these endnotes.

2 Christopher Lockhart, Carla A. Houkamau, Chris G. Sibley, and Danny Osborne, "To Be at One with the Land: Māori Spirituality Predicts Greater Environmental Regard," *Religions* 10, no. 7 (July 2019): 427.

3 For more details, see Natalia Pardo, Hidalene Wilson, Jonathon N. Procter, Erica Lattughi, and Taiarahia Black, "Bridging Māori Indigenous Knowledge and Western Geosciences to Reduce Social Vulnerability in Active Volcanic Regions," *Journal of Applied Volcanology* 4, no. 2 (2015): 1–20.

4 Bernbaum, *Sacred Mountains of the World*, 266.

5 "History and Culture: Tongariro National Park," Department of Conservation, Tongariro, accessed January 19, 2025, https://www.doc.govt.nz/parks-and-recreation/places-to-go/central-north-island/places/tongariro-national-park/about-tongariro-national-park/history-and-culture/.

6 "History and Culture"; Bernbaum, *Sacred Mountains of the World*, 266.

7 Quoted in Paul Star and Lynne Lochhead, "Children of the Burnt Bush: New Zealanders and the Indigenous Remnant, 1880–1930," in *Making a New Land: Environmental Histories of New Zealand*, ed. Eric Pawson and Tom Brooking (Otago, New Zealand: Otago University Press, 2013), 146.

8 The frequency of dispossession of Indigenous peoples to control the land, create national parks, or appropriate natural resources is now recognized across the planet—what happened in my own homeland and across the American West is appalling. New Zealand, among others, is a country that has moved forward in at least trying to right wrongs, addressing issues of social injustice.

9 Snyder, *Practice of the Wild*, 101.

10 Bernbaum, *Sacred Mountains of the World*, 39–42.

11 Pardo et al., "Bridging Māori Indigenous Knowledge," 4.

12 See, for example, Edwin Bernbaum, "Sacred Mountains: Themes and Teachings," *Mountain Research and Development* 26 (2009): 304–9.

13 Edwin Bernbaum, "The Spiritual and Cultural Significance of Mountains," in *Mountains of the World: A Global Priority*, ed. Bruno Messerli and Jack D. Ives (New York: Parthenon, 1997), 42–47.

14 For example, Mount Graham Observatory is on the Apache sacred mountain of Dzil ncha si an.

15 Department of Conservation, *Plan and Prepare: Tongariro Northern Circuit* (Wellington: Department of Conservation, 2015).

16 This was written on the interpretive sign in the third hut of the Tongariro circuit. The quote is as written, including "(god)" in parentheses.

17 From Leonard Cockayne, "A Glimpse into the Alps of Canterbury," in *Canterbury Old and New 1850–1900* (Christchurch: New Zealand Natives Association, 1900), quoted in Eric Pawson and Tom Brooking, "The Meaning of Mountains," in Pawson and Brooking, *Making a New Land*, 166.

18 Susan Forbes, "Nomination of Tongariro National Park for Inclusion in the World Heritage Cultural List," in *Conservation Advisory Science Notes No. 68* (Wellington: Department of Conservation, 1994), 12.

19 Paul Groth and Chris Wilson, "The Polyphony of Cultural Landscape Study: An Introduction," in *Everyday America: Cultural Landscape Studies after J. B. Jackson*, by Chris Wilson and Paul Erling Groth (Berkeley: University of California Press, 2003), 2.

20 Greta Yeoman, "To Summit or Not to Summit?," *Wilderness*, March 19, 2020, https://www.wildernessmag.co.nz/to-summit-or-not-to-summit/.

21 Yeoman; brackets in source. *Pākehā* refers to European descendants.
22 Yeoman.
23 Pardo et al., "Bridging Māori Indigenous Knowledge," 8, 20.
24 M. Stausberg, "The Sacred, the Holy, the Numinous—and Religion: On the Emergence and Early History of a Terminological Constellation," *Religion* 47, no. 4 (2017): 557–90.
25 At the time of writing (2021), the online brochure for the Alpine Crossing day hike shows a very small box next to the map stating in small print, "The alpine lakes and summits of the mountains are sacred to the local Māori tribe Ngāti Hikairo ki Tongariro. Respectfully, they ask that summits are not climbed, waterways are not touched and lakes are not entered." Since I was not doing the day hike, I did not look at the brochure when I was there in 2015 and don't know if this box was included.
26 Atholl Anderson, "A Fragile Plenty," in Pawson and Brooking, *Making a New Land*, 48–49.
27 Te Ahukaramū Charles Royal, "Kaitiakitanga—Guardianship and Conservation," Te Ara: The Encyclopedia of New Zealand, 2007, accessed March 8, 2024, https://www.TeAra.govt.nz/en/kaitiakitanga-guardianship-and-conservation/print.
28 Pardo et al., "Bridging Māori Indigenous Knowledge," 1–20.
29 Pardo et al., 1.
30 Pardo et al., 9.
31 Note also the discussion in chapter 6 on Arne Næss's feelings about fieldwork, where I write that a "field researcher develops a 'respect, even veneration' for all life. It is an understanding that develops through intimate association with the entire ecosystem, creating a connection that reaches beyond humans and a limited array of species." Arne Næss, "The Shallow and the Deep, Long Range Ecology Movement: A Summary," in *The Deep Ecology Movement: An Introductory Anthology*, ed. Alan R. Drengson and Yuichi Inoue (Berkeley: North Atlantic Books, 1995), 4.
32 Interestingly given Māori's view of mountains as ancestors, *kith* in old English referred to one's native land, so the original meaning of *kith and kin* was "one's country and relatives," only later to become "one's friends and relatives." See Oxford Reference, s.v. "Kith and Kin," accessed January 12, 2025, https://www.oxfordreference.com/display/10.1093/oi/authority.20110803100039323.

Chapter 3

1 Christen Girard, *A Short Biography of Margaret and Olaus Murie* (Carlisle, MA: Benna Books, 2019).

2 I found this collection of articles particularly helpful for this chapter: Cosgrove and Dora, *High Places.*

3 Quoted in Andrea Wulf, *The Invention of Nature: Alexander von Humboldt's New World* (New York: Vintage Books, 2015), 88.

4 Robin Patten and Dennis Knight, "Snow Avalanches and Vegetation Pattern in Cascade Canyon, Grand Teton National Park, Wyoming, U.S.A.," *Arctic and Alpine Research* 26, no. 1 (1994): 35–41.

5 Olaus Murie, *Journeys to the Far North* (Nashville: Alaska Northwest Books of Turner Publishing, 2015), 227; quoted in Girard, *Short Biography of Margaret and Olaus Murie*, 16.

6 There is a growing body of academic literature incorporating Traditional Ecological Knowledge. See also Pardo et al., "Bridging Māori Indigenous Knowledge," 1–20; Fikret Berkes, *Sacred Ecology* (New York: Routledge, 2012).

7 Published in five volumes between 1845 and 1862.

8 Humboldt's letter to a friend, 1934, quoted in Laura D. Walls, "Introducing Humboldt's Cosmos," *Minding Nature*, August 2009, 4.

9 See Walls.

10 Bernard Debarbieux, "Mountains: Between Pure Reason and Embodied Experience," in Cosgrove and Dora, *High Places*, 87–104.

11 Margaret E. Murie and Olaus J. Murie, *Wapiti Wilderness* (Boulder: University Press of Colorado, 1987), 187–88.

12 *Sand County Almanac* was originally published in 1948 by Oxford University Press.

13 *The Sense of Wonder* was originally a magazine article published in the 1950s. It was published as a book in 1965 and later reprinted by Harper Collins in 2017.

14 Humboldt, *Views of Nature*, quoted in Walls, "Introducing Humboldt's Cosmos," 9.

Chapter 4

1 This was in a letter to Mrs. Ezra S. Carr, October 8, 1872. The letter was printed in William Frederic Badè, *The Life and Letters of John Muir* (Houghton Mifflin, 1923 and 1924); reprinted online at the Sierra Club, accessed January 12, 2025, https://vault.sierraclub.org/john_muir_exhibit/life/life_and_letters/.

2 Muir went to Alaska seven times, first in 1879.
3 John Muir, "Yosemite Valley," in *Picturesque California* (San Francisco: J. Dewing, 1888); reprinted online at the Sierra Club, accessed January 12, 2025, https://vault.sierraclub.org/john_muir_exhibit/writings/picturesque_california/default.aspx.
4 Donald Worster, *A Passion for Nature: The Life of John Muir* (New York: Oxford University Press, 2008), 253.
5 Kim Heacox, *John Muir and the Ice That Started a Fire: How a Visionary and the Glaciers of Alaska Changed America* (Guilford, CT: Lyons Press, 2014).
6 John Muir, *Travels in Alaska* (Boston: Houghton Mifflin, 1915).
7 Muir, "Sum Dum Bay," in *Travels in Alaska*; reprinted online at the Sierra Club, accessed January 12, 2025, https://vault.sierraclub.org/john_muir_exhibit/writings/travels_in_alaska/chapter_14.aspx.
8 Muir.
9 Muir, "A Cruise in the Cassiar," in *Travels in Alaska*.
10 Walter R. Goldschmidt and Theodore H. Haas, "Possessory Rights of the Natives of Southeastern Alaska" (unpublished file report at Sitka National Historic Park [SITK], 1946), sec. D, 4, quoted in Theodore Catton, *Land Reborn: A History of Administration and Visitor Use in Glacier Bay National Park and Preserve* (Anchorage, Alaska: National Park Service, 1995), https://www.nps.gov/parkhistory/online_books/glba/adhi/index.htm.
11 Edmund Burke, "A Philosophical Enquiry into the Origin of Our Ideas of the Sublime and Beautiful," Eighteenth Century Collections Online, accessed January 9, 2025, https://name.umdl.umich.edu/004807802.0001.000. University of Michigan Library Digital Collections.
12 Yosemite has western Labrador tea (*Rhododendron columbianum*), a different species than what grows in Alaska and Greenland: *Rhododendron groenlandicum*.
13 "Paintings of Yosemite," Yosemite National Park, California, National Park Service, last updated August 26, 2021, https://www.nps.gov/yose/learn/historyculture/paintings-of-yosemite.htm.
14 Simon Bainbridge, "Romantic Writers and Mountaineering," *Romanticism* 18, no. 1 (2012): 2.
15 See Bainbridge for examples.
16 Muir wrote, "But to get all this into words is a hopeless task. The leanest sketch of each feature would need a whole chapter. Nor would any amount of space, however industriously scribbled, be of much avail. To defrauded town toilers, parks in magazine articles are like pictures

of bread to the hungry. I can write only hints to incite good wanderers to come to the feast." John Muir, "The Yosemite National Park," in *Our National Parks* (New York: Houghton, Mifflin, 1901); reprinted online at the Sierra Club, accessed January 12, 2025, https://vault.sierraclub.org/john_muir_exhibit/writings/our_national_parks/chapter_3.aspx.

17 Pussy paws: *Cistanthe monosperma.* Pussytoes: *Antennaria media.*

18 Muir, "Yosemite National Park."

19 John Muir and Chris Highland, *Meditations of John Muir: Nature's Temple* (Berkeley: Wilderness Press, 2001).

20 "The whole landscape showed design, like man's noblest sculptures. How wonderful the power of its beauty! Gazing awe-stricken, I might have left everything for it. Glad, endless work would then be mine tracing the forces that have brought forth its features, its rocks and plants and animals and glorious weather. Beauty beyond thought everywhere, beneath, above, made and being made forever." John Muir, "Through the Foothills with a Flock of Sheep," in *My First Summer in the Sierra* (New York: Houghton, Mifflin, 1901); reprinted online at the Sierra Club, accessed January 12, 2025, https://vault.sierraclub.org/john_muir_exhibit/writings/my_first_summer_in_the_sierra/chapter_1.aspx.

21 "Simplon Pass" was first published in *Poems*, 1845; it was also published in *The Prelude*, 1850; reprinted online at the Poetry Foundation, accessed January 12, 2025, https://www.poetryfoundation.org/poems/45552/the-simplon-pass.

22 See discussion in chapter 3, "The Scientific Mountain."

23 Matthew Fitzgerald, "The Sublime: An Aesthetic Concept in Change," *Collector*, September 23, 2021, https://www.thecollector.com/the-sublime-concept-in-change-philosophy/.

24 Joseph Wood Krutch provides a good source to better understand the difference between naturalist Thoreau and philosopher Emerson in Joseph W. Krutch, *Henry David Thoreau* (New York: William Morrow, 1974).

25 The Wilderness Act of 1964, Pub. L. No. 88-577 (16 U.S.C. 1131-1136).

26 Quoted in Allie Patterson, "Indian Removal from Yosemite National Park," Intermountain Histories, accessed April 5, 2021, https://www.intermountainhistories.org/items/show/339.

27 Patterson.

28 Rebecca Solnit, "John Muir in Native America," *Magazine of the Sierra Club*, March 2, 2021, https://www.sierraclub.org/sierra/2021-2-march

-april/feature/john-muir-native-america.

29 "The 'Last Indian,'" *Witness History*, BBC World Service, September 7, 2012, https://www.bbc.co.uk/programmes/w3ct3c3p.

30 "Unflattering though his descriptions were, Muir accepted blacks as part of the family of man and did not come down on the side of southern or northern racists or white supremacists"; Worster, *Passion for Nature*, 137.

31 George Perkins Marsh, *Man and Nature: Or, Physical Geography as Modified by Human Action* (New York: C. Scribner, 1864), 36.

32 Worster, *Passion for Nature*, 236. Worster notes that Muir's previous teacher, Ezra Carr, quoted Marsh's work.

33 For further information, see Dewey W. Hall, *Romantic Naturalists, Early Environmentalists: An Ecocritical Study, 1789–1912* (Burlington, VT: Ashgate, 2014), 178.

Chapter 5

1 Shepherd, *Living Mountain*, 108.

2 Shepherd, 2.

3 Nan Shepherd's first novel's title was *The Quarry Woods*.

4 Charlotte Peacock, *Into the Mountain: The Life of Nan Shepherd* (Cambridge: Galileo, 2019), 119.

5 Peacock.

6 Shepherd, *Living Mountain*, 106.

7 Shepherd, 3.

8 Shepherd, 4.

9 Shepherd, 23.

10 *Corrie*, *coire*, and *choire* are Scottish terms synonymous with *cirque*.

11 Shepherd, *Living Mountain*, 20, 97.

12 Shepherd, 23.

13 A mountain hut. These are found throughout Scotland.

14 Shepherd, *Living Mountain*, 104.

15 Shepherd, 27.

16 Shepherd, 41.

17 Shepherd, 62.

18 This was in Henry David Thoreau's "Walking," which was first published in essay form in the *Atlantic*: Henry David Thoreau, "Walking," *Atlantic Monthly: A Magazine of Literature, Art, and Politics* 9, no. 56 (June 1862): 657–74.

19 The word *peregrini* refers to "wanderer" or "pilgrim."

20 Thoreau, "Walking."

21 Shepherd, "Fires," 4–5.

22 Shepherd, *Living Mountain*, 96.
23 Shepherd, 105.
24 Shepherd, 11.

Chapter 6

1 Quoted in Gilles Rudaz, “Stewards of the Mountains: The Poetics and Politics of Local Knowledge in the Valaisan Alps,” in Cosgrove and Dora, *High Places*, 147.
2 Limestone and dolostone are similar in composition: both are carbonate sedimentary rocks, limestone composed of calcium carbonate, and dolostone of calcium and magnesium carbonate.
3 The IAT originated in 1993 when Maine conservationist Dick Anderson came up with the idea to create an international trail starting at the Appalachian Trail’s end, continuing on into Canada. Anderson reached out to his friend and current Maine IAT president, Don Hudson; together, they turned the idea into a reality, helped along by other Maine conservationists. It didn’t stop there, and one by one other countries joined the informal organization. Today there are twenty-two IAT chapters, from Maine to Morocco, carrying out the IAT mission: “Thinking beyond Borders,” International Appalachian Trail / Sentier International des Appalaches, accessed January 12, 2025, https://iat-sia.org/about/.
4 Rudaz, “Stewards of the Mountains,” 150.
5 Messerli and Ives, *Mountains of the World*.
6 Thanks to Helen for providing this information.
7 Rudaz, “Stewards of the Mountains.”
8 Henry David Thoreau, “Ktaadn,” in *The Maine Woods* (Boston: Ticknor and Fields, 1864); reprinted online at Project Gutenberg, accessed January 12, 2025, https://www.gutenberg.org/files/42500/42500-h/42500-h.htm#chap01.
9 For further discussion, see J. Nicholas Entrikin, “Afterword: ‘The Unhandselled Globe,’” in Cosgrove and Dora, *High Places*, 216–25.
10 Tenzing Ingty, “High Mountain Communities and Climate Change: Adaptation, Traditional Ecological Knowledge, and Institutions,” *Climatic Change* 145, no. 1 (October 2017): 41–55. Note that the system is apparently changing as tourism and related construction increases.
11 For an example in Tibet, see Li Li, Dieter Thomas Tietze, Andreas Fritz, Zhi Lü, Matthias Bürgi, and Ilse Storch, “Rewilding Cultural Landscape Potentially Puts Both Avian Diversity and Endemism at Risk: A Tibetan

Plateau Case Study," *Biological Conservation* 224 (May 2018): 75–86.

12 Marsh, *Man and Nature*.

13 Norman MacCaig, "A Man in Assynt," in *The Poems of Norman MacCaig*, 3rd ed., ed. Ewen McCaig (Edinburgh: Birlinn, 2010), 221–29.

14 Norman MacCaig, "In Everything," in McCaig, *Poems of Norman MacCaig*, 302–3.

Chapter 7

1 Rothenberg and Næss, *Is It Painful to Think?*, 176.

2 Note that although my interpretations of Næss's ideas are developed from extensive research and study, they are my interpretations. I had hoped to talk to those who worked closely with Næss on deep ecology yet only had the chance to connect with Alan Drengson, who gave my project a "thumbs-up"! But our communication only lasted for a brief time and waned due to his health. Drengson died in 2022.

3 "Deep Ecology Platform," Rainforest Information Centre, accessed January 12, 2025, https://www.rainforestinformationcentre.org/deep_ecology_platform.

1. The well-being and flourishing of human and nonhuman life on Earth have value in themselves (synonyms: inherent worth, intrinsic value, inherent value). These values are independent of the usefulness of the nonhuman world for human purposes.
2. Richness and diversity of life forms contribute to the realization of these values and are also values in themselves.
3. Humans have no right to reduce this richness and diversity except to satisfy vital needs.
4. Present human interference with the nonhuman world is excessive, and the situation is rapidly worsening.
5. The flourishing of human life and cultures is compatible with a substantial decrease of the human population. The flourishing of nonhuman life requires such a decrease.
6. Policies must therefore be changed. The changes in policies affect basic economic, technological, and ideological structures. The resulting state of affairs will be deeply different from the present.
7. The ideological change is mainly that of appreciating life quality (dwelling in situations of inherent worth) rather than adhering to an increasingly higher standard of living. There will be a profound awareness of the difference between big and great.

8. Those who subscribe to the foregoing points have an obligation directly or indirectly to participate in the attempt to implement the necessary changes.

—Arne Næss and George Sessions (1984)

4 At the time of writing, the hytte was owned by the private foundation Tvergastein Arne Næss hytte, https://ut.no/turforslag/118641/tvergastein-rundtur-under-hallingskarvet.

5 Næss noted that "a favored place relentlessly and remorselessly determines the details of one's life"; Arne Næss, Alan Drengson, and Bill Devall, *Ecology of Wisdom: Writings by Arne Næss* (Berkeley: Counterpoint, 2008), 60.

6 Alan Drengson, "Introduction: The Life and Work of Arne Næss: An Appreciative Overview," in Næss, Drengson, and Devall, *Ecology of Wisdom*, 17.

7 Rothenberg and Næss, *Is It Painful to Think?*, 131.

8 Næss, "An Example of a Place: Tvergastein," in Næss, Drengson, and Devall, *Ecology of Wisdom*, 58.

9 I suspect he was referring to *Hallingskarvet: How to Have a Long Life with an Old Father*.

10 Van Boeckel, *Call of the Mountain*. The interview stretched out over five days in June 1995 and was recorded in and around the Tvergastein Hytte.

11 Rothenberg and Næss, *Is It Painful to Think?*, 176.

12 "I do not consider science and above all research incompatible with profound positive feelings towards nature. Tvergastein as 'object' of botanical, zoological, mineralogical, meteorological, and other scientific research did not detract in the least from the immediate experience of togetherness, of identification and appreciation. On the contrary. In **the great naturalist tradition**... the motivation is not mainly cognition, but conative. Feelings are just as much driving the search as is abstract thinking"; Næss, "Example of a Place," 60–61 (emphasis added).

13 Næss, 62.

14 Næss, "Shallow and the Deep," 4.

15 Næss, "Example of a Place," 61.

16 See Næss, "Self-Realization: An Ecological Approach to Being in the World," in Næss, Drengson, and Devall, *Ecology of Wisdom*, 87. In this chapter, Næss notes that "the 'everything hangs together' maxim of

ecology applies to the self and its relation to other living beings, ecosystems, the ecosphere, and the earth, with its long history."

17 See Walls, "Introducing Humboldt's Cosmos."

18 Næss, "Example of a Place," 61.

19 Van Boeckel, *Call of the Mountain*.

20 Rothenberg and Næss, *Is It Painful to Think?*, 16.

21 Arne Næss, "Mountains," *The Trumpeter: Journal of Ecosophy* 21, no. 2 (Autumn 2005): 52, https://trumpeter.athabascau.ca/index.php/trumpet/article/view/56/53. Originally written in a 1992 unpublished work.

22 Næss, 53.

23 Næss, "Modesty and the Conquest of Mountains," in Næss, Drengson, and Devall, *Ecology of Wisdom*, 67.

24 Næss, 67.

25 Aside from a few grammatical corrections for clarity, this is verbatim as I wrote it that last evening at Camp One.

26 Around ten years old, Næss first climbed up to face the rising cliffs of the ridge, feeling even then that the "only dignified way of life would be to remain on the mountain, not to descend"; Rothenberg and Næss, *Is It Painful to Think?*, 60.

27 Barry Lopez, "The Invitation," *Granta*, November 18, 2015, https://granta.com/invitation/.

28 Van Boeckel, *Call of the Mountain*.

29 This is according to Max Oelschlaeger, *The Idea of Wilderness: From Prehistory to the Age of Ecology* (New Haven: Yale University Press, 1991), 145. The journey to Katahdin "was an existential encounter that dealt a death blow to the Emersonian notion that the world existed for humankind."

30 Thoreau, "Ktaadn."

31 Entrikin, "Afterword."

32 Shepherd, *Living Mountain*, 108.

33 Thoreau, "Ktaadn."

34 Rothenberg and Næss, *Is It Painful to Think?*, 154.

35 Rothenberg and Næss, 77–78.

36 Rothenberg and Næss, 60.

37 Rothenberg and Næss, 65–66.

38 Van Boeckel, *Call of the Mountain*.

39 Rothenberg and Næss, *Is It Painful to Think?*, 151.

SELECTED BIBLIOGRAPHY

Badè, William Frederic. *The Life and Letters of John Muir*. Boston: Houghton Mifflin, 1923. https://vault.sierraclub.org/john_muir_exhibit/life/life_and_letters/.

Bainbridge, Simon. "Romantic Writers and Mountaineering." *Romanticism* 18, no. 1 (2012): 1–15.

BBC World Service. "The 'Last Indian.'" *Witness History*, September 7, 2012. https://www.bbc.co.uk/programmes/w3ct3c3p.

Berkes, Fikret. *Sacred Ecology*. New York: Routledge, 2012.

Bernbaum, Edwin. *Sacred Mountains of the World*. Cambridge: Cambridge University Press, 2022.

Carson, Rachel. *The Sense of Wonder*. 1965. Reprint, New York: Harper Perennial, 2017.

Cosgrove, Denis, and Veronica Della Dora, ed. *High Places: Cultural Geographies of Mountains, Ice and Science*. New York: I. B. Tauris, 2008.

Cronon, William. "The Trouble with Wilderness: Or, Getting Back to the Wrong Nature." *Environmental History* 1, no. 1 (January 1996): 7–28.

Department of Conservation, Tongariro. "History and Culture: Tongariro National Park." Accessed January 19, 2025. https://www.doc.govt.nz/parks-and-recreation/places-to-go/central-north-island/places/tongariro-national-park/about-tongariro-national-park/history-and-culture/.

Drengson, Alan R., and Yuichi Inoue, eds. *The Deep Ecology Movement: An Introductory Anthology*. Berkeley: North Atlantic Books, 1995.

Fitzgerald, Matthew. "The Sublime: An Aesthetic Concept in Change." *Collector*, September 23, 2021, https://www.thecollector.com/the-sublime-concept-in-change-philosophy/.

Forbes, Susan. "Nomination of Tongariro National Park for Inclusion in the World Heritage Cultural List." In *Conservation Advisory Science Notes No. 68*. Wellington: Department of Conservation, 1994.

Hall, Dewey W. *Romantic Naturalists, Early Environmentalists: An Ecocritical Study, 1789–1912*. Burlington, VT: Ashgate, 2014.

Heacox, Kim. *John Muir and the Ice That Started a Fire: How a Visionary and the Glaciers of Alaska Changed America*. Guilford, CT: Lyons Press, 2014.

Highland, Chris, ed. *Meditations of John Muir: Nature's Temple*. Berkeley: Wilderness Press, 2001.

Hinton, David. *Hunger Mountain: A Field Guide to Mind and Landscape*. Boston: Shambhala, 2012.

Ingty, Tenzing. "High Mountain Communities and Climate Change: Adaptation, Traditional Ecological Knowledge, and Institutions." *Climatic Change* 145, no. 1 (October 2017): 41–55.

Krutch, Joseph W. *Henry David Thoreau*. New York: William Morrow, 1974.

Leopold, Aldo. *A Sand County Almanac*. New York: Ballantine Books, 1986.

Li, Li, Dieter Thomas Tietze, Andreas Fritz, Zhi Lü, Matthias Bürgi, and Ilse Storch. "Rewilding Cultural Landscape Potentially Puts Both Avian Diversity and Endemism at Risk: A Tibetan Plateau Case Study." *Biological Conservation* 224 (May 2018): 75–86.

Lockhart, Christopher, Carla A. Houkamau, Chris G. Sibley, and Danny Osborne. "To Be at One with the Land: Māori Spirituality Predicts Greater Environmental Regard." *Religions* 10, no. 7 (July 2019): 427.

MacCaig, Norman. *The Poems of Norman MacCaig*. Edited by Ewen McCaig. Edinburgh: Birlinn, 2010.

Macfarlane, Robert. *Mountains of the Mind: A History of a Fascination*. London: Granta, 2004.

Marsh, George Perkins. *Man and Nature: Or, Physical Geography as Modified by Human Action*. New York: C. Scribner, 1864.

Matthiessen, Peter. *The Snow Leopard*. New York: Penguin Random House, 2008.

Messerli, Bruno, and Jack D. Ives, eds. *Mountains of the World: A Global Priority*. New York: Parthenon, 1997.

Muir, John. *My First Summer in the Sierra*. New York: Houghton, Mifflin, 1901.

Muir, John. *Our National Parks*. New York: Houghton, Mifflin, 1901.

Muir, John. *Picturesque California*. New York: J. Dewing, 1888.

Muir, John. *Travels in Alaska*. Boston: Houghton, Mifflin, 1915.

Murie, Margaret E., and Olaus J. Murie. *Wapiti Wilderness*. Boulder: University Press of Colorado, 1987.

Murie, Olaus. *Journeys to the Far North*. Nashville: Alaska Northwest Books of Turner Publishing, 2015.

Murray, W. H. *Mountaineering in Scotland and Undiscovered Scotland*. London: Diadem, 1979.

Næss, Arne. "Mountains." *The Trumpeter: Journal of Ecosophy* 21, no. 2 (Autumn 2005): 51–54. https://trumpeter.athabascau.ca/index.php/trumpet/article/view/56/53.

Næss, Arne, Alan Drengson, and Bill Devall. *Ecology of Wisdom: Writings by Arne Næss*. Berkeley: Counterpoint, 2008.

Pardo, Natalia, Hidalene Wilson, Jonathon N. Procter, Erica Lattughi, and Taiarahia Black. "Bridging Māori Indigenous Knowledge and Western Geosciences to Reduce Social Vulnerability in Active Volcanic Regions." *Journal of Applied Volcanology* 4, no. 2 (2015): 1–20.

Patten, Robin, and Dennis Knight. "Snow Avalanches and Vegetation Pattern in Cascade Canyon, Grand Teton National Park, Wyoming, U.S.A." *Arctic and Alpine Research* 26, no. 1 (1994): 35–41.

Patterson, Allie. "Indian Removal from Yosemite National Park." Intermountain Histories. Last updated December 2, 2022. https://www.intermountainhistories.org/items/show/339.

Peacock, Charlotte. *Into the Mountain: The Life of Nan Shepherd*. Cambridge: Galileo, 2019.

Rothenberg, David, and Arne Næss. *Is It Painful to Think? Conversations with Arne Næss*. Minneapolis: University of Minnesota Press, 1993.

Royal, Te Ahukaramū Charles. "Kaitiakitanga—Guardianship and Conservation." Te Ara: The Encyclopedia of New Zealand, 2007. https://www.TeAra.govt.nz/en/kaitiakitanga-guardianship-and-conservation/print.

Shepherd, Nan. *In the Cairngorms*. Cambridge: Galileo, 2014.

Shepherd, Nan. *The Living Mountain*. 2nd ed. Edinburgh: Canongate, 2011.

Snyder, Gary. *The Practice of the Wild*. Berkeley: Counterpoint Press, 2010.

Solnit, Rebecca. "John Muir in Native America." *Magazine of the Sierra Club*, March 2, 2021. https://www.sierraclub.org/sierra/2021-2-march-april/feature/john-muir-native-america.

Stausberg, Michael. "The Sacred, the Holy, the Numinous—and Religion: On the Emergence and Early History of a Terminological Constellation." *Religion* 47, no. 4 (2017): 557–90.

Thoreau, Henry David. *The Maine Woods*. Boston: Ticknor and Fields, 1864.

Thoreau, Henry David. "Walking." *Atlantic Monthly: A Magazine of Literature, Art, and Politics* 9, no. 56 (June 1862): 657–74.

van Boeckel, Jan, dir. *The Call of the Mountain: Arne Næss and the Deep Ecology Movement*. ReRun Productions, 1997. https://www.deepecology.net/blog/2022/03/16/the-call-of-the-mountain-arne-Næss-and-the-deep-ecology-movement-full-version/.

Walls, Laura D. "Introducing Humboldt's Cosmos." *Minding Nature*, August 2009, 3–15.

Wilson, Chris, and Paul Erling Groth. *Everyday America: Cultural Landscape Studies after J. B. Jackson*. Berkeley: University of California Press, 2003.

Worster, Donald. *A Passion for Nature: The Life of John Muir*. New York: Oxford University Press, 2008.

Wulf, Andrea. *The Invention of Nature: Alexander von Humboldt's New World*. New York: Vintage Books, 2015.

Yeoman, Greta. "To Summit or Not to Summit?" *Wilderness*, March 19, 2020. https://www.wildernessmag.co.nz/to-summit-or-not-to-summit/.

Yosemite National Park, California. "Paintings of Yosemite." National Park Service. Last updated August 26, 2021. https://www.nps.gov/yose/learn/historyculture/paintings-of-yosemite.htm.